THE
CREATIVE
IMAGINATION

THE
CREATIVE
IMAGINATION

◉ PSYCHOANALYSIS *and*
the GENIUS *of* INSPIRATION

EDITED WITH AN INTRODUCTION BY

Hendrik M. Ruitenbeek

CHICAGO

Quadrangle Books / *1965* ◉

To Willem and Kees

ACKNOWLEDGMENTS

THANKS are due the following journals and publishers for permission to reprint copyrighted material:

American Imago, for "The Total Personality in Creative Therapy" by Ernest Zierer.

American Journal of Orthopsychiatry, for "Creative Dance in Therapy" by Lauretta Bender and Franziska Boas.

American Journal of Psychoanalysis, for "Creativity and Encounter" by Rollo May; "The Goal of Creativity in Psychotherapy" by Edith Weigert; "Three Creative Phases in Psychoanalysis: The Encounter, the Dialogue and the Process of Articulation" by Charles R. Hulbeck; "The Growth of Artistic Creativity Through the Psychoanalytic Process" by Paul Lussheimer; and "Creativity and Freedom" by Antonia Wenkart.

American Journal of Psychology, for "The Influence of Creative Desire upon the Argument for Immortality" by Cavendish Moxon.

Bulletin of the Menninger Clinic, for "The Creative Arts as Therapy" by Mary Huntoon.

Bulletin of the Museum of Modern Art, for "Creative Therapy" by Edward Liss.

Bulletin of the New York Academy of Medicine, for "Psychoanalysis and the Study of Creative Imagination" by Ernst Kris.

International Journal of Psycho-Analysis, for "Aesthetics and Psychology of the Artist" by Hanns Sachs; "Infantile Anxiety Situations Reflected in a Work of Art and in the Creative Impulse" by Melanie Klein; "On the Nature of Ugliness and the Creative Impulse" by John Rickman; "Schizophrenic and Creative Thinking" by Robert Wälder; and "On Inspiration: Preliminary Notes on Emotional Conditions in Creative States" by Ernst Kris.

International Universities Press, for "The Childhood of the Artist: Libidinal Phase Development and Giftedness" by Phyllis Greenacre.

Journal of the American Psychoanalytic Association, for "Communication in Psychoanalysis and in the Creative Process: A Parallel" by David Beres.

Alfred A. Knopf, Inc., for "Life and Creation" by Otto Rank (from *Art and Artist*).

Literature and Psychology, for "New Views of Art and the Creative Process in Psychoanalytic Ego Psychology" by Louis Fraiberg.

Psychiatry, for "A Theory Concerning Free Creation in the Inventive Arts" by Harry B. Levey.

FOREWORD

This anthology represents a wide variety of opinions on the topic of psychoanalysis and creativity. An effort has been made to include some of the major schools of psychoanalysis, where it was thought the representatives of these schools had made significant contributions to the subject. I thought it appropriate to start the book with essays by Ernst Kris and Hanns Sachs, who in my opinion have done pioneer work in the area of psychoanalysis and creativity. Kris is represented with two essays, one dealing with the relationship between psychoanalysis and creative imagination, and the other an enlightening essay on inspiration. Hanns Sachs, the founder of the *American Imago* and one of the most important figures in the early years of the psychoanalytic movement, describes the link between aesthetics and the psychology of the artist. Melanie Klein, who during her lifetime was a pioneer in child analysis and an outstanding, if not outspoken, woman in the International Psychoanalytic Association, writes about the influence of infantile anxiety situations on the work of art and creativity. Otto Rank certainly needs no introduction. For a long time he was considered by Freud as his logical successor in the guidance of the psychoanalytic movement, but serious differences between them prevented this. Nevertheless, the "crown prince" of the psychoanalytic movement, as Rank was often called, established himself in his own right. His writings on the psychoanalysis of art and creativity still stand as an example of unique psychoanalytic insight. The essay on life and creation, reprinted here, is certainly one of his finest writings.

John Rickman, who writes on ugliness and creativity, was for years active and outstanding in the British Psychoanalytic

Society and has made valuable contributions to the theory of psychoanalysis.

In the next set of essays there is a wide variety of aspects of creativity and psychoanalysis. Some of these authors represent the school of ego psychology and I especially single out the article by Louis Fraiberg. Phyllis Greenacre, in her excellent essay on the childhood development of the artist (I also think, along this line, of her brilliant study *The Quest for the Father*), and David Beres, on communication in the psychoanalytic and creative processes, certainly make representations for the post-Freudian school. Harry B. Levey, in developing certain theories concerning free creation in the inventive arts, represents those who for a long time have gathered around the Washington School of Psychiatry, in which the Sullivanians play such an important part.

The essays by Edward Liss on creative therapy, Mary Huntoon on the creative arts as therapy, and Lauretta Bender and Franziska Boas' essay on the creative dance in psychotherapy deal with specific applications of the psychoanalytic process to the arts.

The last five essays, which I consider a most important part of this book, are written by those psychoanalysts who have been influenced by the ideas and thoughts of Karen Horney and lately by the existential school of psychoanalysis. The essay by Rollo May on creativity and encounter is a splendid example of the latter; Charles Hulbeck's essay deals with the existential aspects of the creative phases in the psychoanalytic process. While Edith Weigert is concerned with the general goals of creativity in the psychotherapeutic process, the article by Paul Lussheimer deals specifically with the role and growth of artistic creativity through psychoanalysis. Antonia Wenkart, for many years concerned with the application of existential philosophy to psychoanalysis, presents some penetrating insights into the encounter of creativity and freedom.

CONTENTS

THE
CREATIVE
IMAGINATION

□ INTRODUCTION:

NEUROSIS AND CREATIVITY

Hendrik M. Ruitenbeek

"Before you leave today," Freud said in one of his *Introductory Lectures on Psychoanalysis,* "I should like to direct your attention for a moment to a side of fantasy-life of very general interest. There is in fact a path from fantasy back again to reality, and that is—art. The artist has also an introverted disposition and has not far to go to become a neurotic. He is one who is urged on by instinctual needs which are too clamorous. He longs to attain to honor, power, riches, fame, and the love of women; but he lacks the means of achieving these gratifications. So, like any other with an unsatisfied longing, he turns away from reality and transfers all his interest, and all his libido, too, to the *creation* [1] of his wishes in the life of fantasy, from which the way might readily lead to neurosis."

This is probably Freud's definitive statement on the relationship between neurosis and creativity. Art, Freud believed, offered to those who created it and to those who experienced it a gratification which could substitute for the renunciation of instinctual gratification which is the price men pay for being

15

men, human persons living in human societies where sex and aggression both must be reined in, where enjoyment must often be postponed and frustration endured.

Yet Freud did not believe that psychoanalysis offered a complete explanation of creativity. For that is embodied in objective works—poems, plays, pictures, music, the imagined worlds of the novelists, and the carefully wrought structures of the philosophers and scientists. Those works were undoubtedly more than their psychological roots. Yet from those roots sprang the possibility of communication between artist and audience. In *Creative Writers and Daydreaming*, Freud explored the connection between the imaginative play of childhood and the fantasizing of later life and saw how closely the artist and the man in the street might approach each other in their daydreaming. Did they not thus come close, the artist might not be able to convey his visions, and art, as we generally define it, might not exist.

The artist does more than suffer and daydream, however; he enjoys an unusual capacity for sublimating his instinctual desires, Freud argued, and has a gift for repressing his conflicts in flexible fashion rather than in the rigid and compulsive patterns characteristic of the neurotic. Flexibility and sublimation must be objectively embodied, as has been noted, and here Freud acknowledged the limitations of psychoanalysis which, he wrote, must "lay down its arms before the problem of the imaginative writer." Elsewhere, he remarked that analysis "can do nothing toward elucidating the nature of the artistic gift, nor can it explain the means by which the artist works—artistic technique."

Freud himself had faced the problem of expression and those who can read his German know how well he solved it. Ernest Jones is convinced that Freud might have written poetry or fiction had he not found another path. This belief is borne out by Freud's own words in a letter telling his

fiancée, Martha Bernays, how many stories he had imagined
and how he had plotted an Oriental tale, an old-fashioned
genre which has long passed out of fashion but one which
might still be cherished by those who have been enchanted by
the *Arabian Nights*.

Often Freud is cited against himself in attempts to deny the
validity of a psychoanalytic approach to creativity. The sources
of aesthetic feeling, it is argued, are too profound for the
explorations of the analyst: if psychoanalysis should reach the
sources of creativity, they would be destroyed. This attitude,
inconsistent as it may seem when baldly stated, is rooted in
tradition, as is the idea of a link between creativity and neurosis. The primitive shaman, for example, went into trances
and sometimes emerged from his long dream journey with a
new and powerful magic song. Greek and Celtic antiquity
both believed in the divine frenzy that possessed the poet.

Later, romanticism talked of inspiration—the power breathed
into the creative artist from somewhere outside himself. Romantic notions were reinforced, no doubt, by the nineteenth-
century belief that the artist was somehow "unhealthy." This
notion lingers, particularly in cultures where the pursuit of
money is a major social norm. The artist who, by definition,
pursues another goal threatens the social norm. In contemporary America, where the use of psychological terms exceeds the
understanding of them, the artist may be labeled "neurotic."

Since the psychoanalyst may indeed find some links between
creativity and certain neurotic mechanisms, the label cited may
appear more justified than most. Those who contend that
artists should avoid analytic therapy doubt that any analyst
can "understand" an artist; they fear successful therapy might
dissipate the poet's necessary madness. Others contend that
neurosis hampers the artist in creative expression and that
psychoanalysis can free and support the artist in his work.

The late Franz Alexander presented a useful summary of

17

and creativity.[2] Although analysts continue to debate about the contrasting psychodynamics of the two phenomena, they tend post-Freudian thinking on the relationship between neurosis to agree that creativity represents not emotional conflict *per se* but rather effort to resolve such conflict. Neurosis, deriving from unconscious processes, is often an inflexible and ill-adapted attempt at resolution. Creativity, deriving from preconscious processes, tends to be an economic and successful form of resolving emotional conflict. The artist, in other words, is closer to knowing what he is about; thus he can use his psychic energies to shape a work of art out of dream, wish, and daydream, instead of converting that energy into some symptom or some poorly adapted pattern of behavior.

Like Freud, Ernst Kris and Hanns Sachs, two eminent psychoanalytic students of creativity, agree that the essence of artistic creation is form: the ability to combine materials into new artistic shapes and, by communicating through those shapes, to make forbidden wishes acceptable. Wordsworth spoke of poetry as the outcome of emotion recollected in tranquillity. More prosaically, the analyst finds that the artistic work sets feelings which rouse guilt and anxiety at such a distance from the person that they can be experienced vividly, yet with minimal pain.

Alexander himself thought it more fruitful to inquire into the conditions which foster creativity than to try to define the psychological character of the creative act. This opinion implies that creativity is useful for the society as well as pleasurable to the creative person. In concluding his article, incidentally, Alexander notes that contemporary society, bureaucratized as it has become, may find creativity more threatening than serviceable. A number of his fellow analysts seem to have a less somber view. Lawrence Kubie, for example, appears ready to encourage creativity when he observes that creativity is released when the person is relatively free of psychological pressures.[3] He, consequently, would probably tend to deny that neurosis and creativity are positively linked. Artists may have been neurotic, but they were not helped to do their work by their neurotic suffering even if that suffering might, in a sense, have driven them to their labors.

Alexander is somewhat inclined to agree. In contrast to Freud's view, which considers creativity under the aspect of compensation for essential instinctual deprivation, Alexander sees creative effort as akin to play. In his view, play is activity pursued in freedom from the need to act. The fisherman who catches a cod to sell is working; the fisherman who catches a cod for the sheer joy of activity is playing. Play is motivated neither by the demands of the workaday world nor by the pressure to resolve neurotic conflict. The person at play can explore, can set a distance between himself and the material with which he is dealing, can toy with alternatives, and can indulge himself freely in the pleasure of mastering those alternatives. Thus the poet, perhaps frustrated in desire to win a love object, can express his frustration and so put it at an endurable distance. He can play freely with the sound and sense of words until he finds some new turn of rhythm, some fresh metaphor for his unhappiness. Again, the discovery gives him a sense of mastery and so eases his awareness of frustration. Because he finds a new form, and communicates in it, others can share his feelings and so decrease the immediacy and the pain of their own. Thus, psychological suffering may be eased by art, made distant and transmuted by being shared. In the experience of tragedy, particularly, such sharing tends to lessen the individual's burden of guilt and anxiety; to cite Aristotle, he is purged by the "pity and terror" which the poet's words evoke, rouse up, and then diminish.

If we follow the foregoing line of thought, we see that mental illness and neurotic involvement generally have a negative impact upon creativity. Neurotic defenses against anxiety are rigid solutions of inner problems, and rigidity runs counter to the artist's need to treat his materials freely and in novel ways. Many creative persons have been neurotic or even psychotic, but many others have not been. Some institutionalized psychotics produce interesting painting and writing, others do not. And often even the interesting productions are less valuable as art than as raw material for increasing our understanding of psychotic processes.

In his practice, the psychotherapist sees creativity blocked by such problems as neurotic inability to work. Psychoanalysis can operate to free the patient from the compulsion of his "shoulds" and his "claims," as Leon Salzmann labels neurotic rigidities which interfere with the individual's ability to make choices in a spontaneous and appropriate way.

Psychoanalysis itself is something of a creative activity. No longer do analysts regard therapy and cure as a process brought about by proper practice of a special technique, a practice guaranteed through correct training. Rather, as Karen Horney said: "Inherent in man are evolutionary constructive forces which urge him to realize his given potentialities. This means that man, by his very nature and of his own accord, strives toward self-realization and that his set of values evolves from such striving." In contrast and yet in agreement, Martti Siirala describes the way in which the patient is governed by ". . . a feeling of despair, of utterly losing, being rejected, condemned by the law. And the despair contains a convulsive effort to master the law, to be the very master of the law of life."

The mastery to which Siirala refers is not, in my opinion, a drive toward mere adaptation to the demands of the environment. The psychotherapist is not necessarily dedicated to "adjusting" the patient, making him willing to accept the conditions of his social existence rather than to endeavor to change them, if effort at change is not a mere evasion of his need to alter his own life. Instead, in the psychotherapeutic process, the analyst co-operates with a core of creative potentiality in the patient and in himself. Harold Kelman, in his remarkable essay, *Creative Talent and Creative Passion as Therapy*, insists that the therapist must be aware of the *Zeitgeist* and responsive to its subtleties, for the spirit of the time reflects both the discontents and the creative potentialities of the historical moment in which he and his patients try to function. Analyst and patient alike participate in and manifest some of those possibilities even while they suffer from the effects of those discontents. Psychotherapy practiced by a person open to the full range of existence can itself be an art, although now we use the word in its old sense: mastery of a mystery, that is, practical skill carried to a high level of achievement.

In considering the tangled problem of the relationship between neurosis and creativity, it is necessary to take special note that creativity can be dealt with in two aspects: its origins and its expression. By distinguishing between the sources of creativity—which psychoanalysis tends to find in free access to preconscious psychological process—and its concrete objective achievements, we clarify our approach to the relationship between neurosis and creative accomplishment. Psychotherapy is concerned with still another aspect of creativity, the capacity of the individual to realize his potentialities in proportion with his endowment and his opportunities. Highly significant though this may be in clinical practice, it is not our major concern in this anthology. Here we deal with the person who expresses his creative impulse, and resolves certain of his psychological problems, by making works of art. Capacity for creative work, artistic or intellectual—for it should be remembered that philosophies and general scientific theories are aesthetic productions as well as efforts to comprehend truth—may be an inborn gift. In the perfection of that gift, psychoanalysis can play only a minor role, but it may, on occasion, further the creative person's ability to use his gift. Socially more significant, perhaps, psychoanalysts' understanding of the conditions which liberate creativity in the talented person may help those less richly endowed to free themselves and thus encourage them to make greater use of whatever potentialities they may have for bringing a larger measure of creative spontaneity into their daily lives.

NOTES

1. Italics the editor's.
2. "Neurosis and Creativity," *American Journal of Psychoanalysis,* XXIV (1964), 117-29.
3. *Neurotic Distortion of the Creative Process* (New York: The Noonday Press, 1961).

PSYCHOANALYSIS AND THE STUDY OF CREATIVE IMAGINATION

Ernst Kris

"Creative imagination" indicates a mental property which we usually connect with achievements in the arts, in the broadest sense of the word. But scientists and "thinkers" also rely upon creative imagination during certain probably crucial phases of their work; and in one way or another this same mental property may manifest itself in the personal or professional lives of us all.

Common to all manifestations of creative imagination, in the first place, is subjective experience. This tends to be infinitely differentiated in intensity and duration and to appear as an ingredient or accessory in many moods. Three characteristics of this experience seem outstanding.

First: Subjects are aware of the limitation of conscious effort.

Second: They are aware of a specific feeling. It is never a neutral one. There is always some, and frequently a very high emotional charge is involved.

Third: Even if excitement rises, the mind tends to work with high precision and problems are easily solved. If we adopt a broad meaning of the term "problem solving" we can say that some problem solving is always going on, even in art.

A further common element concerns not the subject's experience but the reaction of others to him. Wherever creative imagination is at work, for better or worse it tends to establish some distinction between the one and the many.

This is not, I know, a satisfactory and certainly not an exhaustive description. However, a certain vagueness may not be out of order since we are dealing with a difficult topic. And in the end, the impression must and should prevail that, significant as the contribution of psychoanalysis is, it is limited in various ways. We have started on a voyage with our course largely uncharted.

I shall attempt to characterize the contribution of psychoanalysis to the study of creative imagination with particular reference to art—art in a very broad sense—and loosely follow the guide of the history of psychoanalysis, since its contributions to the study of creative imagination constitute an important part of this history.

The present position of psychoanalysis, its status in science and society, offers a starting point. We shall characterize this status by stressing two aspects. Largely based on psychoanalytic insight for some twenty years a movement has been under way which later historians may well decide to describe as the "Psychiatric Revolution." There is, for one, the rise of psychiatry within medicine, the obsolescence of a rigid distinction between the "physical" and the "mental" in approaches to illness, in the emergence of psychosomatic medicine; there is, moreover, the ever broadening concept of mental health itself, modifying procedures in education and transforming our views on welfare to the point where charity as an institution has come to include considerations of the individual's psychological balance. During the last decade these and other related trends seem to have converged into one direction. It is this: that therapy is gradually being supplemented by prevention; and a program which has existed in a somewhat utopian sense since the earnest days of Freud's work is, thus, being carried further. The second aspect of the current status of psychoanalysis is externally characterized by the growing contact of psychoanalysis with other disciplines. It is not a contact in which psychoanalysis and sociology, anthropology, or political science —to mention only some currently much-emphasized examples —establish an interdisciplinary co-operation, but rather one in which psychoanalysis provides the focal point for a new science of man of which the outlines are here and there visible. Psychoanalytic therapy and psychoanalytic psychiatry in general provide the most essential set of data in the building of this new science.

How did this come about? How could two so far-reaching developments grow out of one root, originally out of the experience of one investigator?

I here turn to a quotation from Freud's earliest writings which describes his own reflections on the first extensive psychiatric case histories which he presented to the public after considerable delay, in the fall of 1895: "I have not always been a psychotherapist, but like other neuropathologists I was educated to methods of focal diagnoses and electrical prognosis, so that even I myself am struck by the fact that the case histories which I am writing read like novels and, as it were, dispense with the serious features of the scientific character. Yet I must console myself with the fact that the nature of the subject is apparently more responsible for this issue than my own predilection. Focal diagnosis and electrical reactions are really not important in the study of hysteria, whereas a detailed discussion of the psychic processes, as one is wont to hear it from the poet, and the application of a few *psychological formulae*, allows one to gain an insight into the course of events."

These words describe the scientist's struggle with a new and particularly challenging subject matter. It was not, as Freud thought at the time, one syndrome or one illness; it was the study of man's psychological conflict, an age-old topic and part of the tradition of Western civilization. Freud's predecessors were not scientists; they were the masters of intuitive insight— poets, writers, and thinkers. Closest to Freud's formulations are those of some of the great men of the century of his own youth, the formulations and approaches of Schopenhauer, Nietzsche, Dostoevsky, and those of some minor and yet very great men, like Samuel Butler; the coincidences which we observe are largely rooted in the similarity of cultural predispositions. This in turn makes us aware of the fact that the demand of the age and the creative effort of the individual must be in some harmony with each other; creative imagination can in some measure anticipate the future, but in empty space, out of tune with at least hidden trends, a genius will not emerge; his work must fit into the structure of the problems which he solves, with which he struggles and which he modifies.

In Freud's work the confines of sciences were widened; an area of phenomena never before approached scientifically was investigated through the formulation and testing of hypotheses. The practical consequences of this step were to be seen in the enlarged orbit of therapeutic intervention, the slow, steady, and uninterrupted progress of the therapeutic technique of psychoanalysis during almost six decades, and the more recent development of psychotherapy in psychoanalytic psychiatry. In one point, at least, these developments were different from those in most other fields of medicine. When unhappiness and self-made destiny proved in some instances to be amenable to therapeutic intervention, not only a cure of illness was offered,

but also a cure where previously the existence of illness had not
of tune with at least hidden trends, a genius will not emerge; his
thus, led to a widening of the confines of medicine itself.

Let me briefly characterize some of the consequences of
Freud's first steps for the development of psychoanalysis as a
theory. The few "psychological formulae" to which he referred in the passage quoted above expanded rapidly into a
cohesive set of propositions. At first, Freud could borrow his
main conceptual tools from the area of his previous interests,
neurophysiology. The general approach, the idea of seeing
human conflicts in terms of an interplay of forces, the distinction of various types of discharge processes and of principles
regulating the economy of psychic energy were derived from
this field. But the therapeutic experience with psychiatric cases
forced upon Freud not only modifications of his early concepts, but also a radical extension of his approach. Two interconnected observations became of decisive importance: the
realization that earliest experiences tend to leave lasting im-
prints on personality development, and the recognition of the
role of instinctual drives, particularly in connection with the
earliest phases of development. The realization of the importance of man's early total dependence on maternal care, unique
among mammals, led Freud to supplement his physiological by
a biological approach. But this biological approach received in
Freud's context a new dimension. It is not limited to the
consideration of generic, biochemical, or physiological forces
within man; it includes also the continuous social influences
upon the growing human organism. In this approach the
dichotomy between the biological proper and the social is eliminated as spurious, a dichotomy which in the past had obscured
many psychological formulations. There are still those who
tend to re-emphasize its existence and thus to support the distinction of two kinds of sciences, natural and social sciences.
The position of psychoanalysis as scientific theory and that of

27

psychoanalytic psychiatry as therapy and hence as source of data illustrate the value of an approach which has made it possible to integrate various fields of investigation around a core of central assumptions.

The psychoanalytic contribution to the study of creative imagination should be seen with this in mind, as a contribution to an inquiry basic to any science of man. This view has determined the selection of the topics which are to be discussed as examples; they deal with phenomena of the nature of art, and art in turn is viewed as a particular, and as the most complex, type of communication in society.

I shall deal with three problems for which I have chosen the following headings:

First: The problem of thematic generalization.

Second: The emotive or aesthetic potential.

Third: Creative communication.

The first topic, the problem of thematic generalization, is concerned with narration whatever the mode of presentation; it is story-centered and hence deals largely with content. The starting point is the relative uniformity of all narration, of myth, folklore, fairy tale, novel, and even drama, or, to put it more cautiously, the very high frequency of recurrent themes.

Previous explanations accounted for this recurrence mainly by two interdependent types of inquiry: thematic similarity was explained by pointing to historical reasons, to the migration of accounts and thus to the influence of one narration upon others. Influence, however, posits a predisposing factor, a universal experience which explains the readiness to accept influence. As such experience, the reactions to cosmological and physiological cycles in nature and man have been most thoroughly investigated. Both the historical and the cyclical explanations are not superseded by the approach of psychoanalysis, which relates the uniformity of themes to the uniformity of conflict-patterns in man's life. This uniformity is rooted in what I mentioned as the biological approach in psychoanalysis. Hence the uniformity of conflict patterns does not refer mainly to the conscious experience of the adult but largely to the experiences and hence also to the thought-processes of the child. Universal human experiences, modified by specific conditions of the cultural environment, account for the extent to which the themes of narration tend to resemble each other.

The typical content of many of these themes was first discovered in the reconstruction of childhood fantasies during the psychoanalytic investigation of adults and later elaborated in the observation of the growing child. We are familiar with the emergence of many such typical fantasies as the response of the child to the riddles of his own existence and to those of the adult world surrounding him: riddles not only in an intellectual sense, although this is part of it. For there is also the inherent conflict of many of the child's most basic strivings with each other and with his environment; there is, moreover, the task of adjusting to a social world in which one is still a child, with wishes and desires no less intense and even more unbending than those of the adult.

The best-known coincidence between myth or great narration and individual fantasy concerns accounts which have the hero of miraculous descent, separated from his original parents, adopted by foster parents up to the day when he splendidly emerges. These accounts, widely spread in Western and particularly Mediterranean tradition, but frequent also in other cultures, have lost nothing of their emotional relevance.

Some 30 per cent of the Americans of this generation are consciously aware of having thought of themselves at some time between the ages of five and fifteen as adopted or foster-children, and of having invented "true" parents of higher or— much more rarely—of lower status. There is hardly a psycho-analytic treatment where some such fantasy fails to play its role. Some of its parts tend to have remained conscious; other, dynamically more significant, parts tend to be repressed. The very fact that I can here quote percentiles of the occurrence of the conscious version is due to a special circumstance: Freud's assertion of the frequent occurrence even within consciousness of a similar fantasy is, to my knowledge, one of the first psychoanalytic hypotheses to have been experimentally tested (by what are called objective scientific methods).

The relation between the individual's fantasy life and the thematic repertory of narrative art opened our eyes to two problems which interact independently. The first concerns the transition from individual fantasy to narrative account. The finding says that the fantasy of the individual, particularly the daydreams of those normal and abnormal individuals who habitually weave their reveries in continued stories, are closely related to the wish for immediate gratification, frequently derived from older, repressed masturbatory fantasies, and have retained some of the characteristics of their origin.

Let me report to you how this problem presented itself to me in my days of apprenticeship. A twenty-year-old youth, interested in many aspects of his medical work, showed by his behavior the wish to impress his teachers as the most gifted and most effective student of a large class, in order to become the one who would, in each of the specialties in which he happened to be interested, make decisive contributions, and thus acquire in the professor a new and more powerful paternal protector. Apart from more obvious and typical dynamics, this behavior repeated the course of a "continued story" which since the age of five or six had dominated the young man's life in many variations. In this fantasy he was the son of the crown prince of Austria, Rudolph, and had been placed as foster-child in a middle-class family. For years the stories which he told himself dealt with the topic of how he would gloriously come forward and rescue his country; how he would meet his grandfather, the emperor, and gain admiration from his own, real parents. This moment, when he would meet *them* was the focal point. Whenever this scene approached, a new setting had to be invented, since the fantasy would start to roll off fast and faster; then the details became unimportant, the "need" to get there dominated his thought, until the whole setting had become unusable and a new version had to be elaborated, soon to become subject to the same fate. The climax had swallowed the plot.

The storyteller, professional or amateur, has liberated himself from similar urgency, can dispose and distribute where the daydreamer is subject to pressures since he cannot delay gratification. Here we have a first and basic precondition to the socialization of what previously was a private experience.

The second problem which impressed psychoanalysts early in their work concerns a finding first established by analytic observation and since corroborated in the study of child behavior. What narrative art offers to the child tends to be treated unconsciously as if it were a fantasy and appears in dreams as its substitute. But a "borrowed" fantasy can be less guiltily used since it comes from outside. The quest for such external stimulation, the need to "borrow" fantasies instead of elaborating one's own, tends to grow under the pressure of certain typical conflicts, particularly those of the phallic phase of psychosexual development.

Among the accounts which stimulate the child's fantasy-life a special place is reserved for those which early in their development the parents or significant substitutes tell or read to their children; these are the stories which tend to remain imbued with the memory of a specific shared experience and to be assimilated with particular ease.

Taking this as an example, we may generalize on the function of the narrator in society. He is the one who under given circumstances, in any specific cultural environment, fulfills a

need of his audience. In primitive society it is the bard's pre-
rogative to speak of the unspeakable, of incest, parricide, and
matricide, of the gods and the demons. However much has
changed, some such prerogatives still remain peculiar to the
professional narrator. We ascribe to him the faculty of adapt-
ing what he knows from personal experience, from his own
fantasy, to the needs of a community. We do not necessarily
assume that what he tells is a tale all his own or all about
himself. His faculty includes the capacity to assimilate many
patterns of conflict, to react to minimal experiences with
emphatic understanding. In speaking of thematic generalization,
I have this set of faculties in mind.

Among the narrator's public there are those who have
remained on the level which we have discussed: they follow
the quest for fantasies which they can borrow. And yet, this
is quite obviously only one of the possible attitudes to narrative art.

To meet the demands of a public may mean a variety of
things and neglect differences as fundamental as those between
the Broadway hit or the pulp magazine and the great work of
literature—differences which can, in some instances, be established by common sense, but which in other instances become
subject to the verdict of the literary critic, whose function I
am not prone to underrate. It is to him that we as psychoanalysts hope to supply some tools. The two contributions of
psychoanalysis to the study of creative imagination, to which
we now turn, may be said to serve this purpose.

The consideration of the emotive or aesthetic potential is
derived from the study of dreams. The texture of dreams,
woven out of the day's unfinished thought and repressed and
reawakened impulses, presents us with an imagery that is only
in rare instances of meaning to the dreamer. Only the psychoanalytic method enables us to understand it.

The overdetermination of single elements in the dream or of

32

whole parts, the condensation of many thoughts into one element, or the representation of one thought in various disguises, these and similar mechanisms are an intimate part of the "dream-work," which produces the manifest dream content. The study of the mechanisms of the dream have suggested that similar mechanisms play a part in the working of creative imagination, in the production of the work of art. But it is a similarity particularly important for its clear differences.

The language of the dream, which is in force when we are asleep, becomes a tool of the creator. The trance or reverie in which it emerges has the capability of most efficient communication. What in the dream impresses us as overdetermination becomes the potential of the art work. This principle has been applied to the study of various media. It is by no means limited to the understanding of narrative creations, and it contributes decisively to our understanding of especially the great masterpieces. The oedipal conflict in *Hamlet* or in *The Brothers Karamazov* is not represented in one but in several versions. There is no one theme that has not its variations; in the relation of several sons to their fathers the central conflict is treated in various interconnected aspects in both these works. Without an understanding of the interaction of those thematic variations, or of the decomposition of one central figure into various characters, of one conflict into its various components, even the most elementary approach to the great thematic compositions cannot be attempted. Such variation of one theme may coexist with the condensation of various different themes into one incident and finally with the condensation of various meanings into one account. When Shakespeare scholars point to the meaning of *Hamlet* in terms of the contemporary Elizabethan scene, this does not contradict other interpretations: contemporary and mythological themes are interwoven. The public is faced with a multiplicity of meanings, integrated into one work and supporting each other.

33

The similarity of art work and dream-work has been best explored and demonstrated in the study of poetry; particularly by William Empson, whose critical writings have been fertilized by psychoanalysis. Poetry is "filled with meaning" more than any other type of verbal communication; words are stimuli to associations which lead in various directions, and when Mr. Eliot, as critic, wishes to appraise the work of one of his contemporaries, of, let us say, Miss Moore, we find him saying that her poems have "a very good spread of associations." Mr. Eliot should know, since the extraordinary richness of his own "spread of associations" seems to have given to his work his unique position in the poetry of this age.

Let me resume. The multiple meaning constitutes richness; the dichotomy between appropriate ambiguity and hidden precision, the latter more stringent as the lines flow into the stanza, becomes an important criterion in the study of poetic language. There are poets who are masters of multidimensional vagueness, without leading finally into the growing precision; there are others whose lines differ from ordinary verbal communication only by meter, rhythm, and setting, by the "music of poetry"—but hardly use the very complexity of meaning. All this seems to have become more understandable to us through our experience with contemporary poetry. Here complexity of words tends to be maximized, multiple meanings abound, and uncertainty of interpretation tends to prevail. There can be little doubt that in this the modern poet is more than accidentally akin to the dreamer; also the phenomenon is not limited to any one artistic medium. It is one of the distinguishing features of much that appears in modern painting. It reveals, I believe, in part the influence of psychoanalysis on modern thought. Not of psychoanalysis as a science, but of some of its findings acting as a social force; there is a trend in modern art to consider the work of art as a documentation of the creative process itself, a tendency which expresses itself in a shift in the traditional or previously existing relation between the artist and his public.

This then brings us to a third area of problems upon which psychoanalysis has thrown light: I propose to refer to it in speaking of creative communication. Psychoanalytic insight has helped to clarify some of the experiences which creators in many fields have described as long as a tradition of introspective writing has existed in Western civilization. These reports can be briefly summarized in the following terms: creation tends to be experienced as a dichronous process; it has two phases which may interact with each other in various ways. They may vary in duration, frequency of occurrence, and intensity. In the first the creator is driven; he is in an exceptional state. Thoughts or images tend to flow, things appear in his mind of which he never seemed to have known.

I quote: "A thought suddenly flashes up like lightning: it comes with necessity. I have never had any choice in the matter. . . . There is the feeling that one is utterly out of hand, with the very distinct consciousness of an endless number of fine thrills and titillations descending to one's very toes. There is a depth of happiness in which the most painful and gloomy parts do not act as antitheses to the rest, but are produced and required as necessary shades of color in such an overflow of light." The sudden character of the experience described in this quotation from Nietzsche's *Ecce Homo* stands in contrast to the second phase of productivity, when all is labor, when the creator looks upon his work, as it were, from the outside, and concentration and endeavor predominate. No one in recent decades has more sharply contrasted these two phases than A. E. Housman, to whom we owe not only one of the most vivid descriptions of creative inspiration, but also of the "hell that is to pay" when the flow has tarried. As the manuscripts of his poems become accessible for study we can watch the difference which he describes, the instances when

35

lines or a stanza flew to the mind, and the others, when ease was absent and purposeful concentration had to substitute.

Psychoanalytic observation of creative individuals leads to a somewhat better understanding of such descriptions. In the state of inspiration the psychic apparatus is in an exceptional condition. The barrier between the id and ego has temporarily become permeable. Impulses reach preconsciousness more easily than under other conditions, and their translation into formed expression can proceed painlessly. Forces previously used for repression are being used by the ego for another purpose. All energy seems to be vested in the process of coming to consciousness; hence the similarity between inspirational experiences and those of a hallucinatory kind, a similarity once more clearest in its difference.

The coming to consciousness in the case of creative effort presupposes a long unnoticed process of shaping: it is this process which, entrusted to preconsciousness, is geared to integration and communication. But the process of creation is not completed during its sudden and inspirational phase.

When the first phase gives way to a second, when the artist steps back to view his work, one might say he identifies with his public; he views what "the spirit" has done. He views it, temporarily, from the outside.

The reaction of the public repeats in reversed order and in infinite variations some of the processes which the artist experienced. These variations are determined by cultural and social factors as well as by individual predispositions. Though these reactions may vary in depth, the core of the process, a gradual moving from the fringe to the center, seems to occur with great frequency. It is impeded when we read the narration as if it were a daydream to be borrowed, or when the art work becomes the pin-up girl, i.e., when we miss the distance from immediate gratification; then we are taken back to more primitive modes of reactions. Clinical observations of such incomplete reactions to the creative effort constitute a promising field of investigation in their own right. It is not of these failures that I intend to speak, but of the successful reaction: then the process from the fringe to the center means that gradually a change in the attitude of the audience is taking place.

This change may have various dimensions. It may lead from the borrowed fantasy stage to the appreciation of the complexity of thematic composition, from what is being said to how it is being said, and here again from the pleasure in rhythm to a gradual understanding of first one, then many interacting and integrated meanings. These changes have one factor in common. They are all changes involving the movement of the audience from passivity to activity. In the end the audience may experience some of the excitement and some of the release of tension which arise when the barriers separating unconscious from preconscious or conscious processes have been loosened: "Next to the seizures and shapings of creative thought—the thing itself—no comparable experience is more thrilling than being witched, illumined, and transfigured by the magic of another's art" (H. A. Murray).

In speaking here of re-creation we stress that the shift in psychic levels which operated in the creative process is repeated, and that in this sense the public identifies itself with the artist. The process of identification to which we refer does not concern the artist as an empirical individual.

How could we assume that biographical familiarity should be essential when the greatest artist's personal life is shrouded in anonymity? And yet, no other compares to Shakespeare as master of creative communication. The identification with the artist's biographical person may be the conscious business of the critic, and re-creation at this point may become reconstruction, the reaction of the connoisseur. What we, here, mean by identification with the artist is an unconscious process in which the audience becomes in its own right creative by being re-creative. It follows the spell of the emotive potential. The understanding then leads to the unconscious mechanisms which the artist had used, to the impulses he had mastered; the audience is with him both in reaching downward and in mastery. We do not assume that the audience's experience need be or can be identical with that of the poet. "A poem," says Mr. Eliot, "may appear to mean very different things to different readers and all these may be different from what the author thought." The readers' reaction may be richer in implication than the creator ever supposed. There is that old word, the core of all psychology of the great, which says: "The genius builds better than he knows."

At this point the psychoanalytic approach may turn out to be useful to the critic in a new sense. It is conceivable that some of the attributes which lend artistic value could be measured by the study of response, and, more particularly, by the survival of great art works as effective stimuli. The study of their emotive or aesthetic potential may account for the lasting appreciation of such unique formulations as that of Sophocles in his Oedipus trilogy, or for many comparable achievements in the arts which seem to triumph over changes in social affairs. Many generations of men repeat what seems to be the fundamental reaction to creative imagination in art; they accept the invitation to an experience of the mind in which a specific and particularly intensive kind of intrapsychic communication is temporarily established, in which controlled regression becomes pleasurable since the experience stands under the firm and unabated control of the ego, which has reasserted its functions: it has become creative, or re-creative.

This outline of some of the problems which occur in creative communication cannot be terminated without, however, a brief mention of two of the sources of insight which have proven particularly valuable. One large field of study which has attracted the attention of many investigators concerns the specific function of creative processes in the therapeutic situation; the creative communication is then limited to the creator and the therapist. Story, poem, or picture facilitates the "coming to consciousness"; the creative experience becomes part of the therapeutic procedure. Whatever the limitations of this technique, even its disadvantages, it has proved, with certain individuals, to be of considerable value. If we try to generalize the conditions under which this is the case, we may say that when free association itself is too threatening, when it might lead to a regressive rush which can no longer be controlled, channelized into production, and shaped by the ego, the onslaught of the repressed can still be organized.

This experience has sharpened our eyes to similar processes outside of treatment situations, in which psychological balance is being re-established by creative activity. When in the course of a particularly intensive conflict narcissistic regression threatens the creative act, an attempt to communicate with others and to establish contact may act as a catalyst. The very intensity of conflict may lend particular impact to the work thus created. This is true of some of the productions of later psychotics produced during the prepsychotic phase of their illness. A normal counterpart to the extraordinary richness and sometimes deceptive fascination of their productions may be found in the expressive ventures of some adolescents who solve the age-specific intensification of their conflicts by sudden and frequently transitory spurts of creative activity.

The second area of clinical experience in which the study of creative communication has become particularly fruitful concerns the artistic productions of the insane; here the variety of meanings which the process of creation gains for the individual becomes apparent; words are not signs but acts, pictures tend to become verdicts, and creation may mean "making" in a literal and magical sense. In extreme cases the artist identifies

39

himself with God, the creator; he destroys and restores, rules and organizes in creating. The delusion of the psychotic artist has its counterpart in the unconscious fantasy of many creative individuals and determines some of the complex attitudes of the artist toward his work—foremost among these, the striving for perfection and the feeling of responsibility in exercising his power as creator. What appears as diffusion of instinctual drives, as magic destruction and reparation in the work of the psychotic, plays its part in many creative processes, but the regression to magical procedure is only partial and temporary. This difference becomes clearest when we realize that the product of the psychotic is created as an act to influence the course of events, while the work of the non-psychotic plays upon an audience from which it aims to elicit responses.

The value of the study of psychotic art for a deepening of our understanding of creative processes in general should not lead us to underestimate differences, a tendency particularly significant in the contemporary scene. The interest of certain artists and of sections of the public in productions of the psychotic has suggested to some a comparison between modern and "psychotic" art, a comparison which points to similarities as evidence of disintegration in our civilization, or of "cultural psychosis." I feel unable to share in, or even to discuss in detail, speculations leading in this direction and find it more useful to refer to what has been briefly suggested before. The fact that productions by psychotic creators have gained aesthetic significance for part of the contemporary public is, I believe, due to the fact that their extreme and often badly integrated ambiguity is experienced as a challenge. "Psychotic art" serves as a screen for a generation to which the exercise of projective power has become to some extent pleasurable in itself. We have spoken of the influence of psychoanalysis on the artists. We have now to add that such influence naturally includes the reaction of the public. The preference for forms which stimulate projection, which enhance the creative activity of the public is not unique in history. Although it seems that it has never been as consistently pursued as during the last decades, it has occurred with varying intensity during various historical periods. Psychoanalysis can only point to the existence of a psychic mechanism, which manifests itself as a partial shift of roles in creative communication. The importance of this shift during various historical periods may be established in studies by experts in cultural change to whom psychoanalysis may have here suggested a new perspective.

The three problem areas which have been reviewed represent only a selection of what psychoanalysis has contributed to the study of creative imagination. Let me now for a moment speak not of what was achieved but of that which we would most like to know; not of results but of questions. All that concerns the typical predispositions of the masters of creative imagination, if such typical predispositions exist, all that concerns the ontogenetic approach to the creator, remains in darkness.

Who are those best equipped for creative work, those whose creative imagination functions with greatest ease and most appropriately? Needless to say that no answer can be offered; we have not been able to solve a problem which during the ages has puzzled all and has evaded even speculative approaches; and we remember Freud's modesty when dealing with it.

When as psychoanalysts we study the artist's personality we are subject to the limitations imposed by the therapeutic situation. Hence most of the statements of psychoanalysts seem to focus on relevant but not on specific factors. There is the impression that in the early history of creative individuals traumatization may play an unusually great part; there is some evidence that there are definite peculiarities in the function of certain defense mechanisms—a problem to which Freud

41

referred when he spoke of "the flexibility of repression" in the artist, which he shares with many severely impaired individuals. With some of them the creative individual is said to share the proclivity to a passive attitude manifest in the high incidence of homosexuality. But again it is the difference which seems most suggestive; the passive abandonment is the matrix of the artist's inspirational experience. Let us at this point turn to speculation: the biological nature of man, one might say, accounts for the fact that on the verge of his greatest and supremely active effort, in creation, his experience tends to be mixed with passive elements; he receives from outside what he is to elicit, he incorporates before he produces and experiences even his own thought as reaching him benevolently tendered from an outside agent.

The quest for the specific confronts us with insight into the limitations of our knowledge. All that we can attempt is to point to certain trends in current research which seem to lead in a definite direction.

When we speak of talent and gift we assume the interaction of inborn endowment and environmental influences. For some decades the first area had been neglected; during the last few years it has resumed some of its importance and gradually more and more investigators in various fields turn in this direction. The psychoanalyst expects most from attempts to study the endowment of the human infant in his earliest stages, to watch how it is molded by the mother and how the mother responds to what appears to be the specific individuality of the newborn. Only after long and painful study may such observations lead into the area where the development of properties in any sense akin to gift and talent may become observable.

Observation here as elsewhere may well follow the path outlined by the clinical impressions gained in psychoanalysis. Let me illustrate this by some examples: The influence of early traumatic experiences on creative activity, their reflection in the artist's work, has been mentioned. In approaching the study of the child's first forming activities in the development of his fantasy life the reaction to and impact of threatening experiences becomes equally apparent. Imagination tries to cope with threats; fantasy arises in part as a defense against danger. Clinical observation in psychoanalysis has pointed to the role which the interplay of libidinous and destructive impulses plays in the artist's work. Observation of children in their creative activities confirms these impressions. Two-to-four-year-olds studied in their behavior at the easel, playing with paint, building blocks, give us a picture of the dynamics of the creative process, more dramatic and richer in detail than expected. There is the child who tentatively approaches the easel, who gingerly puts down line after line, color neatly next to color; then colors are mixed, movements become more rapid, excitement grows, immediate discharge rules. The child has followed the seduction which brush and colors have exercised. Over the months that temptation is gradually mastered. With order, even meaning may accrue to the painting; the impulses to smear may return at times of pressure, and yet the distinction emerges between a completed work and one which is not completed—whatever completion may mean to the child. The child learns to resist the temptation to destroy what he has just produced, and the functions of expression and communication come to the fore. Such observations are far from the realm of art; they describe what, with a term which has grown somewhat loose, we mean by sublimation. But observations of this kind are part of the empirical study of the development of creative behavior as part and parcel of the development of personality.

In one fundamental respect these directions of research and

the first tentative impressions seem to prove that recent progress in psychoanalytic theory may help to clarify even complex
problems. At the outset I stated that the influence of psychoanalysis upon science and social organization as well as its
unique place in medicine was initiated by the scientific study
of conflict. But human faculties emerge from conflict. The
Peeping Tom becomes painter or scientist; children who wildly
and excitedly brush colors on paper may develop highly differentiated skills; their painting activity may successfully
emerge from conflict and may develop into a special aptitude.
Such detachment of activity from conflict, its fundamental
autonomy, is facilitated by certain types of endowment, facilitated further by an infinite range of possible life experiences
and their interaction.

If we look from the battle for creation in the child back
to the clinical data which psychoanalytic investigation reveals,
i.e., to the battle of creation observable in some analytic
patients, a certain affinity becomes apparent. It seems that in
every process of creation the gradual emergence from conflict
plays its part. It may start out in serving a fantasy of the
individual, in meeting an individual's needs, but to the extent
that it emerges from conflict, certain properties may be
acquired which are akin to, and some of them identical with,
gift or skill. We mentioned that themes may be generalized,
the emotive potential may grow, and the process of creative
communication may be initiated. All that is not only the result
of conflict; it is at least in part due to the integrative, and in
this instance autonomous, powers of the ego. And thus creative
imagination may lead to concrete achievements; some of them
art, others devoted mainly and solely to problem solving, to
inventiveness in science, or simply to the enrichment of the
individual's existence. At this point the problem leads back to
the broad stream of our work; for next to therapy stands not
only, as was said, the problem of prevention, but also that

of turning from the infinite variety of the mentally ill to the equally infinite and less explored variety of the healthy. The study of conflict embraces both the well and the sick, it is part of human life, and no basic science of psychopathology can avoid being at the same time basic in the psychology of normal behavior.

1953

☐ AESTHETICS

AND PSYCHOLOGY

OF THE ARTIST

Hanns Sachs

Starting from the fantasies of the individual, psychoanalytic research soon began to investigate the way to the fantasies of mankind.

The first steps on this path were made by Otto Rank, far ahead of all others, with *Der Künstler*. In this book, the turning to the general and historical is not anticipated merely in vague hints, but built up in methodical form a long time before the material of race psychology was used as a new basis.

To deduce a piece of fundamental psychology of the artist from one single, though distinguished, example is the problem Freud solved with his book on Leonardo da Vinci. The second edition is enriched by two findings which fully confirm Freud's hypotheses. One of them, a "mistake," or indeed a number of them, in Leonardo's attempt to represent the sexual act schematically, has been discovered and described by Dr. Reitler; the other, a "cryptographic" presentation of the vulture on the picture of "Saint Anna," is from Pfister.

In a short essay on the poet Dauthendey, Hitschmann demonstrates his father-fixation not only as being important for his poetical production, but as the origin of a phenomenon regarded by the poet as "telepathic." Hitschmann has dealt more fully with Gottfried Keller and drawn an excellent picture of unconscious psychical activity by comparing the poet's typical motives with his behavior toward mother and sister both in social life and in his work. The most important results are as follows: pleasure in looking directed mainly to the female breasts and its repression which allowed the great depicter of human character to paint only landscapes; the motive of "half family," son and mother, daughter and father, living together as a reminiscence of his childhood days after his father's early death, a period the boy longed to return to when a stepfather arrived who lived unhappily with the mother; the inhibited aggression toward women and its inversion into masochistic fantasies, and finally, the mother image in the poet's most interesting female figure, Judith.

A valuable and interesting investigation into the poet's motives is given by Reik on Schnitzler. The main stress is laid upon the delicate psychological understanding of the poet, which arose from his familiarity with his own unconscious, though a familiarity of a quite special kind. Of special interest are the analyses of the dreams which Schnitzler uses in important passages of his works. Interpretation shows that the construction of these dreams is quite on a line with the rules laid down by Freud.

That the connection between unconscious and poetical production is not an achievement of our generation is proved by Dr. Alice Sperber, who deals with Dante's unconscious life. Of special interest is the view, based on rich and well-selected material, that Vergil and Beatrice represent the return of the parent's *imagines*.

The present writer has pointed out that the childhood memories of Spitteler show a striking agreement with the doctrines of Freud as regards the nature and importance of events in childhood.

The investigation of Lorenz into the *Geschichte des Berg-manns von Falun* shows in a very clear way how a simple anecdote, provided it contains the germ, keeps producing ever new fantasies. As the poetical modifications advance, the unconscious complex by which the fantasy was awakened reveals itself more and more distinctly till it appears in clear words (Hofmannsthal's "last modification") just as dreams of one night vary the same unconscious thought with progressive clearness.

In another essay the same author shows that the Oedipus tragedy ends quite in accordance with the fulfillment of the unconscious expectation—union with the mother earth. While the two above-mentioned essays only touched on the complex "the mother's womb," MacCurdy shows a novel by Lytton which is completely built on it and throws light, by analysis of that novel in the most interesting way, on the connections between these fantasies and the "omnipotence of thought."

The idea running through all those essays, namely the return to primitive thinking by apparently original imagination, cannot easily be proved by a better example than the one found by Protze in which a tree exercises all the functions that "savages" are wont to attribute to their totem. Rank's book, *The Doppelgänger*, is based on the same idea, but carried out in a quite different, more complete, and systematic way. Starting from a topic still very attractive to modern literature the author goes back to the superstitions relating to mirrors and shadows, from there to primitive beliefs in the soul connected with mirror images and shadows, and finds at last the psychological resolution of these phenomena in narcissism and in the repression conflict against its radiation leading to object-love. The book contains much material in literary history and

49

ethnology and should become a model through its technical method, never satisfied with mere aphorisms, but always trying to link up connections.

A number of essays deal with two great tragic figures of Shakespeare, Hamlet and Macbeth. The Hamlet essays by Juliusburger and Rank naturally start from the points in Freud's *Interpretation of Dreams,* and what Rank says about the "play" and its position in the drama might be considered as the finishing touch of Freud's conception. More interest still is paid to the figure of Lady Macbeth, previously only touched on in a footnote in the *Interpretation of Dreams.* The most extensive of these essays is one by Jekels; this yields several valuable results, of which only two will be mentioned: the conception of the distribution between two persons of the originally unitary guilt feeling before and after the deed, and the discovery of "Shakespeare's self-reproach," one who left wife and children and lost his only son, as the quintessence of the character of Macduff. Freud starts from this discovery and shows how the problem of childlessness runs below the surface through the whole tragedy. In this complex the old nature myth personified in the tragedy, namely the victory of spring coming with green branches over the sterile winter, coincides with the actual event, the accession of James I as successor of the sterile Elizabeth, who had beheaded his mother. Freud makes it probable also that the night-wandering of Lady Macbeth goes back directly to the last weeks spent in sleepless disquietude of the virgin queen, who once called herself in grief a fruitless stock. Another of Shakespeare's characters is investigated by Freud in the same essay: Richard III, whose personality is developed from the first monologue with logical clearness. He belongs to those who believe they have a special claim on the fulfillment of their wishes because they have been ill-treated by nature at their birth. Among the type of those who break down in success Freud classifies a tragic figure, studied already by Rank: Rebecca West from Ibsen's *Ros-mersholm*. He shows that Rebecca's actual position is the result of a typical fantasy in which the housekeeper sets herself in the place of the housewife. The unconscious root of this fantasy is, of course, to replace the mother in her relation to the father. When Rebecca learns that this tabooed fantasy is reality for her, that is to say, that she is the mistress of her own father, then she becomes unable to enjoy her success and chooses, instead of marriage to Rosmer, death with him.

The essay of Furtmüller's on Schnitzler's *Das weite Land* places striving for power in the center of action, following the author's prepossession for Adler's conception. A more unfortunate choice than one of Schnitzler's plays to prove such theses could not be made. Schnitzler's later works, especially *Casanovas Heimkehr*, have reduced *ad absurdum* the idea of replacing the erotic problem by an egoistic one.

In this writer's essays the attempt is made to trace back to the psychical situation of the author the production of two of the standard works in literature. In both cases the problem of inhibition in production is hinted at, a temporary one in Schiller's case and a final one in Shakespeare's. In reference to Thomas Mann the agreement with dream symbolism and the understanding shown for the basis of homosexuality is pointed out.

An essay on the Moses of Michelangelo by an anonymous author takes quite a distinctive position. Neither the starting point nor the result belong to the domain of psychoanalysis, but the method of the investigation—guessing the past from the present, important things from slight indications, and the psychical tendencies of the artist—answers fully to the psychoanalytic method in its best and purest form.

Among the aesthetic investigations directed to general problems most are based on something or other pointed out by Freud. Their merit lies in the clear presentation and the work-

51

ing out of details. The parallel drawn by Kaplan between tragic hero and criminal is well-proved psychoanalytically and shows this author's right feeling for the new tendency in defining our problems. Through Freud's *Totem and Taboo* we know that it is more than an analogy, that it is the recurrence of the same original crime in different shapes.

A quite uncommon investigation, which in many passages comes very near psychoanalysis, is that by Sperber and Spitzer on the connection between motives and words. Spitzer proves how in the writings of the grotesque poet Christian Morgenstern the word comes before the thing, indeed how the word stimulates the imagination to creativeness. "To treat words like things" is according to Freud a typical quality of childhood, and Morgenstern's humor is based to a great extent on this quality. Still nearer psychoanalysis comes Sperber's shrewd and charming essay on Gustav Meyrink. He shows how certain complexes occur again in this poet's writings, sometimes as a colloquial turn, sometimes as an original comparison. When Sperber speaks about the influence of certain complexes on style and language, the idea arises of completing his investigation in the opposite direction, i.e., instead of working from the complexes to language, from within to without, to feel our way from without to within, to the deep unconscious sources of affect. The "complex of bodily inhibitions" found by Sperber in Meyrink, especially paralysis, blindness, and suffocation, arouses many thoughts in the analytical expert.

Studies on music give us hope that even this difficult subject, lying furthest from psychoanalytic exploration, will perhaps be understood by our methods. The possibility of awakening certain affects by sounds might be explained by their effect on the unconscious. Hitschmann deals, in connection with a dream, with the psychic life of the young Schubert and his family conflict.

The investigation of "uncanniness" by Freud points out

that *heimlich* is one of the ambivalent words which unite two opposite meanings: "homely" and "hidden, dangerous." Of special interest are the explanations of the conditions under which the reawakening of the "omnipotence of thought" causes a disagreeable feeling, this being the reason they are characterized as "uncanny." The complete revival of the childish omnipotence, as in fairy tales, does not give us this impression, but if poetry places itself into reality, then a sudden going back to omnipotence has an uncanny effect, quite the same as in reality itself, when a chance makes us believe for a moment in this possibility. The other root of uncanniness lies in the return of the repressed; the castration complex plays here an important part.

1921

INFANTILE ANXIETY SITUATIONS REFLECTED IN A WORK OF ART AND IN THE CREATIVE IMPULSE

Melanie Klein

My first subject is the highly interesting psychological material underlying an opera of Ravel's. My account of its content is taken almost word for word from a review by Eduard Jakob in the *Berliner Tageblatt*.

A child six years old is sitting with his homework before him, but he is not doing any work. He bites his penholder and displays that final stage of laziness in which *ennui* has passed into *cafard*. "Don't want to do the stupid lessons," he cries in a sweet soprano. "Want to go for a walk in the park! I'd like best of all to eat up all the cake in the world, or pull the cat's tail or pull out all the parrot's feathers! I'd like to scold everyone! Most of all I'd like to put Mama in the corner!" The door now opens. Everything on the stage is shown very large—in order to emphasize the smallness of the child—so all that we see of his mother is a skirt, an apron, and

55

a hand. A finger points and a voice asks affectionately whether the child has done his work. He shuffles rebelliously on his chair and puts out his tongue at his mother. She goes away. All that we hear is the rustle of her skirts and the words: "You shall have dry bread and no sugar in your tea!" The child flies into a rage. He jumps up, drums on the door, sweeps the teapot and cup from the table, so that they are broken into a thousand pieces. He climbs on the window seat, opens the cage, and tries to stab the squirrel with his pen. The squirrel escapes through the open window. The child jumps down from the window and seizes the cat. He yells and swings the tongs, pokes the fire furiously in the open grate, and with his hands and feet hurls the kettle into the room. A cloud of ashes and steam escapes. He swings the tongs like a sword and begins to tear the wallpaper. Then he opens the case of the grandfather clock and snatches out the copper pendulum. He pours the ink over the table. Exercise-books and other books fly through the air. Hurrah! . . .

The things he has maltreated come to life. An armchair refuses to let him sit in it or have the cushions to sleep on. Table, chair, bench, and sofa suddenly lift up their arms and cry: "Away with the dirty little creature!" The clock has a dreadful stomach ache and begins to strike the hours like mad. The teapot leans over the cup, and they begin to talk Chinese. Everything undergoes a terrifying change. The child falls back against the wall and shudders with fear and desolation. The stove spits out a shower of sparks at him. He hides behind the furniture. The shreds of the torn wallpaper begin to sway and stand up, showing shepherdesses and sheep. The shepherd's pipe sounds a heartbreaking lament; the rent in the paper, which separates Corydon from his Amaryllis, has become a rent in the fabric of the world! But the doleful tale dies away. From under the cover of a book, as though out of a dog's kennel, there emerges a little old man. His clothes are made of numbers, and his hat is like a pi. He holds a ruler and clatters about with little dancing steps. He is the spirit of mathematics, and begins to put the child through an examination: millimeter, centimeter, barometer, trillion—eight and eight are forty. Three times nine is twice six. The child falls down in a faint!

Half suffocated he takes refuge in the park round the house. But there again the air is full of terror, insects, frogs (lamenting in muted thirds), a wounded tree trunk, which oozes resin in long-drawn-out bass notes; dragonflies and oleander-flies all attack the newcomer. Owls, cats, and squirrels come along in hosts. The dispute as to who is to bite the child becomes a hand-to-hand fight. A squirrel which has been bitten falls to the ground, screaming beside him. He instinctively takes off his scarf and binds up the little creature's paw. There is great amazement among the animals, who gather together hesitatingly in the background. The child has whispered: "Mama!" He is restored to the human world of helping, "being good." "That's a good child, a very well-behaved child," sing the animals very seriously in a soft march—the finale of the piece—as they leave the stage. Some of them cannot refrain from themselves calling out "Mama."

I will now examine more closely the details in which the child's pleasure in destruction expresses itself. They seem to me to recall the early infantile situation which I have described as being of fundamental importance both for neurosis in boys and for their normal development. I refer to the attack on the mother's body and on the father's penis in it. The squirrel in the cage and the pendulum wrenched out of the clock are plain symbols of the penis in the mother's body. The fact that it is the *father's* penis and that it is in the act of coitus with the mother is indicated by the rent in the wallpaper "which separates Corydon from his Amaryllis," of which it has been said that to the boy it has become "a rent in the

57

fabric of the world." Now what weapons does the child employ in this attack on his united parents? The ink poured over the table, the emptied kettle, from which a cloud of ashes and steam escapes, represent the weapon which very little children have at their disposal: namely the device of soiling with excrement.

Smashing things, tearing them up, using the tongs as a sword—these represent the other weapons of the child's primary sadism: teeth, nails, muscles and so on.

On other occasions I have described this early phase of development, the content of which is the attack made on the mother's body with all the weapons that the child's sadism has at its disposal. Now, however, I can add to this earlier statement and say more exactly where this phase is to be inserted in the scheme of sexual development proposed by Abraham. My result leads me to conclude that the phase in which sadism is at its zenith in all the fields whence it derives precedes the earlier anal stage and acquires a special significance from the fact that it is also the stage of development at which the Oedipus tendencies first appear. That is to say, that the Oedipus conflict begins under the complete dominance of sadism. My supposition that the formation of the superego follows closely on the beginning of the Oedipus tendencies, and that, therefore, the ego falls under the sway of the superego even at this early period, explains, I think, why this sway is so tremendously powerful. For, when the objects are introjected, the attack launched upon them with all the weapons of sadism rouses the subject's dread of an analogous attack upon himself from the external and the internalized objects. I wanted to recall these concepts of mine because I can make a bridge from them to a concept of Freud: one of the most important of the conclusions which he has put before us in *Inhibition, Symptoms, and Anxiety*, namely the hypothesis of an early infantile situation of anxiety or danger. I think that this places analytic work on a yet more exactly defined and firmer basis than heretofore, and thus gives our methods an even plainer direction. But in my view it also makes a fresh demand upon analysis. Freud's hypothesis is that there is an infantile danger situation which undergoes modification in the course of development, and which is the source of the influence exercised by a series of anxiety situations. Now the new demand upon the analyst is this—that analysis should fully uncover these anxiety situations right back to that which lies deepest of all. This demand for a complete analysis is allied to that which Freud suggests as a new demand at the conclusion of his "History of an Infantile Neurosis," where he says that a complete analysis must reveal the primal scene. This latter requirement can have its full effect only in conjunction with that which I have just put forward. If the analyst succeeds in the task of discovering the infantile danger situations, working at their resolution, and elucidating in each individual case the relations between the anxiety situations and the neurosis on the one hand and the ego development on the other—then, I think, he will achieve more completely the main aim of psychoanalytic therapy: removal of the neuroses. It seems to me, therefore, that everything that can contribute to the elucidation and exact description of the infantile danger situations is of great value, not only from the theoretical, but also from the therapeutic point of view.

Freud assumes that the infantile danger situation can be reduced ultimately to the loss of the beloved (longed for) person. In girls, he thinks, the loss of the object is the danger situation which operates most powerfully; in boys it is castration. My work has proved to me that both these danger situations are a modification of yet earlier ones. I have found that in boys the dread of castration by the father is connected with a very special situation which, I think, proves to be the earliest anxiety situation of all. As I pointed out, the attack on the mother's body, which is timed psychologically at the zenith of the sadistic phase, implies also the struggle with the father's penis in the mother. A special intensity is imparted to this danger situation by the fact that a union of the two parents is in question. According to the early sadistic superego, which has already been set up, these united parents are extremely cruel and much dreaded assailants. Thus the anxiety situation relating to castration by the father is a modification, in the course of development, of the earliest anxiety situation as I have described it.

Now I think that the anxiety engendered in this situation is plainly represented in the libretto of the opera which was the starting point of my paper. In discussing the libretto, I have already dealt in some detail with the one phase—that of the sadistic attack. Let us now consider what happens after the child has given rein to his lust for destruction.

At the beginning of his review the writer mentions that all the things on the stage are made very large, in order to emphasize the smallness of the child. But the child's anxiety makes things and people seem gigantic to him—far beyond the actual difference in size. Moreover, we see what we discover in the analysis of every child: that things represent human beings and therefore are objects of anxiety. The writer of the review writes as follows: "The maltreated things begin to live." The armchair, the cushion, table, chair, etc., attack the child, refuse to serve him, banish him outside. We find that things to sit and lie upon, as well as beds, occur regularly in children's analyses as symbols for the protecting and loving mother. The strips of the torn wallpaper represent the injured interior of the mother's body, while the little old number-man who comes out of the book cover is the father (represented by his penis), now in the character of judge and about to call the child, who faints with anxiety, to his reckoning for the damage he has done and the theft he had committed in the mother's body. When the boy flees into the world of nature, we see how it takes on the role of the mother whom he has assaulted. The hostile animals represent a multiplication of the father, whom he has also attacked, together with the children assumed to be in the mother. We see the incidents which took place inside the room now reproduced on a bigger scale in a wider space and in larger numbers. The world, transformed into the mother's body, is in hostile array against the child and persecutes him.

In ontogenetic development sadism is overcome when the subject advances to the genital level. The more powerfully this phase sets in, the more capable does the child become of object-love, and the more able is he to conquer his sadism by means of pity and sympathy. This step in development is also shown in the libretto of Ravel's opera; when the boy feels pity for the wounded squirrel and comes to its aid, the hostile world changes into a friendly one. The child has learned to love and believes in love. The animals conclude: "That is a good child— a very well-behaved child." The profound psychological insight of Colette—the author of the libretto of the opera—is shown in the way in which the conversion in the child's attitude takes place. As he cares for the wounded squirrel, he whispers: "Mama." The animals around him repeat this word. It is this redeeming word which has given the opera its title: *Das Zauberwort* ("The Magic Word"). But we also learn from the text the factor which has ministered to the child's sadism. He says: "I want to go for a walk in the park! I want most of all to eat up all the cakes in the world!" But his mother threatens to give him tea without sugar and dry bread. The oral frustration which turns the indulgent "good mother" into the "bad mother" stimulates his sadism.

I think we can now understand why the child, instead of peaceably doing his homework, has become involved in such an unpleasant situation. It had to be so, for he was driven to

61

it by the pressure of the old anxiety situation which he had never mastered. His anxiety enhances the repetition compulsion, and his need for punishment ministers to the compulsion (now grown very strong) to secure for himself actual punishment in order that the anxiety may be allayed by a chastisement less severe than that which the anxiety situation causes him to anticipate. We are quite familiar with the fact that children are naughty because they wish to be punished, but it seems of the greatest importance to find out what part anxiety plays in this craving for punishment and what is the ideational content at the bottom of this urgent anxiety.

I will now illustrate from another literary example the anxiety which I have found connected with the earliest danger situation in a girl's development.

In an article entitled "The Empty Space," Karin Michaelis gives an account of the development of her friend, the painter Ruth Kjär. Ruth Kjär possessed remarkable artistic feeling, which she employed especially in the arrangement of her house, but she had no pronounced creative talent. Beautiful, rich, and independent, she spent a great part of her life traveling, and was constantly leaving her house, upon which she had expended so much care and taste. She was subject at times to fits of deep depression, which Karin Michaelis describes as follows: "There was only one dark spot in her life. In the midst of the happiness which was natural to her, and seemed so untroubled, she would suddenly be plunged into the deepest melancholy. A melancholy that was suicidal. If she tried to account for this, she would say something to this effect: 'There is an empty space in me, which I can never fill!' "

The time came when Ruth Kjär married, and she seemed perfectly happy. But after a short time the fits of melancholy recurred. In Karin Michaelis' words: "The accursed empty space was once more empty." I will let the writer speak for herself: "Have I already told you that her home was a gallery

62

of modern art? Her husband's brother was one of the greatest painters in the country, and his best pictures decorated the walls of the room. But before Christmas this brother-in-law took away one picture, which he had only lent to her. The picture was sold. This left an empty space on the wall, which in some inexplicable way seemed to coincide with the empty space within her. She sank into a state of the most profound sadness. The blank space on the wall caused her to forget her beautiful home, her happiness, her friends, everything. Of course, a new picture could be got, and would be got, but it took time; one had to look about to find just the right one.

"The empty space grinned hideously down at her.

"The husband and wife were sitting opposite one another at the breakfast table. Ruth's eyes were clouded with hopeless despair. Suddenly, however, her face was transfigured with a smile: 'I'll tell you what! I think I will try to daub a little on the wall myself, until we get a new picture!' 'Do, my darling,' said her husband. It was quite certain that whatever daub she made would not be too monstrously ugly.

"He had hardly left the room when, in a perfect fever, she had rung up the color-shop to order the paints which her brother-in-law generally used, brushes, palette, and all the rest of the 'gear' to be sent up at once. She herself had not the remotest idea of how to begin. She had never squeezed paint out of a tube, laid the ground-color on a canvas, or mixed colors on a palette. While the things were coming, she stood before the empty wall with a piece of black chalk in her hand and made strokes at random as they came into her head. Should she have the car and rush wildly to her brother-in-law to ask how one paints? No, she would rather die!

"Toward evening her husband returned, and she ran to meet him with a hectic brilliance in her eyes. She was not going to be ill, was she? She drew him with her, saying: 'Come, you will see!' And he saw. He could not take his eyes from

63

the sight; could not take it in, did not believe it, *could* not believe it. Ruth threw herself on a sofa in a state of deadly exhaustion: 'Do you think it at all possible?'

"The same evening they sent for the brother-in-law. Ruth palpitated with anxiety as to the verdict of the connoisseur. But the artist exclaimed immediately: 'You don't imagine you can persuade me that you painted that! What a damned lie! This picture was painted by an old and experienced artist. Who the devil is he? I don't know him!'

"Ruth could not convince him. He thought they were making game of him. And when he went, his parting words were: 'If *you* painted that, *I* will go and conduct a Beethoven symphony in the Chapel Royal tomorrow, though I don't know a note of music!'

"That night Ruth could not sleep much. The picture on the wall had been painted, that was certain—it was not a dream. But how had it happened? And what next?

"She was on fire, devoured by ardor within. She must prove to herself that the divine sensation, the unspeakable sense of happiness that she had felt could be repeated."

Karin Michaelis then adds that after this first attempt, Ruth Kjär painted several masterly pictures, and had them exhibited to the critics and the public.

Karin Michaelis anticipates one part of my interpretation of the anxiety relating to the empty space on the wall when she says: "On the wall there was an empty space, which in some inexplicable way seemed to coincide with the empty space within her." Now, what is the meaning of this empty space within Ruth, or rather, to put it more exactly, of the feeling that there was something lacking in her body?

Here there has come into consciousness one of the ideas connected with that anxiety which I have described as the most profound anxiety experienced by girls. It is the equivalent of castration anxiety in boys. The little girl has a sadistic desire, originating in the early stages of the Oedipus conflict, to rob the mother's body of its contents, namely, the father's penis, feces, children, and to destroy the mother herself. This desire gives rise to anxiety lest the mother should in her turn rob the little girl herself of the contents of her body (especially of children) and lest her body should be destroyed or mutilated. In my view, this anxiety, which I have found in the analyses of girls and women to be the deepest anxiety of all, represents the little girl's earliest danger situation. I have come to see that the dread of being alone, of the loss of love and loss of the love object, which Freud holds to be the basic infantile danger situation in girls, is a modification of the anxiety situation I have just described. When the little girl who fears the mother's assault upon her body cannot *see* her mother, this intensifies the anxiety. The presence of the real, loving mother diminishes the dread of the terrifying mother, whose introjected image is in the child's mind. At a later stage of development the content of the dread changes from that of an attacking mother to the dread that the real, loving mother may be lost and that the girl will be left solitary and forsaken.

In seeking the explanation of these ideas, it is instructive to consider what sort of pictures Ruth Kjär painted since her first attempt, when she filled the empty space on the wall with the life-sized figure of a naked negress. Apart from one picture of flowers, she confined herself to portraits. She twice painted her younger sister, who came to stay with her and sat for her, and, further, the portrait of an old woman and one of her mother. The two last are described by Karin Michaelis as follows: "And now Ruth cannot stop. The next picture represents an old woman, being the mark of years and disillusionments. Her skin is wrinkled, her hair faded, her gentle, tired eyes are troubled. She gazes before her with the disconsolate resignation of old age, with a look that seems to say: 'Do not trouble about me any more. My time is so nearly at an end!'

"This is not the impression we receive from Ruth's latest

work—the portrait of her Irish-Canadian mother. This lady has a long time before her before she must put her lips to the cup of renunciation. Slim, imperious, challenging, she stands there with a moonlight-colored shawl draped over her shoulders; she has the effect of a magnificent woman of primitive times, who could any day engage in combat with the children of the desert with her naked hands. What a chin! What force there is in the haughty gaze!

"The blank space has been filled."

It is obvious that the desire to make reparation, to make good the injury psychologically done to the mother and also to restore herself was at the bottom of the compelling urge to paint these portraits of her relatives. That of the old woman, on the threshold of death, seems to be the expression of the primary, sadistic desire to destroy. The daughter's wish to destroy her mother, to see her old, worn out, marred, is the cause of the need to represent her in full possession of her strength and beauty. By so doing the daughter can allay her own anxiety and can endeavor to restore her mother and make her new through the portrait. In the analyses of children, when the representation of destructive wishes is succeeded by an expression of reactive tendencies, we constantly find that drawing and painting are used as means to restore people. The case of Ruth Kjär shows plainly that this anxiety of the little girl is of greatest importance in the ego development of women, and is one of the incentives to achievement. But, on the other hand, this anxiety may be the cause of serious illness and many inhibitions. As with the boy's castration dread, the effect of his anxiety on the ego development depends on the maintenance of a certain optimum and a satisfactory interplay between the separate factors.

1929

▣ LIFE AND CREATION

Otto Rank

Before we trace the rise and significance of "artist's art," if one may so call it, as it grows out of the primitive art ideologies, it is perhaps desirable to characterize more clearly its essential precondition: namely, the creative personality itself. In spite of all "unconsciousness" in artistic production (a point to which we shall return later), there can be no doubt that the modern individualist type of artist is characterized by a higher degree of consciousness than his earlier prototype: the consciousness not only of his creative work and his artist's mission, but also of his own personality and its productiveness. If, as it should seem, the instinctive will-to-art (Riegl), which creates abstract forms, has in this last stage of artistic development become a conscious will-to-art in the artist, yet the actual process which leads a man to become an artist is usually one of which the individual is not conscious. In other words, the act which we have described as the artist's self-appointment as such is in itself a spontaneous expression of the creative impulse, of which the first manifestation is simply the forming of the personality itself. Needless to say, this purely internal process does not suffice to make an artist, let alone a genius, for, as Lange-Eichbaum has said, only the community, one's contemporaries, or posterity can do that. Yet the self-labeling and self-training of an artist is the indispensable basis of all creative work, and without it general recognition could never arise. The artist's lifelong work on his own productive personality appears to run through definite phases, and his art develops in proportion to the success of these phases. In the case of great artists the process is reflected in the fact that they had either a principal or a favorite work, at which they labored all their lives (Goethe's *Faust*, Rodin's *Porte d'enfer*, Michelangelo's Tomb of Julius, and so on), or a favorite theme, which they never relinquished and which came to be a distinct representation of themselves (as, for example, Rembrandt's self-portraits).

On the other hand, this process of the artist's self-forming and self-training is closely bound up with his life and his experiences. In studying this fundamental problem of the relation between living and creating in an artist, we are therefore again aware of the reciprocal influence of these two spheres. All the psychography and pathography (with its primary concern to explain the one through the other) must remain unsatisfactory as long as the creative impulse, which finds expression equally in experience and in productiveness, is not recognized as the basis of both. For, as I already showed in my essay on Schiller (written in 1905), creativeness lies equally at the root of artistic production and of life experience. That is to say, lived experience can only be understood as the expression of volitional creative impulse, and in this the two spheres of artistic production and actual experience meet and overlap. Then, too, the creative impulse itself is manifested first and chiefly in the personality, which, being thus perpetually made over, produces art work and experience in the same way. To draw the distinction quite drastically between this new standpoint and earlier ones, one might put it that the artist does not create from his own experience (as Goethe, for instance, so definitely appears to do), but almost in spite of it. For the creative impulse in the artist, springing from the tendency to immortalize himself, is so powerful that he is always seeking to protect himself against the transient experience, which eats up his ego. The artist takes refuge, with all *his own* experience, only from the life of *actuality*, which for him spells mortality and decay, whereas the experience to which he has given shape imposes itself on him as a creation, which he in fact seeks to turn into a work. And although the whole artist psychology may seem to be centered on the "experience," this itself can be explained only through the creative impulse— which attempts to turn ephemeral life into personal immortality. In creation the artist tries to immortalize his mortal life. He desires to transform death into life, as it were, though actually he transforms life into death. For not only does the created work not go on living; it is, in a sense, dead—both as regards the material, which renders it almost inorganic, and also spiritually and psychologically, in that it no longer has any significance for its creator, once he has produced it. He therefore again takes refuge in life, and again forms experiences, which for their part represent only mortality—and it is precisely because they are mortal that he wishes to immortalize them in his work.

The first step toward understanding this mutual relation between life and work in the artist is to gain a clear idea of the psychological significance of the two phenomena. This is only possible, however, on the basis of a constructive psychology of personality, reaching beyond the psychoanalytical conception, which is a therapeutic ideology resting on the biological sex impulse. We have come to see that another factor must be reckoned with besides the original biological duality of impulse and inhibition in man; this is the psychological factor par excellence, the individual will, which manifests itself both negatively as a controlling element, and positively as the urge to create. This creator impulse is not, therefore, sexuality, as

Freud assumed, but expresses the antisexual tendency in human beings, which we may describe as the deliberate control of the impulsive life. To put it more precisely, I see the creator impulse as the life impulse made to serve the individual will. When psychoanalysis speaks of a sublimated sexual impulse in creative art, meaning thereby the impulse diverted from its purely biological function and directed toward higher ends, the question as to what diverted and what directed is just being dismissed with an allusion to repression. But repression is a negative factor, which might divert, but never direct. And so the further question remains to be answered: what, originally led to such repression? As we know, the answer to this question was outward deprivation; but that again suggests a merely negative check, and I, for my part, am of the opinion that (at any rate from a certain definite point of individual development) positively willed control takes the place of negative inhibition, and that it is the masterful use of the sexual impulse in the service of this individual will which produces the sublimation.

But even more important for us than these psychological distinctions is the basic problem of why this inhibition occurs at all, and what the deliberate control of the vital impulse means to the individual. Here again, in opposition to the Freudian conception of an external threat as the cause of the inhibition, I suggest that the internal threatening of the individual through the sexual impulse of the species is at the root of all conflict. Side by side with this self-imposed internal check, which is taken to be what prevents or lessens the development of fear, there stands the will as a positive factor. The various controls which it exercises enable the impulses to work themselves out partially without the individual's falling completely under their influence or having to check them completely by too drastic repression. Thus in the fully developed individual we have to reckon with the triad Impulse-Fear-Will, and it is the dynamic relationship between these factors that determines either the attitude at a given moment or—when equilibrium is established—the type. Unsatisfactory as it may be to express these dynamic processes in terms like "type," it remains the only method of carrying an intelligible idea of them—always assuming that the inevitable simplification in this is not lost sight of. If we compare the neurotic with the productive type, it is evident that the former suffers from an excessive check on his impulsive life, and, according to whether this neurotic checking of the instincts is effected through fear or through will, the picture presented is one of fear-neurosis or compulsion-neurosis. With the productive type the will dominates, and exercises a far-reaching control over (but not check upon) the instincts, which are pressed into service to bring about creatively a social relief of fear. Finally, the instincts appear relatively unchecked in the so-called psychopathic subject, in whom the will affirms the impulse instead of controlling it. In this type—to which the criminal belongs— we have, contrary to appearances, to do with *weak*-willed people, people who are subjected to their instinctive impulses; the neurotic, on the other hand, is generally regarded as the weak-willed type, but wrongly so, for his strong will is exercised upon himself and, indeed, in the main repressively, so it does not show itself.

And here we reach the essential point of difference between the productive type who creates and the thwarted neurotic; what is more, it is also the point from which we get back to our individual artist type. Both are distinguished fundamentally from the average type, who accepts himself as he is, by their tendency to exercise their volition in reshaping themselves. There is, however, this difference: that the neurotic, in this voluntary remaking of his ego, does not get beyond the destructive preliminary work and is therefore unable to detach the whole creative process from his own person and transfer

71

it to an ideological abstraction. The productive artist also begins (as a satisfactory psychological understanding of the "will-to-style" has obliged us to conclude) with that re-creation of himself which results in an ideologically constructed ego; this ego is then in a position to shift the creative will power from his own person to ideological representations of that person and thus to render it objective. It must be admitted that this process is in a measure limited to the individual within himself, and not only in its constructive, but also in its destructive, aspects. This explains why hardly any productive work gets through without morbid crises of a neurotic nature; it also explains why the relation between productivity and illness has so far been unrecognized or misinterpreted, as, for instance, in Lombroso's theory of the insanity of genius. Today this theory appears to us as the precipitate left by the old endeavors to explain genius on rational psychological lines, which treated such features as depart from the normal as pathological. How-ever much the Italian psychiatrist's theory is an exaggeration of the materialism of nineteenth century science, undeniably it had a startling success, and this I attribute to the fact that genius itself, in its endeavor to differentiate itself from the average, has probably dramatized its pathological features also. But the psychologist should beware of deducing from this apparent factor any conclusions as to the production or total personality, without taking into account the feeling of guilt arising from the creative process itself; for this is capable of engendering a feeling of inferiority as a secondary result, even though the primary result may be a conviction of superiority. As I have said elsewhere, the fundamental problem is individual difference, which the ego is inclined to interpret as inferiority unless it can be proved by achievement to be superiority.

Even psychoanalysis in its turn did not succeed in surmount-ing Lombroso's materialist theory of insanity or supplementing his rational explanation by a spiritual one. All it did was to substitute neurosis for insanity (which was at bottom Lombroso's own meaning), thus tending either to identify the artist with the neurotic—this is particularly the case in Sadger's and Stekel's arguments—or to explain the artist on the basis of an inferiority feeling. (Alfred Adler and his school took the latter view.) It is characteristic that during the last few years the psychiatrists (such as Lange-Eichbaum, Kretschmer, Plaut) who have contributed most toward clearing up the position of genius are precisely those who have managed to keep clear of the one-sidedness of these psychoanalytical schools. And if these researches have not made any important contribution to the understanding of the process of creating, psychoanalysis, even in its exaggerations, must at least be credited with having discovered that experience, in so far as it is the antithesis of production, embraces not only the relations of love and friendship, but also those morbid reactions of a psychic and bodily nature which are known as neurotic. A real understanding of these neurotic illnesses could not, however, be satisfactorily obtained as long as we tried to account for them in the Freudian sense by thwarted sexuality. What was wanted in addition was a grasp of the general problem of fear and of the will psychology going therewith which should allow for the exercise of the will, both constructively and destructively, affecting the ego and the work equally. Only through the will-to-self-immortalization, which rises from the fear of life, can we understand the interdependence of production and suffering and the definite influence of this on positive experience. This does not preclude production being a creative development of a neurosis in objective form; and, on the other hand, a neurotic collapse may follow as a reaction after production, owing either to a sort of exhaustion or to a sense of guilt arising from the power of creative masterfulness as something arrogant.

Reverting now from the production process to experience, it does not take long to perceive that experience is the expression of the impulse ego, production of the will ego. The external difficulties in an artist's experience appear, in this sense, but as manifestations of this internal dualism of impulse and will, and in the creative type it is the latter which eventually gains the upper hand. Instinct presses in the direction of experience and, in the limit, to consequent exhaustion—in fact, death—while will drives to creation and thus to immortalization. On the other hand, the productive type also pays toll to life by his work and to death by bodily and spiritual sufferings of a neurotic order; and conversely in many cases the product of a type that is at bottom neurotic may be his sole propitiatory offering to life. It is with reason, therefore, that from the beginning two basic types of artist have been distinguished; these have been called at one time Dionysian and Apollonian, and at another classical and romantic. In terms of our present dynamic treatment, the one approximates to the psychopathic-impulsive type, the other to the compulsion-neurotic volitional type. The one creates more from fullness of powers and sublimation, the other more from exhaustion and compensation. The work of the one is entire in every single expression, that of the other is partial even in its totality, for the one lives itself out, positively, in the work, while the other pays with the work—pays, not to society (for both do that), but to life itself, from which the one strives to win freedom by self-willed creation whereas for the other the thing created is the expression of life itself.

This duality within one and the same type is of outstanding significance in the psychology of the productive type and in the work it produces. For, while in the two classes of neurotics (frustrated by fear and by the will respectively) the form of the neurosis is of minor matter compared with the fact of breaking down the inhibition itself, by the curative process of dynamic equilibration, in the productive type the dynamism itself determines not only the kind but the form of his art. But this highly complicated problem is only mentioned here with

74

a view to discussion later, and we will turn from the two artist
types, which Müller-Freienfels, in his *Psychologie der Kunst*
characterizes as expressive artists and formative artists, back to
the problem of experience which is common to both. This
problem, as was pointed out at the beginning of this chapter,
only becomes intelligible through the conception of immortality. There appears to be a common impulse in all creative
types to replace collective immortality—as it is represented biologically in sexual propagation—by the individual immortality
of deliberate self-perpetuation. This is, however, a relatively
late stage of development in the conception of immortality,
after it has already become individualized—a stage preceded by
attempts to create conceptions of collective immortality, of
which the most important is religion. I have tried in another
connection to show how, within religious development itself, the
idea of the collective soul was gradually transformed into the
idea of the individual god, whose heir the artist later became.
The initial conception of an individual god, subsequently to be
humanized in the genius, had itself been helped on, and perhaps even only rendered possible, by art. But there was an
early stage of artistic development, which was at the same time
the climax of religious development, in which the individual
artist played no part because creative power was still the pre-
rogative of the god.

The individual artist, whose growth from the creative conception of a god has been sketched out, no longer uses the
collective ideology of religion to perpetuate himself, but the
personal religion of genius, which is the precondition of any
productions by the individual artist type. And so we have
primitive art, the expression of a collective ideology, perpetuated by abstraction which has found its religious expression in
the idea of the soul; classical art, based on a social art concept,
perpetuated by idealization, which has found its purest expression in the conception of beauty; and, lastly, modern art, based

75

on the concept of individual genius and perpetuated by con-
cretization, which has found its clearest expression in the personality cult of the artistic individuality itself. Here, then, in
contrast to the primitive stage, it is the artist and not art that
matters, and naturally therefore the experience of the individual
takes on the significance characteristic of the romantic artist
type. Here, obviously, not only do we see the tendency—in
our view the basic tendency—of the artist type to put oneself
and one's life into one's creative work, but we see also how, in
the eyes of this type, the problem of the relation between
experience and creation has become an artistic (aesthetic) one;
whereas it is really only a psychological one, which discloses,
indeed, important points of contact with art (considered as an
ideological conception), but differs from it in essence.

For the romantic dualism of life and production, which
manifests itself as a mixture of both spheres, has, as a typical
conflict within the modern individual, nothing to do with art,
although obliged like art to express itself creatively. This romantic dualism of life and creation, which corresponds to our
psychological dualism of impulse and will, is, in the last resort,
the conflict between collective and individual immortality, in
which we have all suffered so acutely since the decay of religion and the decline of art. The romantic type, flung hither
and thither between the urge to perpetuate his own life by
creating and the compulsion to turn himself and life into a
work of art, thus appears as the last representative of an art
ideology which, like the religious collective ideology, is in
process of dying out. This does not prevent this final attempt
to rescue the semicollective "religion of genius," by taking it
into modern individualism, from bringing forth outstanding
and permanently valuable works of art; perhaps, indeed (as
Nietzsche himself, the ultra-romantic, recognized), it requires
that it should. On the other hand, it is just the appearance of
this decadent type of artist which marks the beginning of a

new development of personality, since the tendency to self-perpetuation is in the end transferred to the ego from which it originally sprang.

On this issue the romantic becomes identical, as a psychological type, with the neurotic—this is not a valuation, but merely a statement of fact—and for that matter the comparison may even be reversed, since the neurotic likewise has creative, or, at least, self-creative, forces at command. We can thus understand the experience problem of the individualist type of artist also only by studying the nature of neurosis, just as the therapy of the neurotic requires an understanding of the creative type. Now, the neurotic represents the individual who aims at self-preservation by restricting his experience, thus showing his adherence to the naïve faith in immortality of the primitive, though without the collective soul ideology which supports that faith. The productivity of the individual, or of the thing created, replaces—for the artist as for the community —the originally religious ideology by a social value; that is, the work of art not only immortalizes the artist ideologically instead of personally, but also secures to the community a future life in the collective elements of the work. Even at this last stage of individual art creativity there function ideologies (whether given or chosen) of an aesthetic, a social, or a psychological nature as collective justifications of the artist's art, in which the personal factor makes itself more and more felt and appreciated.

If the impulse to create productively is explicable only by the conception of immortality, the question of the experience problem of the neurotic has its source in failure of the impulse to perpetuate, which results in fear, but is also probably conditioned by it. There is (as I have shown) a double sort of fear: on the one hand the fear of life which aims at avoidance or postponement of death, and on the other the fear of death which underlies the desire for immortality. According to the compromise which men make between these two poles of fear, and the predominance of one or the other form, there will be various dynamic solutions of this conflict, which hardly permit of description by type labeling. For, in practice, both in the neurotic and in the productive type—the freely producing and the thwarted—all the forces are brought into play, though with varying accentuation and periodical balancing of values. In general, a strong preponderance of the fear of life will lead rather to neurotic repression, and the fear of death to production—that is, perpetuation in the work produced. But the fear of life, from which we all suffer, conditions the problem of experience in the productive type as in other people, just as the fear of death whips up the neurotic's constructive powers. The individual whose life is braked is led thereby to flee from experience, because he fears that he will become completely absorbed in it—which would mean death—and so is bound up with fear. Unlike the productive type, who strives to be deathless through his work, the neurotic does not seek immortality in any clearly defined sense, but in primitive fashion as a naïve saving or accumulation of actual life. But even the individualist artist type must sacrifice both life and experience to make art out of them. Thus we see that what the artist needs for true creative art in addition to his technique and a definite ideology is life in one form or another; and the two artist types differ essentially in the source from which they take this life that is so essential to production. The classical type, who is possibly poorer within, but nearer to life, and himself more vital, takes it from without; that is, he creates immortal work from mortal life without necessarily having first transformed it into personal experience as is the case with the romantic. For, to the romantic, experience of his own appears to be an essential preliminary to productivity, although he does not use this experience for the enrichment of his own personality, but to economize the personal experiences, the burden of which he would fain escape. Thus the one artist type constantly makes use of life other than his own—in fact, nature—for the purpose of creating, while the other can create only by perpetually sacrificing his own life. This essential difference of attitude to the fundamental problem of life throws a psychological light on the contrast in styles of various periods in art. Whatever aesthetic designation may be applied to this contrast, from the spiritual point of view the work of the classic, more or less naturalistic, artist is essentially *partial*, and the work of the romantic, produced from within, *total*. This totality type spends itself perpetually in creative work without absorbing very much of life, while the partial type has continually to absorb life so that he may throw it off again in his work. It is an egoistical artist type of this order that Ibsen has described in so masterly a fashion. He needs, as it were, for each work that he builds, a sacrifice which is buried alive to ensure a permanent existence to the structure, but also to save the artist from having to give himself. The frequent occasions when a great work of art has been created in the reaction following upon the death of a close relation seem to me to realize those favorable cases for this type of artist in which he can dispense with the killing of the building's victim because that victim has died a natural death and has subsequently, to all appearances, had a monument piously erected to him.[1]

The mistake in all modern psychological biography lies in its attempt to "explain" the artist's work by his experience, whereas creation can be made understandable only through the inner dynamism and its central problems. Then, too, the real artist regards his work as more important than the whole of life and experience, which are but a means to production—almost, indeed, a by-product of it. This refers, however, to the classical type only, for to the romantic type his personal ego and his experience are more important than, or as important as, his work; sometimes, indeed, production may be simply a means

79

to life, just as to the other type experience is but a means to
production. This is why romantic art is far more subjective,
far more closely bound up with experience, than classical,
which is more objective and linked to life. In no case, however,
will the individual become an artist through any one experience, least of all through the experiences of childhood (which
seem pretty universal). The becoming of the artist has a particular genesis, one of the manifestations of which may be some
special experience. For the artistic impulse to create is a dynamic factor apart from the content of experience, a will problem which the artist solves in a particular way. That is, he is
capable of forming the given art ideology—whether of the collective kind (style) or the personal (genius idea)—into the
substance of his creative will. He employs, so to say, personal
will power to give form or life to an ideology, which must
have not only social qualities like other ideologies, but purely
artistic ones, which will be more closely specified from the
point of view of aesthetics.

The subjective character of modern art, which is based on
the ideology of a personal type of artist, imposes also a special
outlook in the artist toward his own creative power and his
work. The more production is an essential means to life (and
not just a particular ideological expression of it), the more will
the work itself be required to justify the personality—instead
of expressing it—and the more will this subjective artist type
need individuals to justify his production. From this point of
view as well as others it is easy to see that experience, in its
particular form of love experience, takes on a peculiar significance for the romantic artist, whose art is based on the personality cult of the genius concept. The primitive artist type finds
his justification in the work itself; the classical justifies the
work by his life, but the romantic must justify both life and
experience by his work and, further, must have a witness of
his life to justify his production. The fundamental problem of

the romantic artist is thus the self-justification of the individual raised above the crowd, while the classical artist type expresses himself in his work—which receives a social justification by way of general recognition. But the romantic needs, further, whether as contrast or as supplement to this social approval, a personal approbation of his own, because his feeling of the guilt of creation can no longer be allayed by a collective ideology any more than he can work effectively in the service of such an ideology. In this sense his artistic work is rather a forcible liberation from inward pressure than the voluntary expression of a fundamentally strong personality that is capable of paralyzing the subjective element to a great extent by making collective symbolism his own. The artist who approximates more nearly to the classical type excels less, therefore, in the creating of new forms than in perfecting them. Further, he will make much more frequent use of old traditional material, full of a powerful collective resonance, as the content of his work, while the romantic seeks new forms and contents in order to be able to express his personal self more completely.

Thus, as the artist type becomes more and more individualized, he appears on the one hand to need a more individual ideology—the genius concept—for his art, while on the other his work is more subjective and more personal, until finally he requires for the justification of his production an individual public, also: a single person for whom ostensibly he creates. This goes so far in a certain type of artist, which we call the romantic, that actual production is possible only with the aid of a concrete muse through whom or for whom the work is produced. The "experience" which arises in this manner is not, like other sorts of experience, an external phenomenon set over against creative work, but is a part of it and even identical with it, always providing that the muse—in practice, usually a real woman—is suited to this role or at least makes no objection to it, and so long as the artist can maintain such a relation on the ideological plane without confusing it with real life. It is this case, in which the conflict between life and creation reaches extreme intensity, that we so often see actualized in the modern type of artist. Here the woman is expected to be muse and mistress at once, which means that she must justify equally the artistic ego, with its creativeness, and the real self, with its life; and this she seldom (and in any case only temporarily) succeeds in doing. We see the artist of this type working off on the woman his inward struggle between life and production or, psychologically speaking, between impulse and will. It is a tragic fate that he shares with the neurotic, who suffers from the same inner conflict. Another way out of the struggle is to divide its elements between two persons, of whom one belongs to the ideological creative sphere, and the other to the sphere of actual life. But this solution also presents difficulties of a psychological as well as a social order, because this type of artist has a fundamental craving for totality, in life as in work, and the inner conflict, though it may be temporarily eased by being objectivized in such an outward division of roles, is as a whole only intensified thereby.

The same applies to another solution of this ego conflict which the artist has in common with the neurotic, and one which shows, more clearly even than the complicated love conflict, that it is at bottom a question not of sexual but of creative problems. From the study of a certain class of neurotic we have found that in many cases of apparent homosexual conflicts it is less a sexual perversion than an ego problem that underlies them, a problem with which the individual can deal only by personifying a portion of his own ego in another individual. The same applies, it is true, to heterosexual love relations, from which the homosexual differs only in that the selfward part of this relation is stronger, or at any rate more distinct. If the poet values his muse the more highly in proportion as it can be identified with his artistic personality and its ideology, then self-evidently he will find his truest ideal in an even greater degree in his own sex, which is in any case physically and intellectually closer to him. Paradoxical as it may sound, the apparently homosexual tendencies or actual relationships of certain artists fulfill the craving for a muse which will stimulate and justify creative work in a higher degree than (for a man) a woman can do. It is only as the result of the artist's urge for completion, and his desire to find everything united in one person, that it is mostly a woman that is taken as, or made into, a muse, although instances of homosexual relations between artists are by no means rare.

Greece, in particular, with its high development of purely intellectual ideologies in art and philosophy, was of course the classical country of boy love; and there is nothing contradictory in this, particularly if we understand the boy friendship in the Greek spirit. For it was in the main, or at least collaterally, a high spiritual relation which had as its basis and object a pedagogic training for the boy. The master—whether philosopher or sculptor, or, in other words, artist in living or in shaping—was not content to teach his pupil or protégé his doctrines or his knowledge; he had the true artistic impulse to transform him into his own image, to create. And this, by the way, was the form of personal immortality characteristic of Greek culture at its height, which not only found expression in works of art or spiritual teaching, but sought fulfillment in a personal, concrete successor. This successor was no longer (or not yet, if we think of Rome) the physical son, but the like-minded pupil. This is why the spiritual relation of pupil and master—which Christianity was to set up again as the center of its doctrine of life—has remained a more important thing to the creative artist than the juridical father-and-son relationship which psychoanalysis seeks to regard as fundamental, whereas it is spiritually of a secondary order. And in Greece, therefore, the state of being a pupil did not mean the

83

mere acquiring of a certain discipline and the mastery of a certain material knowledge, as in the civilization of father right, but the forming of a personality—which begins by identification with the master and is then "artistically" developed and perfected on the pupil's own lines. In this sense the Greek was creative before he arrived at creating works of art, or, indeed, without ever shaping anything but himself and his pupil. Socrates is the best known of many examples of this.

This educative ideology of the artistic Greek nation, which is manifested also in boy love in all its aspects, brings up the question: Did that Greek art, which may seem to us today the main achievement of the Greek civilization, perhaps represent to the Greek a mere by-product thereof, an auxiliary, in fact, to the education of the men, who as the real vessels of the culture were thus enabled *inter alia* to practice art for its own sake? This brings us to another question: Was not every great art, whether of primitive or cultivated peoples, bound up with some such cultured task, which lies beyond the bounds of aesthetics, but also beyond all individual artist psychology? In any case, there are numerous literary proofs of the high degree to which the Greeks were conscious of this national importance of their art. They said that men should learn from works of art and try themselves to become as beautiful and perfect as the statues around them. This gives us an insight into the characteristic way in which the Greeks extended their own creation of individual personalities to include a whole nation, which was not content to produce works of art for their own sake but strove to create an artistic human type who would also be able to produce fine works of art. Seen in this light, boy love, which as Plato tells us aimed perpetually at the improvement and perfection of the beloved youth, appears definitely as the classical counterpart of the primitive body art on a spiritualized plane. In the primitive stage it is a matter of physical self-enhancement; in the civilized stage, a spiritual perfecting in the other person, who becomes transferred into the worthy successor of oneself here on earth; and that, not on the basis of the biological procreation of one's body, but in the sense of the spiritual immortality symbolism in the pupil, the younger.

Christianity took over this ideal of personal character formation in the symbol of the Exemplar Master, but, in proportion as it became a worldwide religion of the masses, it was unable to carry it out at the personal level. The collective immortality dogma, which became symbolized in Christ, relieved the individual of this task of personal self-creation; Christ instead was no longer a model, but became a victim who took upon himself voluntarily the development of everyone's personality. Correspondingly, Christian art remained stationary in the abstract collective style of the religious ideology, until in the Renaissance it was freed by the emergence of a new type of personality. It was not mere imitation of classical Greece, but the expression of a similar ideology of personality that led the artists of the Renaissance to try to reexperience the Greek ideal of boy love. We see, for instance, two of the really great artists, of entirely different social environment, expressing the identical spiritual ideology, with such far-reaching similarity that the notion that the mere accident of a personal experience produced both cases must be dismissed. Both Michelangelo and Shakespeare found almost identical words in their famous sonnets for the noble love which each of them felt for a beautiful youth who was his friend. Michelangelo's case is the simpler in that we at least think we know to whom his sonnets were addressed, although it might equally well be the short-lived Ceccino Bracchi or Tommaso de Cavalieri, the object of a lifelong adoration. It is not even clear in some of his later sonnets whether his "idol" refers to his young friend or to Vittoria Colonna, whose platonic friendship came later. The content of Shakespeare's sonnets is a far more complicated matter. His ideal has been sought among the widely differing persons among the aristocracy of his day. His adoring friendship for the youth in question was not, as with Michelangelo, followed by a soothing maternal friendship, but was broken in upon by a young and beautiful woman. Here, as in his dramas, woman figures as an evil, disturbing demon that the Elizabethan dramatist never succeeded in transforming into a helpful muse, but always felt to be an obstacle to creative work; whereas in his young friend he found the ideal which spurred him on and aided him. But whatever the decision reached by zealous scholars concerning the identity of the person addressed in his immortal sonnets, this biographical fact seems to me unimportant as compared with the psychological evidence that this glorification of a friend is, fundamentally, self-glorification just as was the Greek boy love. In this sense, not only are the sonnets in fact self-dedicated—as is creative work of every description—but they reveal that peculiar attitude of the creative instinct toward the creative ego which seeks to glorify it by artistic idealization and at the same time to overcome its mortality by eternalizing it in art.

The fact that an idealized self-glorification in the person of another can take on physical forms, as in the Greek boy love, has actually nothing to do with the sex of the beloved, but is concerned only with the struggle to develop a personality and the impulse to create which arises from it. This impulse is at bottom directed to the creator's own rebirth in the closest possible likeness, which is naturally more readily found in his own sex; the other sex is felt to be biologically a disturbing element except where it can be idealized as a muse. But the likeness to himself will not only be found in the bodily form of his own sex, but also be built up with regard to the spiritual affinity, and in this regard the youthfulness of the beloved stands for the bodily symbol of immortality. In this manner does the mature man, whose impulse to perpetuate himself drives him away from the biological sex life, live his own life over again in his youthful love; not only seeking to transform him into his intellectual counterpart, but making him his spiritual ideal, the symbol of his vanishing youth. The sonnets of both these Renaissance artists are full of such laments over the vanishing youth of the beloved, whose glorious picture it is the duty of the poem to preserve to all eternity. Just as we know, from the psychology of the creative genius, that his impulse to create arises from precisely this tendency to immortalize himself in his work, so we can be in no doubt as to whose transitoriness it is that the poet deplores with almost monotonous reiteration. In these sonnets there is so complete a revelation of the meaning and content of the whole output of their authors, and indeed of the nature of the artist's creative instinct in general, that their high valuation and, no less, their intriguing ambiguity, become comprehensible. Yet they are easy to understand if we regard them as the subjective completion of their author's objective creations, for in their naïve self-projection they admit their own transitoriness to be the reason for their own perpetuation in poetry.

From this point of view, then, the biographical presentation, even when it can be done with certainty, seems to us inessential. We are by no means cast down when this method fails, for we can understand that beyond a certain point failure is unavoidable, since the creation of a work of art cannot be explained even by the reconstruction of an inspirer. Thus the factual and concrete biography of Michelangelo or Shakespeare does not enable us to understand their work the better; rather we are left more amazed than before at their coincidence. Vasari, anyhow, declares that the one and only portrait by Michelangelo which was true to nature was that of his young friend Tommaso Cavalieri, "for he detested copying the actual appearance of anyone who was not completely beautiful." The same ideal fashion in which he immortalizes the beloved in poetry corresponds exactly with Shakespeare's attitude to *his* ideal. For the English poet also has the conscious intention of immortalizing his friend's beauty at least in his verse, if time is bound to destroy his bodiliness. This is the constantly reiterated theme in the Shakespeare sonnets, and Michelangelo had the same feeling in the presence of the beloved youth: that his beauty should be incorporated into eternity. Not only is it evident from this self-immortalization in the work that the matter is at bottom one of self-immortalization expressed in another (in the ideal) but both these artists have expressed with great clearness, and to the point of monotony, the idea of oneness with the friend. Shakespeare says:

> What can mine own praise to mine own self bring?
> And what is't but mine own when I praise thee?

And Michelangelo in one of his sonnets not only says that a lover "transforms himself" into the beloved, but in a letter presses this transformation of the beloved into his own image, so far as to call his friend Tommaso "a genius who is a stranger in this world."

This psychological solution of the much-disputed sonnet problem shows how experience, and still more the whole attitude toward life, grows out of the struggle to create and so reduces the problem of experience to the problem of creativity. For the extent to which the artist succeeds in actualizing his love ideal, in the service of his own self-immortalization, is of minor importance compared with the basic attitude that his work discloses—namely, one originating in dissatisfaction with artistic creation and so urging the creator in some form or other toward life—that is, toward the actual experiencing of his fundamental self. In any case his impulse to form man in his own image or in the image of his ideal inevitably brings him into conflict with real life and its conditions. These conditions are not artistic, but social conditions, in which one individual has to respect another and is not permitted to remake him.

Now, a certain measure of conflict is, of course, necessary to creative work, and this conflict is, in fact, one of the fields in which an artist displays his greatness, or, psychologically speaking, the strength of his creative will power. By means of it he is able to work off a certain measure of his inner conflict in his art without entirely sacrificing the realities of life or coming into factual conflict with them. In any case, the destructive results of this ensemble of realities upon the neurotic, as we are able to observe them in his neurosis, show that what distinguishes him from the artist is that the latter constructively applies his will power in the service of ideological creation. A certain type of artist, for whom Goethe may stand as the model, will learn to deal with his experiences and conflicts economically and in the end wisely, while another type exhausts his strength in chasing after stimulating experiences so that his conflict does not come out in production. For the artist himself the fact that he creates is more immediately important than what he produces, although we are inclined to make his classification as a particular type depend upon the result, his art work. Here again, we find ourselves at a point where art as the result of production must be sharply differentiated from the artist as a creative individual. There is, in fact, no norm for the artist as a type, although we are constantly tempted to set up more or less precisely formulated norms both for art and for the individual work of art. Production is a vital process which happens within the individual and is independent at the outset from the ideology manifested in the created work. On the other hand, the work can show an equal independence toward the artist who has created it, and can in favorable instances be compared with other works within the categories of art; but it can never be compared with its author or with the artist as a psychological type. Between the two—artist and art—there stands life, now dividing, now uniting, now checking, now promoting.

89

Here we must return once more to the relation of the artist to woman (or to the opposite sex). In the life of many an artist this is a disturbing factor, one of the deepest sources of conflict, indeed, when it tends to force or beguile him into closer touch with life than is necessary or even advantageous to his production. To make a woman his muse, or to name her as such, therefore, often amounts to transforming a hindrance into a helper—a compromise which is usually in the interest of productiveness, but renders no service to life. Here, again, everything naturally depends on the artist's dynamic type and his specific conflict over life and production. There are artists for whom even a feminine muse represents nothing but a potential homosexual relation; for they see in her not so much the woman as a comrade of like outlook and like aims, who could equally well—and possibly better—be replaced by a male friendship. On the other hand, there is an artist type which is totally unable to produce at all without the biological complement of the other sex and indeed depends directly on the sexual life for its stimulus. For the type which is creative in and by means of sexual abstinence has its opposite in another type which, strange to say, is not only not exhausted by the sexual act but is definitely stimulated to create thereby. Schulte-Vaerting has described this type as the "sexual superman," but it seems to me rather that here, too, some hidden mechanism of fleeing from life is involved, which impels the artist from biological mortality to individual immortality in production after he has paid his tribute to sexuality.

This leads us to the profoundest source of the artistic impulse to create, which I can only satisfactorily explain to myself as the struggle of the individual against an inherent striving after totality, which forces him equally in the direction of a complete surrender to life and a complete giving of himself in production. He has to save himself from this totality by fleeing, now from the Scylla of life, now from the Charybdis of creation, and his escape is naturally accomplished only at the cost of continual conflict, both between these two spheres and within each of them separately. How this conflict and the triumph over it is manifested in creative working I seek to show elsewhere. For the moment we are dealing only with manifestations and attempted solutions within the sphere of life, irrespective of whether these are concerned with persons of the same or of the opposite sex. In every case the artist's relation to woman has more an ideological than a sexual significance, as Emil Lenk has demonstrated in a study on creative personalities (*Das Liebesleben des Genies*). Usually, however, he needs two women, or several, for the different parts of his conflict, and accordingly he falls into psychological dilemmas, even if he evades the social difficulties. He undoubtedly loves both these persons in different ways, but is usually not clear as to the part they play, even if—as would appear to be the rule—he does not actually confuse them one with the other. Because the muse means more to him artistically, he thinks he loves her the more. This is seldom the case in fact, and moreover it is psychologically impossible. For the other woman, whom, from purely human or other motives, he perhaps loves more, he often enough cannot set up as his muse for this very reason: she would thereby become in a sense defeminized and, as it were, made into an object (in the egocentric sense) of friendship. To the muse for whom he creates (or thinks he creates), the artist seldom gives himself; he pays with his work, and this the truly womanly woman often refuses to accept. But if his relation takes a homosexual form, this giving is still more obviously a giving to himself; that is, the artistic form of giving through production instead of surrendering the personal ego.

True, from the standpoint of the ego, the homosexual relation is an idealizing of oneself in the person of another, but at the same time it is felt as a humiliation; and this is not so

91

much the cause as the actual expression of internal conflicts. For, in the dynamism which leads him to create, the artist suffers from a struggle between his higher and his lower self, which manifests itself equally in all the spheres and utterances of his life and also characterizes his attitude to woman. She can be for him at once the symbol of the highest and the lowest, of the mortal and the immortal soul, of life or of death. The same applies too, as we shall see, to the work itself or to creation, for which the artist is prepared to sacrifice everything, but which, in the hour of disappointment and dejection, he frequently damns and curses. There is in the artist that fundamental dualism from which we all suffer, intensified in him to a point which drives him with dynamic compulsion from creative work to life, and from life back to new and other creativity. According to the artist's personal structure and spiritual ideology, this conflict will take the form of a struggle between good and evil, beauty and truth, or, in a more neurotic way, between the higher and the lower self. It is a struggle which, as we shall presently see, determines the cultural genetic start and development of the creative instinct itself. In the personal conflicts of the individual artist the fundamental dualism which originally led to cultural development and artistic creation persists in all its old strength. It cannot, however, be reconstructed and understood as a matter of individual psychology from an analysis of the artist's personal past, because the modern individual not only comes into the world with humanity's fundamental dualism, but is also potentially charged with all the attempts to solve it, so that his personal development no longer provides any parallels with the development of the race.

For if we inquire into the relation between work and production in the artist, we must bear in mind that there are two kinds of experience, just as there are at least two ways of artistic production. Whereas in preanalytical biography it was chiefly the artist's later and proportionately more active experience that was brought into relation with his creativeness, psychoanalysis, with its emphasis on the decisive importance of infantile impressions, brought this more passive stage of experience into the foreground. This conception got no further, however, than the banal statement that even the artist was not immune from those typical experiences of childhood which one had come up against in analyzing the adult. Just as Freud saw the cause of neurosis in these typical childhood experiences themselves and not in the individual's particular reaction to them, so did his school claim to see in those same childhood impressions the experiences which led to artistic creativity, though without being able to explain the difference between one outcome of them and another. An inexplicable remainder had therefore to be admitted, but this remainder embraced no more and no less than the whole problem of artistic creativity. Beyond this statement analytical psychography has to this day not progressed. And although the Oedipus complex, and the sexual problem of the child that is bound up with it, still forms the center, this is rather the sign of a fatal stoppage than a proof of the superlative importance of this family problem. The whole of analytical pathography has battened for more than a quarter of a century on the Oedipus problem, which was first applied to artistic creation by Freud in his *Interpretation of Dreams*, without, however, reaching even the point at which I came out when I published my book, *Das Inzest-Motiv in Dichtung und Sage.*

In this book, as already mentioned, the Oedipus problem is treated mainly as a motive and only in a minor degree as an individual complex; hence its ideological significance was considered as well as its psychological. Although, under the spell of the Freudian idea, I gave pride of place to the individual as against the collective psychology (which I have since learned to appreciate as "ideology"), yet with respect to the latter, too, I certainly did not steer clear of psychological premises

93

in dealing with this collective motive which we find in myth
and saga before the poets made a theme of it. But, be this as
it may, the book has even now not been superseded; indeed,
analytical art criticism has not yet faced its problems—to which
I must at this point return. That the poets struggled so intensely with the Oedipus complex was regarded at the time as
a proof of its ubiquity, and so it actually was so far as concerned individual psychology. But from the standpoint of the
psychology of artistic production, the poets' wrestling with the
Oedipus experience seems to me to mean something essentially
different: namely, that the artist reacts more strongly than,
and certainly in a different way from, the normal person to
this unavoidable average experience of the parental relation.
This is not, however, because of the experience, but because
of his peculiar reactivity, which in the case of artistic expression we call creative. Now, from the comparison that I drew
in my generalized formulation of "the artist" between artist
and neurotic, it results that the latter also reacts differently
from the average person to these and similar experiences.
Only, this distinctive reaction does not, with him, lead to
production, but to inhibition or to fixation. The artistic reaction is thus distinguishable from the neurotic by an overcoming of the trauma or of the potentiality of inhibition resulting
therefrom, no matter whether this is achieved by a single effort
or is spread over the whole lifework. This overcoming, however (so far as my researches have taken me), is only possible—
or at any rate only psychologically explicable—in one way,
and this, as we have learned from the therapy which helps to
overcome these development inhibitions, is through volitional
affirmation of the obligatory, which in every case not only
works usefully, but is also definitely creative. Applied to the
special case of the Oedipus conflict, it appears to me that it is
the willed affirmation of the inhibitive family ties that is the
creative and at the same time liberating factor. But this affirma-

tion of the given, which in relation to family symbols manifests itself as erotic desire (toward mother and sister) and thirst for battle (with father or brother), corresponds on the one hand to creative appropriation and on the other to a constructive victory over it.

And with this we are back again at the fundamental process of artistic production, which consists in just this deliberate appropriation of that which happens and is given (including passive experiences) in the form of individual new creation. The Oedipus complex forms one of the cultural symbols of this conflict because it synthesizes the biological, psychological, and characterological sides of it. But, even so, it only symbolizes—even in the case of a child, for whom the Oedipus complex is already the expression of an inner experience and not merely adaptation to an outward destiny. It even seems to me as if the Oedipus myth itself, if taken in the Greek spirit, were an experience of this same striving for independence in human development: namely, the deliberate affirmation of the existence forced on us by fate. That which is dimly but unequivocally preordained for the hero by his birth, in the mythical account, he deliberately makes his own by embodying it in action and experience. This experience is a creative experience, for it serves to create the myth itself, and the sagas, poems, and tragedies based on it, whose various representations of the one theme are determined by the collective ideological outlook of the moment and the interpretation appropriate thereto. But the life of the individual hero himself will inevitably be destroyed, whether this human destiny be interpreted in terms of heroism, fatalism, or tragedy.

1932

NOTE

1. Shakespeare's *Hamlet* and Mozart's *Don Juan* are familiar examples of the reaction after a father's death, while Wagner's *Lohengrin* followed on the death of the composer's mother. These works are supreme examples of artists negotiating with the problem of the beyond. To these instances may be added Ibsen's epilogue *When We Dead Awaken;* here the death is that of the artist himself.

ON THE NATURE OF UGLINESS AND THE CREATIVE IMPULSE

John Rickman

The study of aesthetics presents difficult problems and the solution of them is made more arduous if the field of observation is unduly constricted. So long as aesthetics is confined to an examination of beauty, research is likely to prove as sterile as is a study of behavior which confines itself to the single factor of pleasure. Human psychology made greater progress when it gave recognition to the factors of mental pain, anxiety, and guilt; it would therefore seem prudent to accord more significance than is commonly done to these disturbing but powerful forces in our aesthetic inclinations, and to see whether the underlying impulses of destructiveness, which give rise to these painful feelings, do not provide a substratum to art as they do to everyday life. It is even possible that by representing in a neutral medium the interplay of creative and destructive instincts the artist can help us to comprehend a better solution of the conflicts that press within us than we could do for ourselves unaided, with nothing interposed between us

97

and our passions but the medium of our unstable flesh. The artist provides more than a momentary consolation for our miseries; he goes behind the veil which screens the source of our dejection and brings back evidence for the triumph of the creative impulse over the forces of destruction; he can do this not by the denial of pain but by facing it with a determination to master it. If we are to learn anything about aesthetics we must be ready to follow the path he takes.

It cannot be said of the psychoanalysts that they study only the pleasant things of this life, and we should expect that their contributions to aesthetics would be full of the struggle between the contending forces in the mind. Oddly enough, the subject has suffered a relative neglect and, when mentioned, attention is given in the main to those factors which have contributed to the content of a work of art rather than to the meaning to the artist and his audience of the underlying forces of love and hate, of creativeness and destruction, which possess us in the depths of our being; perhaps it would be more correct to say that the deeper strata of conflict are implied rather than made explicit. The strain that man suffers from the double task of adjusting his love and hate to two objects at a time, both being loved and both hated, and, what is more, both being related to one another—a difficulty in orientation and emotional adaptation which analysts call the Oedipus complex—has, of course, found much exemplification in our literature. Ernest Jones's *Hamlet* is an excellent instance; and the way in which, owing to the unbearable nature of our unconscious ideas, if appearing undisguised in consciousness, our minds disguise the crude and horrible, so that these will not disfigure the more gracious intentions of our thoughts, has been often illustrated; again we can refer to Ernest Jones's work, particularly his *Madonna's Conception*. The lead in this direction of research was given by Freud in his *Delusion and Dream* and *Leonardo da Vinci*; he also wrote the only paper by a psychoanalyst which deals solely with the aspect of aesthetics that is usually neglected—*The Uncanny*.

The research into our mental life which takes into account not only man's double orientation and ambivalence to objects, but which also brings into prominence the employment of projection and introjection, not as mere and occasional expurgatory or masterful acts, but as the basic behavior of the immature psyche, and stresses the continuing activity of the extroject and the introject in the outer or inner world respectively, and the interplay of these in the mind, and, as it seems, the body of the infant and of our unconscious grown-up selves—these new researches, which we owe to Melanie Klein, throw fresh light on aesthetic problems, and are illustrated in her *Infantile Anxiety Situations Reflected in a Work of Art and in the Creative Impulse*. What follows here is a marginal note to that paper, and to her *Contribution to the Psychogenesis of Manic-Depressive States*.

Etymology and Uses of the Word "Ugly"

Skeat tells us something which at once carries us deep into our subject. He defines *ugly* as *frightful, hateful*. It comes from a root connected with *ugg-* (Icelandic), meaning *fear*, and with *-ligr*, meaning *-like*. The main root is traced in the Gothic *ogan*, again meaning to *fear*, and *ogjan*, meaning *to terrify*. The Scandinavian *oga*, meaning *dread*, is connected with the Gothic *agis* which means *fear*, *anguish* and the Irish *aegal*, meaning the same thing. These words are derived from the same root as the Greek ἄχος, meaning *anguish* and *affliction*.

In the columns of the Oxford English Dictionary under *ugly* we find the following: "Having an appearance or aspect which causes dread or horror; frightful or horrible, especially through deformity or squalor . . . offensive or repulsive to the eye . . . morally offensive or repulsive, base, degraded, loathsome, vile, later used in weaker sense as offending against propriety, highly objectionable . . . offensive or unpleasant to taste or smell . . . causing disquiet or discomfort, of a troublesome awkward nature . . . somewhat hazardous, perilous . . . suggestive of trouble or danger . . . cross, angry, ill-tempered."

An Experiment on the Feeling of Disgust

Although in this paper we shall not refer again to the contributions of experimental psychology or experimental aesthetics to the solution of the problem of ugliness—nor for that matter to any other work but psychoanalytic—the researches of Petö (Budapest, 1935) cannot pass unnoticed. They are valuable not only because they deal with the rather neglected field of osmics, but chiefly because they show that the subjective response may vary with the age of the subject, a point that does not find much mention in works on aesthetics:

Various substances (spices, flowers, fruit, resin, fumes, and smells of putrefaction—asafetida, polysulphides) were exhibited to nearly three hundred children, aged from one month to sixteen years, who were divided into three groups, under five, five to six, and over six years old. Eighty-nine out of ninety-two under five showed no disgust or disagreeable feeling, one showed disgust toward some smells, two reacted as grown-up people would have done. Of the thirty-nine in the five-to-six-year group eleven behaved with indifference or said that disagreeable smells were good ones, nineteen showed disgust like grown-up people, nine showed partly a satisfied or indifferent, partly a dissatisfied reaction. In the over-six group of one hundred sixty-four children one hundred twenty-seven showed dissatisfaction or strong disgust, thirteen indifference, twenty-four a mixed behavior. Only the children of five years and over distinguished between agreeable and disagreeable smells; before that age there was no aversion; over six years children made the adult distinctions.

Petö rightly points out that in view of the light which psychoanalysts have thrown on the latency period and also on the building up of the superego, with accompanying changes in the mental outlook, at least among civilized peoples, the main alteration in aesthetic response in this instance may be ascribed to changes in the *vita sexualis* and to consequent altered outlook of the mind.

Some Factors Which Influence Aesthetic Appreciation

A missing part. Some people feel uncomfortable in the presence of ancient statues which are incomplete; they say that these would be beautiful if they were not mutilated, but as now seen they are horrible and sometimes in their injured state they are even called ugly.

When such people come as patients to us for analysis— usually, of course, for other reasons than a disturbance of their aesthetic sense—we have an opportunity of finding out some of the factors which influence their appreciation or disappreciation of these objects. Analysis does not provide much material for aesthetic study, but the smallness of the number of individuals who bring forward material bearing directly on these problems is compensated for by two factors: first we observe the aesthetic judgment or appreciation in the same setting as we observe all other mental activities of the patient, i.e., in the framework of his free associations in analysis, and secondly we are able to observe the changes in aesthetic appreciation running parallel with the changes in mental outlook in other directions—in the patient's love life, work, and sublimations generally.

Returning to the statues, it appears that the subject identifies himself with these objects, i.e., he has thought of himself as a mutilated person, or he has identified the statue with someone whom he has in his thoughts mutilated. It would be more correct to say that the sight of the statue rouses unconscious fantasies of remutilation, because the fantasy is not roused for the first time by the statue. Its injury awakens the impulse to carry the destruction a stage further. These fantasies can be traced back to the patient's early years and have undergone many modifications, submergences, and resuscitations. An important fact confronts us at this point: the re-awakened fantasy is more disturbing than the defects in the object itself; the fantasy, which is one of aggressive action, remains unconscious, the affect of fear or horror becomes attached to the external object so that the person does not realize his secret wish; the fantasy is kept from consciousness at the expense of the richness of the subject's emotional relation to an external object.

The reason for thinking that the affects roused by the fantasy are more disturbing than those roused by the defects in the object is found in the effects of treatment; when the wish-fantasy of mutilation is brought to consciousness and the patient is able to bear an examination of it, and has traced its origin in its relation to loved persons, it is also found that his contemplation of mutilated statues is now not affected by his anxieties; he can enjoy them as a "composition" or a "unity" and is not distracted by the defective or defaced parts. It is perhaps hardly necessary to say that the change does not come about through discussing the statues, nor from any talk about aesthetics, but solely as a by-product of work necessary for the treatment of a neurotic trouble.

It may be objected that this first example is a trivial and neurotic reaction and that it cannot be made the basis of a general criterion of ugliness. I should consider the objection sound were the response to mutilation not so very widespread; mutilation fantasies play a large part, for instance, in the inhibitions of love life, and I should be loath to exclude them from a discussion of aesthetics, because their elaboration in the unconscious part of the mind and the impetus they give to exertions of an opposite character—restorative and creative—

may on further examination be fruitful in our understanding not only of aesthetics but of our social life.

The attitude to deformity, to defective growth, to a "foreign body," and to unfinished work. It is not regarded as surprising when people say that they regard deformity of body or defect in growth, whether generalized or localized, and whether seen in the flesh or in a representation, as ugly. Though we accept the statement readily enough, the reason for this view may be quite complicated. There is a component derived from the anxiety about personal mutilation which comes from an identification with the victim of the distortion; but since the mind resists the idea that the self is ever horrible this factor of identification with a dreaded sight cannot in itself lend much strength to the feeling that the object is ugly. There is, however, sometimes another component derived from an identification with the aggressor who has produced the distortion; such pleasure as is harbored in the unconscious on this account is manifest in consciousness as discomfort due to guilt, the direct perception of guilt feelings as such being suppressed. In the case of a work of art the aggressor is clearly the artist, so that the contemplation of his work puts us in a position where we are faced in our fantasy with two objects at the same time, the producer and the object produced, which in the unconscious is always regarded as a person. It is possible that the production and enjoyment of art is dependent on this capacity to cope simultaneously with ambivalence to two intimately related but yet separate objects. The eagerness in the young to produce what in any other animal would be properly regarded as a biologically useless activity, the drawing and plastic work, rhythmic noises and tunes, and the variation in intensity of these impulses with the phases of sexual development, suggest that a close connection exists between the employment of art work and the personal and social problems derived from this double orientation, because in the young the task of experimental manipulation of love and hate impulses toward objects, internal as well as external, is almost its sole occupation. (Those who apply the theory of dialectical materialism to art and who emphasize the dependence of creative art upon the social impulses have also to consider the possibility that these spring from a common root; those who hold true to the theory will readily accept this; those whose inner strains call for immediate application of their views in political action commonly overlook it.)

Returning to the distortions and to unfinished work, these have in common the effect of rousing in the imagination the thought of what might have been. Just as the distortion rouses guilt at our complicity in the deed or anger at a potential good thing being deformed, so on contemplating unfinished work some feel cheated by the artist and react to the frustration with hostility—using the judgment of ugliness as a cover for their resentment. Others of course respond in the opposite way, feel grateful to the artist for that part which he has given them and enjoy the opportunity to share with him, in their fantasy, in the completion of a lovely production. There is another characteristic which sometimes excites the judgment of ugliness, viz., where the onlooker finds what he regards as a "foreign body" in an otherwise acceptable work. If this particular figure was not in the composition or this cloud was not in the sky the picture would be all that could be desired; as it is, it is spoiled by this alien thing and the picture is reckoned ugly. This is the antithesis to the "missing part" objection; it is the presence of something bad which renders the whole intolerable—a neurotic reaction, surely.

Fettering of interest to periods, cultures, and antiquity. The foregoing considerations have roused in our minds the impression that these factors which limit aesthetic appreciation are neurotic manifestations, and that perhaps no true art lover is influenced by them; in a word that the investigation of those things which produce aversion is calculated to disclose neurotic behavior, and that it does not take much gumption to surmise that neurosis is likely to disturb art appreciation in some way or other. Maybe this is so; nevertheless the way in which the disturbance comes about should not be neglected by psychology.

Leaving aside the aversions, let us consider some factors which limit the scope of what is felt to be attractive in works of art. Certain periods in history and certain cultures have, as we say, an appeal for us; we think we should have felt at home in them, and anything which reminds us of them gives us pleasure so that we readily respond to their influence. If we examine this attitude more closely we commonly find that there is a connection between the conception of the culture or period and the daydreams or fantasies which serve as the background of our mental life. The links between the culture chosen and the daydream can be traced if we follow the history of the significant content through the course of development of the patient's fantasies, but the awakening of the association by a work of art need not be direct nor of course need it disclose its oedipal roots; indeed, it need not be direct at all, e.g., the general treatment or style of a picture may evoke some echo of that world we people in our daydreams. An artist seems to be able both to convey by an economy of means denied to lesser folk a wide range of associations, more particularly of the emotions, which the whole composition and the details of his work evoke, and to control them so that they shall not scatter wide but by subtle focusing reinforce one another and penetrate deeper and deeper into the mind of the onlooker; at least I take it that some such process occurs, analogous to the interplay of elements in a dream.

These preferences for particular periods or cultures are apt of course to pass over to a possessive appreciation of the chosen field with depreciation of others—a characteristic of nursery preferences, but one which leads directly to interest in external objects. In contrast there is the type which can only enjoy or venerate the antique. One patient whose family was of a "respectable antiquity" was fascinated by any work (artistic or political) of the period when his family "began." I think the reason which some antique-fetishists put forward, viz., that objects which have been preserved through the ages against the carelessness and resentment of succeeding generations must have some merit in them, contains a truth, but a truth which they use as a rationalization. In this connection we must remember those who are unable to see in an ancient work of art anything that commends it to their favorable notice, i.e., a quality as intrinsically irrelevant as antiquity is used as a mark against it. The truth is that there is a fashion in these matters, and to a far greater extent than they are aware people are influenced in their aesthetic appreciations by social habits. Another instance of this is the relatively recent enjoyment by civilized nationals of the art of primitive tribes; it would seem likely that this is a case of diminution of aesthetic inhibition coinciding with a greater tolerance of other sexual customs and social codes than their own and resulting in an increased aesthetic enjoyment. Anxiety is the chief inhibition of enjoyment, whether it be aesthetic or other.

The relation of limitation of aesthetic appreciation to inhibitions in love life. The parallel between these two kinds of restriction is striking—the preference for newness or for age, the satisfaction in completeness and intolerance of a missing part, deformity, a foreign body, the pleasure in private possession of the prized object and numbing of the senses in a public collection, the proneness to be disturbed from the enjoyment of the whole if anxiety is roused by a part—all these peculiarities are in the person approaching an object, whether it be artistic or sexual. The legend of Pygmalion reminds us that from classical times the connection between the two impulses

106

was recognized and that a bridging of the gap might be abnormal. And yet there is a ready transfer of emotion from loved persons to works of art in normal people, and many feel a refreshment of spirit from a work of art similar to that which they experience when they make the acquaintance of an inspiring person. It seems to be stronger than a mild narcotic and provides more than "a temporary refuge for us from the hardships of life" (Freud). Though its influence may "not [be] strong enough to make us forget real misery"—the same may be said of love—yet it has the power to penetrate beneath the surface of our minds and both assist us in our struggle with despair and help us to grasp those things which seem to triumph over death.

It seems that since we left the illuminating pages of Skeat we have drifted away from the subject of ugliness and have hardly touched on the creative impulse at all. Perhaps that will come later, but we must consider first some more general problems connected with what may be going on in the artist's mind when he is engaged in his work.

Dream-Work and Art Work

Dream-work is the best known instance of the interplay between unconscious impulses on the one hand and perceptions and memory traces on the other. In the dream the unconscious wish uses sensory perceptions and memory traces in order to express thoughts that cannot come to consciousness on account of repression; the dream-work consists in transforming the arrangement of images so that they have one meaning for the unconscious part of the mind and they may or may not have another sort of significance or interest for the conscious layer of the mind. Since the aim of the dream is to provide unconscious satisfaction to the dreamer it is as a rule a matter of relative indifference whether the manifest content of the dream makes sense for anyone else; there is the familiar analogy of the play written by and performed for an audience of one— the dreamer.

Dreams differ in the degree to which the manifest content shows the influence of the primary processes of thought (condensation, displacement, absence of contradiction, etc.), or "perception identity," or reveals the influence of the secondary processes of thought, or "thought identity." Perhaps this difference in dreams could be employed also in aesthetics. Some works of art give the appearance at first meeting of being confused and formless (surrealist pictures for example); others show, at first sight at any rate, the opposite tendency, viz., an effort to achieve exact representation of detail (Frith's "Derby Day" is an instance of this). Just as orderliness of the manifest content of the dream is not its most important characteristic for the analyst, so conventional forms are not the most important thing to the artist. The surrealists deliberately imitate the dream, but only, of course, the visible characteristics of the manifest content. On the analogy now being pressed, their work will be strong only so long as the force attaching to the latent content can be given full scope. Also on this analogy it would be as rash to judge an artist's work by the standard of his own theories as to value the significance of a dream (as a thing giving a key to important aspects of the dreamer's inner life) by the importance he attaches to its neat arrangement or its incoherence.

Both dreamer and artist strive to reduce mental tension, an important difference between the two work processes lying in the different "audiences" for whom the elaborate fantasy is produced.

We should try to relate the aphorism "A dream is a play with an audience of one," to the saying that an artist does not produce for himself but for the whole of humanity. Ferenczi, in one of his brilliant asides, put the question, "To whom does one relate one's dreams?" and quotes Lessing's couplet:

Alba mihi semper narrat sua somnia mane,
Alba sibi dormit; somniat Alba mihi.

(It is just as charming in English: "Alba always tells me her dreams in the morning; she sleeps for herself, but she dreams for me.") Sachs, recalling our attention to the fact that the daydream is a preliminary stage of poetry, considers that "daydreams in common," in which two or more persons co-operate by giving up their closest ego-interests, should further our understanding of the production of poetry. He found that a common feeling of guilt leads the players of the storytelling game to seek and to find "relief in the working-out of a daydream, since in it lay an unconscious admission of the same guilt of the other party. . . . The artist's own person has to step into the background for the sake of the effect of the work!"

We could therefore arrange the dream series as follows: first the dreams for oneself alone, then the dreams for a particular person, then the daydreams-in-common for the group playing that particular game. To apply this to art is no great step, but our explanation must also take into reckoning that the artist feels that his work is for the whole of humanity and for all time. We achieve a simplification if we say that the inner audience for whom the artist works is the superego. This may influence his work on three levels: the least important superego element is derived from the art school where his technical accomplishment was in some measure shaped, where his work had to pass muster. It is a late acquisition, a conscious or preconscious level of mental operation, which guides the hand rather than fires the spirit. Another audience is that of the cultured people of his generation whose influence he absorbed during his formative years. The first influences his

109

technique, the second commonly influences his choice of subject; neither have much to do with that which will make his work live. I suggest as a guess that there is a third kind of audience composed not of memory traces of actual people's actual behavior, but of those compounds of external experience and inner fantasy which, following Melanie Klein, we call "inner objects." A work of art is composed for them in the sense (to be elucidated more fully later) that they are the objects who are intended to be influenced; they both give impetus to the creation of the work and are the objects to be influenced by it. Before we deal with this there is a general question to be touched on.

What Is It That Is Satisfying in Art?

Three answers to this question will be discussed: first the factor of sensuous pleasure, secondly the relief of tension that comes when a conflict is solved, and thirdly an aspect which we may call an "eternal" factor, borrowing the term from common usage.

Sensuous pleasure. It is usually held that the mere representation of a sensually attractive object does not constitute great art. The wide diversity of object-choice in the love life of man, and in its derivative the beauty-loving life, is so great that the attractiveness of a particular object exactly reproduced is bound to have a restricted appeal. At best this so to say photographic representation of the attractive recalls past gratifications; what "movement" it possesses is retrogressive, and even the recall of past pleasures is limited. Its effect is psychologically unstable, it cannot recall a moment from the past without recalling all of it, its pain and its guilt as well as its joys; the avoidance of discomforting aspects of experience does not reanimate experience but fosters illusion. Such art is a "flight to beauty"; it reminds us of the struggles of the psychotic to conceive of a world more and more saturated with goodness so that he may cherish the illusion that evil does not exist in it at all. But anxiety and guilt cannot for long be denied; the attempt to evade them leads to an ever-increasing emphasis on the charms of the object, till the point is reached when—in the case of a work of art—the observer can feel neither identification nor loving object-relation with the thing represented and dismisses it—as he would dismiss a person who has such a one-sided disposition—as insipid and uninteresting.

And yet sensuous pleasure lies at the very center of art. It is clear that sensuous pleasure of the positive or attractive kind is not enough; the artist who is in flight to beauty creates an illusory world and does not help us much to face the pain of the real world nor does he endear it to us. I take it that I have been describing "escape art" and its limitations.

The solution of conflict. In work where this plays a large part the artist faces the problem of anxiety and guilt. The mind finds rest when it has first mastered pain and then turns to pleasure. This factor is easier to state than to demonstrate, but an example is seen in *Hamlet,* in which, as Ernest Jones pointed out, the playwright carries us into the painful situation of the Oedipus conflict and depicts various aspects of its solution. Drama deals with the tensions of triangular situations in the medium of the relation of living people; in the case of other arts the analogous interaction would be that of part-objects and the interplay of constructive and destructive tendencies. There is little I can say in support of this notion beyond the statement that it strikes me as somewhat plausible. Just as our adult emotional life is a great elaboration and synthesis of the primitive fantasies of childhood, so one would expect our adult art to be a similar elaboration and synthesis of the graphic impulses which in our early years gave expression to our need to exercise power over objects with the magic of

111

drawing, and our need to externalize and fix those ever-changing images and moods which disturbed our peace of mind. To the child's fantasy a line is a parent figure, another line crossing it is the other parent, or is a knife hewing the first in two. The pencil is a magic wand giving power over the figures to do good or ill as the mood is at the moment. This is a primitive expression of what the infantile artist *feels*, it bears no relation to what he *sees*. When a higher stage of graphic skill is reached there is a desire to bring under the dominion of the magic pencil objects seen in the outer world.

One might hazard a guess about the development of the graphic impulse having three phases: first, the expression in the magical action—drawing—of primitive impulses directed against external objects, without regard to the accuracy of the representation of those external objects in the drawing—a depicting of inner fantasy, perhaps of the relation of inner objects to one another. In the second phase attention is paid to the depiction of the form of the external object, interest being driven to it perhaps through anxiety as to the fate of its inner counterpart, but the treatment of details is governed by part-object interests. In the third phase the element of composition, always present even in the first phase, though then rudimentary, now develops, perhaps as a result of the increasing capacity to separate the elements in the combined-parent figure; this is the phase in which the interaction between inner and outer objects ceases to be wholly magical and acquires some of the characteristics of thought—delayed discharge of mental tension allowing for the matching of the product of the mind with the objects dealt with, whether these are external events and processes to be co-ordinated by the formulation of a law (as in science) or the matching of the feelings experienced on viewing an object after its exteriorization with those experienced by the ego, resulting from maybe unconscious introspection (as in art). Composition is probably always a synthesis of elements which the mind has decomposed or torn asunder, an effort of construction after a mental act of destruction.

We may get a little further if we consider the nature of the instrument in the unconscious fantasy by means of which this magical control is exercised, and by considering the artist's relation to it. Sometimes we hear an artist say, "If I am an artist, I live; if not, I am dead. Unless I am creating, I am nothing!" There is felt to be something inside but separate from the self which is essentially creative; it produces "art-children" out of the artist, who is in a way passive to its power but active in response to it. If we follow carefully the early history of this mental experience we find it expressing a passive relation to a creative image of infancy, the father figure, and to the part of him which is capable both of creating and of entering another person. The creative power is in fantasy an inner possession because in fantasy its corporeal prototype was originally desired by the child for the purpose of incorporating it in the self, and thereby he could obtain control over his world, father, mother, and all future children and rivals. But the incorporating process cannot be selective against the inclusion of the unpleasant; the ambivalence felt against the external object follows it into the inner sanctuary. Hate jeopardizes it in the one place as in the other. "If I am an artist, I live" can be interpreted, "Unless I have evidence that this object within me is alive and active in the creation of good things, there is nothing to live for, since my hate against it will extinguish the producer of all that is good and desirable." In such a case—perhaps in all—the production of a work of art takes away the sense of guilt arising from the fact that death wishes are streaming toward and stifling the good object which was once external and now in fantasy is harbored within the self. Artists sometimes feel that they are the trustees of a great treasure; this accounts for their modesty. At times they feel so close an identification with the great force within them that they reckon themselves as gods. In this connection and in view of the infantile origin of the notion of God and of creativeness the arrogance of some artists is not a thing to be wondered at.

The eternal factor. Of one thing an artist is certain when he has achieved his highest purpose: that its power to affect the heart of man will last for ever. It is not a sufficient explanation that his work will give satisfaction beyond his lifetime and that in the reckoning of time after our death we count a thousand years as but a day; the imperviousness of the unconscious to thoughts of personal extinction and to the gauging of time does not bring us to the correct position, as it seems to me, to value this feeling of the eternal in art. Nor, I think, should we lean overmuch on the thought that through the most intimate contact of the artist's mind with generation after generation of men he extends the duration of his influence to timeless dimensions. Such a preconscious thought may make an artist the readier to speak of his own or another person's art as of everlasting value, but the same motive cannot influence us who merely look at and appreciate his work.

A work of art appeals to us in proportion to the depth of the emotional level which is stirred in our minds; the artist cannot take us where he himself has never been. If we limit ourselves to what might be called the biographer's life of the artist we cannot explain the power these people have to affect nearly the whole of mankind. But if we take into consideration the intensity of infantile pain, the enormous courage and endurance of the child in the face of what it feels to be great dangers to itself and to loved ones, its passionate belief that in spite of the fact that its world is reduced to chaos nevertheless it will and can put things right, its good humor due to its belief that in spite of its own evil impulses it has the power to restore and re-create a good world again and that its good objects will remain; if we reckon with the fact that the child goes through periods when the face of familiar things is changed and all that it loves and trusts is crushed by its own violence and befouled by its hate; and if with all this we reckon with the influence and power of infantile fantasy and experience upon our adult perception and emotion—then we may see how the artist can lead us into and out of the world of suffering. His creative activity is the beginning of a new world built on the ruins of the old; those strokes of the brush in his fantasy build up bit by bit the good objects which he has destroyed and make them come to life. (I do not mean to imply that all great art is done in a paroxysm of nervous break-down, but that unless the artist can reach down to the experience of deep anxiety and find the way out his work will not give us a deeper understanding of ourselves or a fuller enjoyment of life.)

But to return to our question. Time is not really the point of discussion, *death* is the thing referred to. The immortal work of art is not one which has merely survived through the ages from the carelessness and indifference of other people, but is a living proof that the artist himself has stayed the course of havoc and has himself made life come out of dust and confusion. In all nature death is the only irreversible reaction; the triumph and the illusion of art is that it can turn back the dead into the world of the living.

It is not so really. It is believed to be so. But artists feel this way, and because we wish for the same outcome we give currency to the conception about the eternal value of a great work of art. At least this much is true, that these treasures are the nearest to the eternal that man can make, and in fact both in antiquity and in the reverence they compel they can meet the challenge of the everlasting hills.

We have been speaking about works of art to the neglect of that to which the term beauty is most applied—the human face. Of its beauty we say that it contains an undying loveliness, though we know that half a dozen decades will end it. Do we mean only that we hope that the satisfaction we get from the contemplation of the beautiful face will never be erased from our memory by pain or destroyed by hate?

I would like at this point to refer to a curious experience. A patient in deep depression came for analysis. She was dressed in black and wore knotted round her neck a long scarlet rope of silk, her face was hooded with a large black hat. She wore black gauntlets of shiny kid, but her fingers, which kept up a twisting angular movement, seemed too small for the gloves so that the thin leather creased and bent as if it were the loose scaly covering of a bird's claw. Her face was made up in the livid purplish coloring of a corpse; her mouth was curved almost to deformity and was usually drawn in, but it opened and closed slowly as the tip of the black kid claw pulled down the lower lip. Her brow was drawn and her eyes stared intently at nothing. All this while she uttered soft groans, saying to herself, "Oh! Oh! Oh!" In the course of a session a commonplace interpretation was made; instantly she changed to a new creature. The angular movements of her fingers gave place to a smooth stroking of her body, the claw turned to a soft caressing hand, the hunched shoulders relaxed, her brow smoothed, her eyes brightened, the hollows in her face filled with smiling cheeks, her expression was radiant. The thought crossed my mind, "Why, my goodness, she is beautiful!"

Reflection showed that in repose (I am not speaking of the expression in melancholy) and even smiling, when she had great charm, the attribution of beauty might perhaps be an exaggeration. My first idea was that my mind followed the quick return of animation, and, possibly in relief of strain, overshot the due mark of appreciation. But to that view another and less psychomechanical explanation can be added. For the moment my words—so I then regarded the episode, or so my unconscious fantasy ran—had brought this living corpse to life. It was a miracle, and the description "beautiful" was applied because that is what we think of life when we expect death, that is what we think when we see the signs of triumph over death.

Since having this experience I have wondered whether some of the special power to hold a lasting position in the memory which a film actress possesses, I think of one in particular, is not due to the fact that in repose she has at times the appearance of enduring an almost unbelievable burden of inner misery and mental pain, and not once but several times in each film we see that "miracle" occur; under the influence of her partner or from the upwelling of her own emotion that bare skull grows soft and human.

One of the characteristics of beauty is its power to convey the feeling that struggle is over, that peace has come at last. Though we may go into the depths of pain and depression again and again we carry with us the assurance that through all violence and evil there has remained this marvellous witness to the endurance of life over death. Once deathless is deathless evermore!

In all this only one aspect of beauty is touched on, that which leads to the reduction of anxiety and pain, not that which leads to the heightening of pleasure and desire. Or should one say that which leads directly to the heightening of pleasure and desire? It is doubtful whether the direct paths of the mind are as straight and simple as they seem; maybe we only wish they were so, so that we need take no reckoning of the way our mind is shaped by pain.

What, it may be asked, has all this talk of beauty to do with our topic—ugliness? Only this, that it does not do to try to answer oversimple questions in the terms of reference which wishful thinking too readily provides. This paper serves merely to emphasize a possible genetic connection between the pain due to destructive impulses and the paramount need to create lasting goodness and wholeness from what had been in fantasy injured and rendered bad. The urge to reparation is, owing to the strange nature of human mental development, probably an integral part of creative activity; the horror of the ugly and the wish to change it is that *vis a tergo* which thrusts us into constructive work in art, in science, and even in the humble tasks of our daily round.

What Is Ugliness?

Ugliness has power over us, we cannot treat it with indifference. It rouses our deep-set emotions and its horror lingers in the memory. The etymology of the word shows that it is closely connected in men's minds with fear; but we also find on closer viewing that it rouses anxiety and guilt. A sailor may call a cloud ugly but he means only that it forebodes the dangers of a storm; as an artist (on land) he might regard its splendor with admiration because its threats will not assail him; as an ordinary being he might find relief, as many do, in watching the development of an external tempest, which being none of his making can be viewed without rousing inner alarm or misgiving. If there should be horror we can safely say that it is due to the arousal of early phobias and fantasies in which the raging elements are surrogates for persons whom he himself has lashed to fury, and that he dreads to witness the external fulfillment of his own secret wishes or to see spread out before him the awful chaos which lies within himself.

The case of a cloud called ugly is really too simple to help us much; but what do we mean by an ugly face? Is there a face that all mankind would call ugly, an awfulness that strikes chill into the heart of every soul? A configuration of chaos, a sense of something destroyed, of hate embodied in or indelibly marked upon human flesh, that we have no power to transform? As eternal beauty is a challenge to destruction and a triumph, is ugliness a challenge and a victory, but to the other side? Ugliness is not merely displeasing in the highest degree, a cause of mental pain, giving no promise of peace; it is something which stirs fantasies so profoundly that our minds cannot let the object alone; it does not feel as if this thing has merely happened, but that it is something done to hurt. I believe that the fear which ugliness rouses is due to the irrefutable evidence which it provides that the will to destructiveness has been let loose; and we turn from it in part through dread of the temptation of complicity, in part because we cannot bear to contemplate what in our unconscious fantasy we have already done to something that was and might again be good. Those whose lives have been shaped by restitutive impulses, the sisters of mercy, nurses, and those who minister to the incurables, and those who are fortified by the desire to fulfill a special office, the priest giving extreme unction or relatives attending to the wants of the dying, do not notice or are seemingly unaffected by appearances which all others would call the ugliest manifestations of deformity and disease; and such is the power of affection—often supported, it is true, by the process we call "denial"—that persons whose character and conduct seem of the ugliest are those dear to them people who are only troubled in spirit and struggling with difficulties.

The word "ugly" is used as a judgment upon an object or as the expression of an emotional response to it, and always denotes a disturbance, present or latent, of equanimity in the presence or at the thought of the object. If we are dissatisfied with a description or definition of the term which allows for so much subjective bias, it means, I think, that we are trying to make our intellectual judgments an absolute criterion, like an act of mensuration where both end points can be tested with complete freedom. But if we must be content, as I think is the case—and we can only be satisfied with it if we are convinced that it is true—that in the emotional life of man there is always a point of reference, a zero on the measuring scale, that lies in the unconscious part of the mind, then we must adapt our mode of research, or at least one part of it, to a closer understanding of the unconscious factors which influence, if they do not govern, our aesthetic judgment and appreciation.

(If one end of the measuring scale is buried out of sight we must forgo absolute standards and use the concept of quantity only so far as it applies to what we can observe. In this connection I have made no attempt to apply the dialectical conception of a change of quantity producing a change in quality; this cannot for long be ignored in respect to the problem of anxiety, though so far few analysts have dealt with this.)

Man, it has often been said, is a religious animal; this notion is used to support the view that there must therefore be a God, an absolute of creativeness and initiation, toward which we poor mortals must inevitably turn in our moments of need and to whom we must give thanks for our blessings. Man, it is less often said, is an art-needing animal, and by the same process of ratiocination it is thought that there must be an absolute of beauty to which as the lodestone draws iron we half-blind mortals turn for a criterion and for refreshment. Both views express a lofty if rather childish aspiration, but they are hard to reconcile with man's position in animal creation. If we were oriented, as I imagine the animals are, in a relatively simple way to the objects which excite our interest; if we desired without doubting our love and hated without qualm; if our periods of rut and non-rut were more or less separated, and the sexual impulse only thrust itself upon us when we were independent of parental care and capable of achieving coitus and reproduction after the manner of those who produced us; if the litter in which we were born were not confused and encumbered with the still-dependent but vigorous offspring of the litter before us, and we had no ground for jealousy of those that came after us—if all these things were so, I doubt if we should have deep rooted in our mental life our load of anxiety and guilt. But then we should not be human, and, as Freud said, none of us would change places with the creatures in an animal community however much we might feel discontented with our human civilization. The reason for this, I surmise, is that, these experiences having become engrained, we need to work over the tangle until it is straightened out. There is a limit to the process of denial; under strain or throughout weakness we can deny a part of the reality of our inner life, but not all of it. Born into a human world we shoulder a burden characteristically human that cannot be laid down.

The mark of our humanity is the depth of our capacity to love and the agony which overwhelms us when our loved ones lie in danger from our own aggression. The strongest passions arose when we were weak and least able to control them, and our minds were flooded with fantasies which roused —and still rouse—our horror, and excite our sensual cravings. On this foundation our mental lives and our civilization are built.

In the works of man, as in those which we separate and call the products of nature, we see creative and destructive forces in active interplay. When we discern the influence of creation predominating we are moved by something we call beauty, when we see destruction we recoil at the ugly. Our need for beauty springs from the gloom and pain which we experience from our destructive impulses toward our good and loved objects; our wish is to find in art evidence of the triumph of life over death; we recognize the power of death when we say a thing is ugly.

1940

121

▣ SCHIZOPHRENIC AND
CREATIVE THINKING

Robert Wälder

Up to the present time psychoanalysis has not been applied to the psychology of thought. This is due to the nature of the psychoanalytic method, which was developed for the purpose of investigating unconscious content, that is, of examining the mode of function of mental strata which, phylogenetically older, underlie the layer of co-ordinated thought processes. This more archaic function can be observed in dream processes and in schizophrenia. From this point of view psychoanalysis is not called upon to make any comment on the laws regulating thought, which is a matter for experimental research; the relation of the individual phenomena of thought to unconscious processes is, however, a subject which concerns it, as is also the expression of instinctual functioning through the creation of thought images.

For the purposes of this brief study, the intention of which is mainly to point out certain problems, we shall adopt the familiar procedure of examining pathological manifestations. We do so, not because we share the general impression that there is only a quantitative difference between the normal and the pathological or that a pathological state merely magnifies what can be observed in normal life. On the contrary, we believe that, although they are often difficult to formulate, there are many important qualitative differences on both sides which are easily overlooked on account of the quite striking analogies. We start from pathological data because we hope in this way to elucidate some aspects of the problem, not because we hope to explain all its aspects.

Considering first of all schizophrenic forms of thought, we find that paranoidal and hebephrenic forms, although not the only types, are nevertheless the most striking and the most fully described. To illustrate the paranoidal type we shall select the most thoroughly analyzed example of paranoia, Freud's dissection of Schreber's delusional system.

The main element of Schreber's paranoidal system was his belief that he had been turned into a woman who was to play an important part in the regulation of cosmic affairs, who would in fact be essential for the world's salvation. Unhampered by any considerations of general validity, we may proceed to study this very typical example apart from the other elements in the delusion.

The first point to be recognized concerning this pathological idea is the feminine attitude; regarded from the point of view of instinctual life, the fantasy is a homosexual one. As Freud has shown, this change of attitude had already been indicated in various ways before the outbreak of the actual psychosis. We can therefore regard a regression to homosexuality as the first phase in the formation of Schreber's delusional idea. At this stage there are obviously many avenues open: a regression of this type can be seen in the case of obvious perversions as well as in some neuroses, and to indicate how these paths diverge it is necessary to single out certain specific manifestations in the development of the delusion.

A second point in the formation of the paranoiac idea is

the manner in which this mode of instinctual functioning is experienced: it is not regarded as a process occurring within the individual's own personality, if we may use the term, but as a result of external influence. By displacement of the ego boundaries, to adopt the current phraseology, a variation in object-cognition occurs: an internal manifestation is regarded as external. An analogous mechanism of projection is seen in the normal individual, where instinctual activity is often regarded as something foreign to the ego, as an influence to which one submits or which one rejects. Familiar expressions, e.g., "it came over me," "it carried me away," betray this attitude, and psychoanalysis has found an apt term for this in designating instinctual life as the "it" (id). The analogy is, however, too limited: the id of a normal person is more foreign to his ego than his conscious will; it is less a subject than an object. Notwithstanding this, a normal person always knows that he should not seek for "it" outside his own personality. The paranoiac does so.

So far we can recognize in the formation of the delusional thought-system a regressive outbreak of passive homosexuality and the variation in object-relations characteristic of schizophrenia. Taken by itself the first would run: "I become—instinctually—a woman"; the second is modified to: "I am changed—by external means—into a woman." To this formula is added a subjective interpretation which expands an isolated thought into a religious system: "this sexual change in me will bring about the world's salvation."

This third step discloses the paranoiac's desire to co-ordinate his experience with his cosmology. He cannot bear simply to accept the situation; he must immediately fashion some theory to explain it. His idea of world redemption and the part played by his change into a woman is a theory produced in order to co-ordinate and satisfactorily explain his new experience. This dovetailing of experience into a wider concatenation brings about the specific paranoidal reaction. Borrowing an expression from the psychology of "shape" (*Gestalt*), we may speak of structures being "seen into" (*hineinsehen*) the outer world (or of internal processes being experienced externally). We would suggest that any hypertrophy of this tendency should be called hypergnosis in contradistinction to agnosis, or diminished perception of "shape."

Hypergnosis must be present to give the impression of a paranoidal picture: in its absence the displacement of ego boundaries is suggestive merely of schizophrenia, never of paranoia. The significance of hypergnosis as a *differentia specifica* of paranoia can be illustrated by a case reported by Kronfeld: a catatonic patient remarked, concerning the confused and chaotic impressions he had experienced in the catatonic state, that the chaos had been outside him and not inside him. In this case definite experiences and the perception of them existed outside the ego boundary, yet the third stage of delusional formation was absent, viz., the "seeing into" (*hineinsehen*). Had he been hypergnostic he would have co-ordinated the experiences projected into the outside world, either as well-regulated sensory perceptions (visual and auditory hallucinations) or as theoretical elaborations (a delusional system). Mere displacement of ego boundaries without hypergnosis brings about a schizophrenic but not a paranoidal state.

So far we have distinguished in the development of a paranoid system the stages of experience, of the process of its projection, and of a hypergnostic co-ordination of it into a cosmology. Our presentation is so far incomplete that it takes no account of paranoid systems dealing ostensibly with abstractions and not, as in Schreber's case, with his own person. Apart from paranoiacs with delusions of persecution, jealousy, or redemption, there are cases with inventive mania, cosmological theories, ideas of world reformation, physical discoveries, and many more. The connection between these forms and the forms previously described lies in the word "ostensibly." As a matter of fact, analysis shows that judgments on matters external to the ego represent in deeper layers judgment concerning personal experiences. Paranoiac theories are not concerned immediately with the original material but with presentations which by a process of displacement are substituted for the original material. The idea can then be kept from consciousness, whereas in the simpler type first described, e.g., Schreber's case, the ego-dystonic content, fantasies of passive homosexual outrage, appears directly in consciousness. As an example of the second type let us analyze briefly a distorted idea from a confusional case.

A patient with mild schizophrenia is entirely absorbed with the subject of parental conflict. Hardly any other idea occurs to him except by way of his parents' attitude to it. The origin of this conflict was the son's rebellion against the strict religious and patriarchal views of his parents, particularly of his mother. His life is one constant repetition of situations of rupture and reconciliation with them. On occasions of rupture he is usually stuporose and ceases all activities, but after successful reconciliation his energies return, merely to prepare for the next catastrophe.

This patient has elaborated a philosophical system which absorbs most of his activity and which he regards as of the first importance. In such a highly educated person (a physician) his philosophical system must appear doubly trivial, barren, and crazy. His main idea runs that fundamentally there can be nothing but agreement between science and religion; this has always been apparent to him and he seems to have regarded the idea almost as a revelation.

From what sources does he derive his evidence? He may at some time or other have heard of the scholastic theses on this subject; but how can this truth be accompanied with such intense conviction unless it is related to some equally profound experience? The experience, it seems, must be his perpetual bondage to his parents, above all to his mother. He feels in some dim way that love alone could control his peculiar and often extremely reprehensible conduct and has a foreboding that, unlike other men, his bondage will never yield to that degree of independence which is a prerequisite of tender feeling. And this experience of compulsive dependence which he does not admit—it is manifested by open revolt and by violent accusations against his parents, colored largely with guilt feeling—becomes apparent to him only in the distorted form of his main thesis. Religion represents the pious and strict mother, who implanted profound conscientious scruples in her son with regard to his adoption of the profession of medicine; he himself represents natural science. The unity of religion and science is for him no mere shibboleth; his is a lasting conviction, because it is based on experience—not of course an "experience" of the unity between science and religion, but of the unity of the persons from which this allegory is built up.

Here then is an example of the instinctual language being translated into terms of cultural life; one of the factors in the process seems to be the wish to repudiate the facts of instinctual life, hence a kind of repression. The thought we have just analyzed is not actually paranoid in nature: the element of projection of the fundamental experience into the outer world is lacking. Had such an element been present the experience would not have been formulated as "my parents and myself constitute an indissoluble unity" but rather "external forces compel me to be one with my parents." The thought translation would then run somewhat as follows: "scientific principles are modified by external influences, perhaps by some apparatus, in such a way that they are at one with religion"; the thought would then be definitely paranoiac. Although not paranoiac in the strict sense of the term (the fundamental experience does not appear to be homosexual), this analyzed thought will serve to illustrate the process of translation.

We are now in a position to reduce the processes of delusion-formation to their elements. Some definite experience is internally objectivated and, owing to the individual's hypergnostic tendency, becomes the foundation of a system; either foundations are formed to support the experience or the experience is converted into a generalization. In this way the experience itself may not be represented, its place being taken by translations, seemingly different in content, derived from any suitable spheres of ideation. In this instance the seemingly paranoiac formation is merely a copy of the original one.

We may now attempt to differentiate between the mechanisms of obsessive thoughts and delusional thoughts respectively. We cannot do so in terms of content, since typical delusional ideas, e.g., of redemption or persecution, can appear as true obsessive thoughts in cases of pure obsessional neurosis. The obsessive and the delusional form are distinguished phenomenologically by the existence of evidence of the experience. In the latter instance evidence is advanced and there exists a state of complete refractoriness to corrective modification; in the former the thought obtrudes itself in a compulsive way, but is discredited by the subject who exhibits ambivalence and doubt. We believe that underlying this difference there is another concerning the unequivocal nature of the experience. The other processes of paranoidal thought-formation are also observed in obsessional neuroses (with certain minor differences) but the underlying experience appears to be contradictory and in no sense unequivocal instinctually. In Schreber's case, had a complete breakthrough of homosexuality not occurred, had the opposing tendencies been strong enough to lead to open conflict, the experience would *ceteris paribus*— variation of experience of object and hypergnosis—have led to the presentation of the content of his delusion in the form of obsessive thoughts, fantasies of homosexual assault of an extremely compulsive nature, fantasies of redemption recurring persistently in spite of repudiation, etc.

It would be quite wrong to attempt to explain the difference between obsession and delusion on the grounds of a stronger sense of reality-testing. For in the presence of other characteristic factors, an unequivocal experience invariably routs the reality-censor (one has only to think how frequently delusional thoughts persist in personalities otherwise completely intact). To put the matter more correctly, every delusional thought has passed the reality-censor and is based on a true experience. The generalization and theoretical superstructures are alone false. We must not of course ignore the fact that the degree of capacity for generalization and theoretical naiveté is not much in excess of that displayed in daily life by most other people of the same cultural development.

The distinctions we have drawn between obsession and delusion enable us to explain why obsessional thoughts frequently acquire a delusional form, and why an obsessional neurosis may develop into paranoia. In all such cases, an experience originally contradictory, associated with conflict and represented in obsessive thoughts, is gradually divested of conflict and comes to be accepted *in toto* by the individual. We shall shortly have occasion to describe the modifications in the ego ideal which precede this change.

The factors in delusional formation which we have so far described seem to be essential ones but do not cover the whole ground. For when Schreber was looking for some construction by means of which he could co-ordinate his altered instinctual life into a cosmic scheme, there were undoubtedly numerous possibilities open to him. It still remains unexplained why his theoretical venture took the particular form of a delusion of redemption having a characteristic megalomaniac pattern. It is only by study of the alterations taking place in the ego ideal that we can get a more precise idea of the course of events.

That the homosexual tendencies forced their way into action and consciousness implies a breakdown of the corresponding part of the ego ideal; the prohibition "I must not love men" must first of all be removed. Does this imply a breakdown in the ego ideal?

One gathers that the process is not one of demolition but rather of an internal rearrangement of layers. The original prohibition of homosexuality is not swept aside in the rush of the instinctual drive without substitution; in fact it secures a considerable amount of compensation. The moral component of the ego ideal certainly comes greatly weakened out of the conflict, but only after the narcissistic component has been developed in a highly civilized manner as a compensation. To Schreber himself the new demand of the ego ideal ran "I must be the savior of humanity"; so that he could afford to be easy over the breakdown of his ideal in another direction: "Even if I have homosexual ideas, they do not signify the same for me as for others; in my case it is no mere instinctual gratification, but a fate which falls on me along with this, my function of savior."

It is perfectly clear from a study of Schreber's ideas that this compensatory process played a decisive part in forming the content of his delusion. As Freud has shown, Schreber did not in the first instance explain his experience on the savior hypothesis but connected it with the much more direct assumption that he was molested sexually. This tendency did not, however, develop any further; it lacked the narcissistic compensation necessary for a breakdown of the moral ideal. Schreber's idea was that all attempts to change his sex for unnatural purposes (i.e., in order to satisfy some person's sexual desire) had completely miscarried, whereas his castration for purposes in keeping with natural law (i.e., as a method of world redemption) seemed to him a quite reasonable outcome of the conflict.

This compensation, which itself proves the existence of narcissistic fixations, alone enabled the instinctual drive to break through; moreover, this process in the ego ideal explains why among many possible theories this particular delusional idea arose in his mind. The ultimate form of the delusion must reproduce this process in the ego ideal; the new delusion must be made to tally with fresh demands on the part of the ideal. Hence we must amplify our original presentation of the origin of delusional thinking, in that the content of the idea is definitely decided by a rearrangement of the elements in the ego ideal permitting the fundamental experience to be worked out.

We have already exceeded the limits of a description of paranoid thought formation; the example we have given in illustration of "translation" of an instinctual situation and our investigation of obsessive thoughts have carried us beyond our original theme. They enable us, however, to arrive at a generalization which brings us to the real thesis of this paper. In our opinion this mechanism of paranoid thought formation can be regarded as a prototype of the mechanism of creative thinking and of normal thought processes generally.

We believe that it is in keeping with psychoanalytical experience to assume that non-delusional true creative thinking is also based on an experience. The inclination for some particular subject and fixation on these thoughts arise solely from the experience; contradiction in the experience gives rise to doubt concerning the thought formations, while what is unequivocal in the experience produces the evidence for the thought processes and the unalterable conviction regarding them.

We can also observe in non-delusional thought the second factor, projection. A certain degree of objectivation is present in all thought, although of course in normal cases it does not go beyond the boundaries of the ego. It is our belief that objectivation is not a result of thought operations but that objectivation of the experience is a prerequisite of the appearance of thought elaboration.

Hypergnosis invariably plays a part in the development of creative thinking: a hidden connection must be grasped. We might call this a developed perception of "shape." This can be correlated with the usual form of perception of "shape" by means of a simple observation. In the case of visual thinkers productive ideas are often perceived in optical "shape" forms while analogous "shape" experiences are recorded by auditory and motor types.

The translation of experience into thought content must, in accordance with our theory, also occur in normal thinking. At any rate this certainly happens when the thoughts relate to matters other than the subject's own instinctual life.

Hence we must assume that certain displacements also occur normally within the ego ideal. The possibility of experience, its ultimate translation and transferred representation imply very slight retrogressions and compensatory formations in the ego ideal, although these are not so archaic in nature or so obvious as in the simple case of the Schreber delusion.

And this outline must serve also as a basis for the normal processes of thought, in so far as these are concerned with completed thought-presentations. We may assume that in such instances there is some variation in the intensity and perhaps in the content of the fundamental experience, that there are minor degrees of difference in objectivation, and that the process of hypergnosis is less marked.

We are now in a position to consider the difference between paranoidal and true creative thinking, and this leads to the further question whether in psychological mechanisms of thought formation it is possible to distinguish between true and false. The latter problem is beyond the scope of our present discussion, since it takes us from the region of psy-

chology to theories of cognition and cannot be clearly formulated without some such theoretical basis. As we are limited
here to purely psychological considerations, we can only present certain common, possibly typical differences between paranoidal and correct thinking, without of course claiming that
these have universal application or are incapable of other
interpretation.

In the first place, can it be said that a preference for one
definite form of experience (the homosexual form) is typical
of paranoidal thinking only? This could be decided only after
abundant analytical investigation of the processes of creative
thinking. Again, may there not be some typical difference in
the degree of projection which determines whether only relative objectivation of the experience takes place without over-
stepping ego boundaries or whether displacement into the outer
world occurs? We may hazard the guess that projection of
the latter sort is the basis of any weakening of the reality
censorship. It disturbs the whole context of the experience,
which then appears to the individual to be purely environmental and yet in opposition to external reality. A condition
has arisen which we describe as a case of reality censorship,
since the external world as experienced by the individual no
longer coincides with the actual external reality. The basis for
this profound variation of objective experience appears to be
a regression to the early period of development in which
numerous isolated ego instincts had not yet been unified by
more developed ego instincts and when ego boundaries were
correspondingly vague.

Our assumption that damaged reality-testing is due to the
injury of ego boundaries in the process of experiencing individual experience gains some support from an analogous process
occurring in normal life. Whenever a minor injury of ego
boundaries occurs in a normal person and makes him seek for
the explanation of his fate outside his own person, a weakening

of the reality-testing faculty occurs. Actual facts are reinterpreted and external reality is seen in a false light.

Moreover, typical differences between paranoidal and normal thinking appear to relate to the functioning of the ego ideal. Disintegration of the ideal is never so extensive in the case of normal thinking, and above all compensation formation never involves the same primitive narcissistic stages as it does in paranoia.

We have so far dealt more with paranoidal and creative thinking, approaching the latter problem by way of the former. We have still to consider two varieties of schizophrenic thinking, paranoid and heboid. We term "heboid" that form of disordered and confused thinking which flies from one idea to another. The pathological form of this is seen in the hebephrenic "flight of ideas," which is in curious contrast to the ordered thinking of paranoia. In our opinion this manifestation can be best understood on the assumption that it consists of numerous fragments of paranoidal formation, each one rapidly displacing the last, none of them being carried to a conclusion. We may take it that there is here a rapid change of significant experiences and that the source of this change is to be found in a kind of dissipation of libido. Heboid thinking is then to be regarded (with the differences noted above) as a pathological prototype of that variety of normal thought which is called inconsequent, never keeping to one subject for any length of time.

In sharp contrast to the schizophrenic types is a variety of thinking seen in a pathological form in amentia. In contrast to the types already described the fragmented thought formations of such patients indicate a reduced appreciation of "shape," or, to keep to our terminology, a kind of hypergnosis. It is characterized by an incapacity to synthesize experience. This, too, has its counterpart in normal life.

Within the limits of this contribution we have not been able to deal with every form of pathological thinking nor to give a full description of the corresponding normal types. We have had to content ourselves with provisory formulations of a theory concerning the functional dependence of thought processes on instinctual life. The results of investigation of the processes of ordered thinking which have been reached by thought psychologists have not been referred to here. Doubtless there are many points of view common to both methods of approach which will have to be considered and given proper valuation in any future comprehensive theory of thought.

1926

◻ THE INFLUENCE
OF CREATIVE DESIRE
UPON THE ARGUMENT
FOR IMMORTALITY

Cavendish Moxon

Human curiosity first serves the self-centered impulse to seek objects which cause pleasure and to avoid objects which threaten pain. In proportion to the growth of ethical repressions of crude impulse and cultural sublimations of infantile desire, curiosity has been diverted to problems in the external world. Civilization has involved a severe limitation of the open play of fantasy and the direct satisfaction of desire. Only by means of elaborate religious, artistic, and scientific disguises can the primitive desires escape. Indeed the aim of scientists is to discover fact even when fact contradicts the deepest desire.

Since many precious wishes have been hidden below consciousness, it is clear that the psychological study of the unconscious inevitably arouses great affective opposition. This is an obvious factor in some of the adverse criticisms of Freudian theories. In some cases the unconscious opposition is strong enough to prevent the severe renunciation of pleasure involved in accepting the new hypotheses. In other cases the admission of unwelcome facts has to struggle against the rationalizations and moralizations of primitive impulse and self-centered desire. The struggle is strongly marked in the artistic temperament which delights in new symbolic representations of unconscious desires and in imaginary association of preconscious impressions. The creative artist has a strong will to live which is symbolized by belief in survival of death. Moreover the artist tends to be conscious of the poverty of his expressions in comparison with the wealth of his impressions. He will therefore be almost overwhelmed by the smallness of his productions when he learns that all his previous experiences have been impressed and preserved in his subconscious mind.

Such, it would appear, is the feeling of Maeterlinck, who has published his views about the preservation of impressions in what he terms the subconscious mind. The poet accepts the facts which he uses as a new way of rationalizing the belief in survival which satisfies his deepest desires. The weight of these desires may be estimated by their power to obscure the poet's critical judgment on matters of fact. Maeterlinck's reason for belief in survival is similar to the argument based on the premises that justice is supreme and that an enormous amount of conscious ability is destroyed by death before it is able to do its good work for the world. Maeterlinck modifies this argument by putting his emphasis on the waste of unconscious mental energy, and by substituting natural economy for divine justice. The poet as psychologist knows that the conscious waste of material represents but a small part of the vast mass of unused subconscious material in even the longest human life.

Maeterlinck has argued that man's unconscious soul survives his conscious and bodily death. His argument appears to rest on two premises—a fact about the extent of man's wasted unconscious life, and a belief about the nature of organic life in general. The fact is proved by a very large number of observations made by hypnotists and psychoanalysts. A countless number of sensations are preserved at subconscious levels of the mind, either in temporal succession or in more elaborately associated groups. The subconscious part of the psyche is therefore enormously larger than the conscious organ of perception and memory. From the immense and ever increasing subconscious accumulation there rise to consciousness only a few fragments, as memories, fantasies, jokes, automatisms, intuitions, or symbolic images. Maeterlinck stands in wonder before the store of psychic material revealed by research. With his vivid imagination the poet pictures the boundless possibilities for mental creation that are involved. His aesthetic conscience refuses to contemplate the final loss of so great a hidden treasure. Even the most productive genius cannot use every impression that has sunk into forgetfulness for lack of the appropriate stimulus for its recollection and use. Therefore, argues Maeterlinck, the retention of so many impressions is a useless mental process under the conditions of bodily life on earth.

At this point the poet seems to have been carried away by his emotional reaction to the new knowledge, and to have made an exaggerated statement about the uselessness of subconscious impressions. Certainly not every impression returns through the normal memory of even the oldest and busiest thinker. But the majority of subconscious impressions are at any time available for conscious use if required. The only exceptions are a few unpleasant or disgusting impressions which have been so deeply pressed into the unconscious that neither they nor their associated impressions can be recalled by memory. The unemployment of such undesirable images, however, is surely no loss which calls for a compensatory opportunity in a future life. Of the vast majority of impressed experiences that lie

139

within the limits of conscious recall, it is possible that any one
may become a valuable memory in order to serve some individual or social purpose—to save a life, to compose a poem, to
make a joke, to construct a theory or a machine. Any selective
process in the subconscious might fail to include and preserve
ideas or images that could be used again to preserve or enrich
the personal and the collective life. Nature is a bountiful pro-
vider. No expenditure is extravagant if only it is directly or
indirectly a means to the preservation and transmission of life.
Millions of seeds are produced in order that a small minority
may survive. It is better that countless germs should perish
than that one should be lacking when required to subserve the
instinct for the preservation of the species. Likewise it is worth
Maeterlinck's keeping a subconscious packed full of idle words
and images if, by a stroke of genius, some few may rise to conscious life as the elements of a poem or a play.

We are now in a position to estimate the validity of Maeterlinck's second premise, which he asserts as if it were an undis-
puted scientific law: "It is admitted that nature does nothing
that is useless." This unqualified negative proposition is certainly
not admitted by the present writer. There spring to his mind
pictures of many monstrous products of nature—useless additional limbs, innate morbid impulsive tendencies and instinctive
disharmonies which have no value for the organism or the
species as a whole. No doubt such entirely useless structures
and modes of behavior are exceptions. The majority of organs
and functions in nature have at one time some degree of usefulness to the species. The appendix was not always a dangerous relic. And the tendency of organisms to produce a sudden
variation of form or instinct usually promotes survival though
it occasionally makes a self-destroying monster.

Maeterlinck's argument would be stronger if he could show
that all the subconscious impressions are useless for earthly life.
But he knows the loss to be only partial—thanks to memory

and creative intuition. Now if many seeds are wasted in order that a few may be used, the natural inference of a mind unbiased by unconscious desire would be that a host of subconscious impressions may be held in readiness to form a useful thought or a beautiful deed. Maeterlinck's premise is so inaccurate as to invalidate his argument from the supposed uselessness of the subconscious impressions that a strictly utilitarian nature must provide another sphere of usefulness for the unconscious after death. Moreover, the usefulness of a subconscious impression is not wholly dependent upon its regaining consciousness. The psychoanalytical study of behavior has made it probable that subconscious impressions when they become the images of desire indirectly play an important determining part in every act of judgment, choice, creation, and appreciation. The capability for attention, no doubt, strictly limits the recall of images; but Bergson showed forgetfulness to be useful for practical life. If memory were complete, choice and action would have an impossible task.

The biologist might be satisfied to have shown the weakness of Maeterlinck's argument. The psychologist's interest is by no means exhausted till he has gone a step further and explained the use of so weak an argument by so strong a mind. Maeterlinck is indeed only one instance of the paradox that eminent men often give illogical reasons for their belief in immortality. We must therefore generalize our inquiry and ask what it is that leads even men of genius to overlook the inadequacy of their reasons for this particular belief. The answer is given by the psychoanalysts, who have proved that men's reasons for belief in survival are unconsciously influenced by the desires they imperfectly conceal. The basic motives for the refusal to contemplate the annihilation of the ego are neither logical nor moral. The fact is, as Dr. Ernest Jones declares, that "in the unconscious everyone believes in the omnipotence of his thoughts, in the irresistibility of his charms, and in the immor-

141

tality of his soul." The unconscious is not concerned with moral and metaphysical reasons for survival. The unconscious feels the primitive will to live. Death has no meaning for this level of the psyche, which refuses to think of the extinction of itself and of the objects to whom its love and interest have been transferred. In the unconscious dream-thoughts men appear to be alive many years after their death; time is abolished and the ego "dies" or disappears only in order to be reborn. The conscious arguments are therefore afterthoughts or rationalizations of the primitive wishes. The great unconscious weight of lowly psychobiological desires accounts for the acceptance of many an argument, that, without this support, would be spurned by all intelligent men. Likewise the will to believe in survival without proof is due to the unbounded egoism of the unconscious mind. Religious faith in the eternal moral values of the soul has its roots in the supreme worth of the unconscious ego in its own estimation; and belief in immortal life is a barrier against the fearful thought of wasted powers—powers which seem immense and are checked and limited by an indifferent world. A rationalistic psychology has supposed that the original cause of belief in immortality was the false reasoning of primitive man who believed he saw his dead friends alive in the world of his dreams. The new psychology, which seeks for wishes beneath thoughts, declares that the savage saw his dead living in dreams because he could not conceive the intolerably unpleasant thought of the annihilation of those who ministered to the pleasure of his beloved and immortal self. The nonexistence of time for the unconscious mind is proved by the fact that for many years after their death some parents continue to exercise a repressive and harmful influence over their families, who only consciously accept the fact of their freedom, and show their bondage and fear in the dream-products of their unconscious life. An expression of the adult's unconscious refusal to face the fact of death sometimes openly appears upon the lips of the child. The following conversation reported by Jung makes this clear.

Anna, aged three, asks: "Grandmama, why have you such faded eyes?"
Grandmama: "Because I am old now."
Anna: "But that means that you will be young again."
Grandmama: "No, I shall get older and older, you know, and then I shall die."
Anna: "Yes, and then?"
Grandmama: "Then I shall be an angel."
Anna: "And then will you become a little child again?"

In night-dreams and to some extent in daydreams is realized the desire of the self-centered psyche for a free and endless exercise of its powers in a perfect world. In metaphysical opinions and religious hopes the unconscious wishes have to compromise with the scientific interest in external reality. In men of poetical imagination like Maeterlinck, we see the fight of self-love for dominance, and the consequent imperfect rationalization of unconscious desire. Maeterlinck, we conclude, is led to use bad reasons in support of his belief in immortality because this belief is a necessary symbol of his unconscious desires, which dominate the thoughts in his conscious creed.

1922

143

ON INSPIRATION:

PRELIMINARY NOTES ON

EMOTIONAL CONDITIONS

IN CREATIVE STATES

Ernst Kris

The present paper is devoted to an attempt at understanding some of the psychological problems connected with inspiration. For reasons of space I cannot quote at length the clinical, biographical, and anthropological evidence on which this essay is based. It will, however, be given in full on another occasion, in a study of the nature of creative processes on a broader basis.

Let us take the spirit of language as a guide for our first steps. The various meanings of the word "inspiration" show a single conception developing along a progressive scale. The literal meaning is best illustrated by the narrative in Gen. 2:7: "And the Lord God formed man of the dust of the ground and breathed into his nostrils the breath of life; and man became a living soul." The usage of the word "inspiration" in modern times is, however, twofold. It comprehends the action of inhaling as well as the action of blowing on, or into, the passive as well as the active part of the process.

145

The metaphorical usage to which I shall mainly refer transposes the bodily action onto the mental plane. The action of inspiring and the condition of being inspired refer to the mind. "A special immediate action or influence of the spirit of God or some divine and supernatural being" (*Shorter Oxford Dictionary*, 1936) takes hold of a person. He becomes an instrument of the divine, and his works are inspired in the same way as those books of the Bible which are thought to have been written under divine influence and have retained a special place in the religious belief of man. From this conception, which, for the purpose of this paper, I shall call the "full metaphorical meaning of inspiration" and which is based upon the immediate substitution of spiritual influence for breath, all other figurative meanings of the word derive. Two of them, however, are further differentiated. We sometimes call spontaneous ideas, visions, or conceptions, "inspiration" and speak of the inspiring influence of a person upon others. I shall refer to these meanings as the second and third stages of metaphorical usage. Divergent as they undoubtedly are, they still have a common basis. They both describe changes in the attitude of man, the first a change in his mind which arises suddenly, the second a change in his emotional life, mostly due to the influence of another person. Both these changes, however, are characteristic of states of inspiration in the full metaphorical sense. But in the latter the alteration of the normal attitude is not limited to the mental and emotional condition of the person; it also embraces his physical state. This alteration generally arises suddenly and is ascribed to the influence of some spirit. The concept of inspiration is intended to account for these states: it is an explanation on the animistic level. In order to replace it by a scientific explanation we shall have to enumerate some of the characteristics of such states.

In their purest form they are found in primitive society. They appear mainly in the religious sphere, which includes almost all productive mental activities. The inspired persons are mainly priests, medicine men, or prophets. At a large stage —if we can speak of evolution where such uncertainty still prevails—the poet and, in exceptional cases, men of action join them. These men of action, however, are not the mythical heroes, not the great revolutionaries; they are rather of the type of "the prophet as leader." The states of inspiration are not permanent. They take hold of the individual for a certain time. They are mostly connected with a partial loss of consciousness and are almost habitually accompanied by various sorts of more or less unco-ordinated motor activities.

The clinical classification of these states is not always easy. They sometimes show characteristics of epileptic or—perhaps more frequently—hystero-epileptic states (*morbus sacer*) or else a more or less complicated hysterical symptom formation. But while there seems to be a certain variety of clinical syndrome which may predispose to these states, the psychological conception of the belief in inspiration and of the processes occurring in it aims at a solution that will not be limited to any one of these clinical conditions. These highly complex processes may be described as phenomena of regression. In clinical cases this regression is likely to lead to a withdrawal of ego control from many of the higher mental activities. As an example we have mentioned that the co-ordination of motor activities is frequently affected. To add another most characteristic feature, in states of inspiration speech becomes automatic. It is not the subject who speaks but a voice from out of him. The pronouncements of this voice from him are unknown before the state of inspiration has arisen. It is the voice of his unconscious, he communicates it to others, and he himself becomes part of the public.

In such communications the unconscious is supreme. They are always prophecy or poetry of some kind. The vision of the future is, of course, largely based upon the interaction of wish and fantasy (the main contents of the unconscious) with the preconscious understanding of the needs and desires of the community. The essence of vaticination has in fact always been the unconscious connection between the prophet and the client, the forecast of the future being based upon the experience of the past. The poets of old were hardly distinguished from priests and prophets. Their main province was myth, that is to say the past of the tribe or the common fantasy about that past, in which terrible deeds occurred, incest and murder, similar to those which mold the fantasy life of early childhood. The story of this past is not entrusted to consciousness. In a state similar to that of intoxication, elated, in a trance, not conscious of what he does—thus Plato, to whom we owe this first description of the state of inspiration—the poet sings his song. The voice of God speaks through him to men. Obviously all similar states, when the prophet acts as leader, when he codifies the law or writes down what has been revealed to him, are based upon analogous mental experiences. We are perhaps thus justified in saying that the inspired leadership of primitive society consists of individuals who, among other qualities which do not enter into the framework of our present deliberation, are distinguished by a certain disposition to communicate with the repressed wishes and fantasies in themselves by the use of special mechanisms. These mechanisms are in the nature of projection and introjection. What comes from inside is believed to come from without. The voice of the unconscious is externalized and becomes the voice of God, who speaks through the mouth of the chosen. This process of externalization constitutes one decisive element of the phenomenon of inspiration, but not the whole of it.[1] The knowledge which the voice communicates is not only derived from God, but literally given by him. The awareness itself is a result of inspiration as well as a part of it, and thus the driving of the unconscious toward consciousness, the process of becoming conscious, is attributed

148

to the influence of the divine. In other words, an alteration of cathexis inside the person, the bursting of the frontiers between the unconscious and the conscious, is experienced as an intrusion from without. We may therefore say that the conception of inspiration is connected with two emotional experiences. Though they are intimately interwoven with each other and may, therefore, not always be distinguished by the individual himself, they may be separated here for the sake of our presentation: in the concept of inspiration impulses, wishes and fantasies derived from the unconscious are attributed to a supernatural being and the process of their becoming conscious is experienced as an action of this being upon the subject, and thus activity is turned into passivity.

Before we attempt to carry this trend of thought any further we shall have to consider some of the conditions which may account for the universality and the tenacity of the belief in inspiration. Two main purposes seem to be served by that belief: one concerns its social and the other its individual aspect. Through the idea of inspiration the communication gains in authority, and the person who communicates it is relieved of the burden of responsibility. The increase in authority is best exemplified if we think of the concept of revelation. The revealed truth is of a quality other than that of truth acquired through human effort. It is beyond criticism as well as beyond doubt. The problem of responsibility, however, is more complicated; it is intimately linked with anxiety and guilt. In speaking of archaic social conditions we may say that the tale the poet tells derives from or touches upon the forbidden sphere of wishes, desires, and impulses. Under the assumption of inspiration not he but the divine is acting; he is not responsible, his feelings of guilt are relieved, and no anxiety need arise.

The full metaphorical meaning of inspiration, however, underwent an alteration even in the ancient world, and thus it became a term designating special conditions of creation,

149

though without losing the whole of its original meaning. Just as the prerogatives conceded to the man of genius are still derived from the days in which *ingenium* had its full mythological meaning, so the consideration granted to those who are in this special state of creativeness still reflects the older conception. This relation does not exist for the public only; it is not only a sociological one, but it remains true of the creators themselves; it has a full psychological sense.

In many autobiographical descriptions, especially by poets or artists, we hear that the creative states are states of special excitement. This excitement may be favored by certain conditions and may be evokable by certain stimuli, but as a rule it cannot be controlled altogether. In these conditions the individual may feel more or less elated or depressed, extremely vital or ill. The act of creation becomes extremely easy, sometimes progressing at great speed, and a feeling arises that "the real work is done by some unseen collaborator" (R. L. Stevenson).

Out of a great variety of autobiographical descriptions I want to choose one which impresses me by its moderation and prudence. In his Leslie Stephen Lecture at Cambridge on *The Name and Nature of Poetry* (1933), A. E. Housman describes what one might fittingly call his individual experience of poetic inspiration: "I think that a production of poetry is less an active than a passive and involuntary process." He compares it with human or animal secretion and stresses the fact that it is painful and accomplished in a state near to illness: "Having drunk a pint of beer at luncheon—beer is a sedative to the brain and my afternoons are the least intellectual portions of my life—I would go out for a walk. As I went along, thinking of nothing in particular, there would flow into my mind with sudden and unaccountable emotion, sometimes a line or two of verse, sometimes a whole stanza at once, accompanied, not preceded, by a vague notion of the poem as a whole. Then there would usually be a lull and perhaps the spring would bubble up again. I say bubble up, because the source of the suggestion thus proffered to the brain was an abyss." This abyss Housman is inclined to locate in "the pit of the stomach."

While here the veil of understatement disguises the emotional upheaval of the creative state under a cover of self-irony, we may imagine that other less critical minds would be inclined to describe analogous though less fruitful experiences in terms of the full metaphorical meaning of inspiration. In Housman's words, however, another meaning of that word is implied: that which I suggested should be called the second stage of metaphorical usage. In this sense inspiration designates, as we said, the sudden arising of visions or thoughts, and in this sense inspiration may be called almost the everyday version of the creative process which we all know as a flash of thought.

I should like to discuss this phenomenon in connection with scientific thinking, where the sudden experience concerns some step in the attempt to solve a problem. Summarizing some of the results of psychological research, we may emphasize the following points: The work of the mind in research and discovery does not consist only in a continuous application to the quest for a solution. A part of the work is done in preconscious elaboration, the result of which comes into consciousness in sudden advances. It is almost always possible to find traces of an interrelation between some external stimuli and this preconscious process.[2]

Some of the greatest scientific discoveries are attributed to chance by the discoverers themselves, just as Newton's observation of a falling apple is alleged to have been the source of his discovery of the law of gravitation. A closer analysis of such cases, which play a considerable part in typical biographies of scientists, has, as Paulhan has shown, proved beyond all doubt that what appears to be chance is in fact an observation impregnated with previous preconscious experiences. The making of the observation is in itself a part of the preconscious process. In the words of Louis Pasteur: "Le hasard ne favorise que les esprits préparés." The idea, however, that the discovery originated from the observation which chance offered and that the whole of the mental process involved was indeed started by chance, through an inspiration, deserves some further comment. Chance is always tinged by the conception of fate. It stands for what in religious terms may be called the will of God, in the last analysis for God himself.[3] And thus our path seems to have led us back to the problem of inspiration. The belief in the part played by chance in scientific discoveries repeats on another plane the idea of the voice of the unconscious which is externalized and attributed to God. In order to account for this similarity several arguments may be adduced. Scientific thinking is in itself never sharply separated from the realm of the unconscious, and the psychoanalysis of inventors and research workers shows that there is an intimate connection between these higher mental functions and unconscious wishes and desires and their infantile roots. This argument concerning the id aspect of scientific thought may be supplemented by another which might be called the superego aspect. Any research or discovery may, in some sense, be an attempt to trespass across established boundaries and thus be related to infantile situations in which such attributes were forbidden and dangerous. But a third argument may still be added; it concerns the aspect of ego psychology. The working of our mind in productive thinking is, as we have said, not based on steady application only. It is most probably connected with changes of cathexis which may take the character of sudden, as it were eruptive, processes. The part attributed to chance would then properly be described as rationalization. But this description is true only in a somewhat superficial sense. It does not take into account one further element: that

of the excitement sometimes connected with productive thinking, even if that excitement is less noticeable than with any
other sort of creative activity. Such excitement is of a libidinal
nature. Evidence is easily accessible in so far as "normal" conditions of creative activity are concerned.[4] The evidence, however, which I should like to mention here, as shortly as possible, concerns its pathological aspect, i.e., states of excitement
connected with unsuccessful creative activity in thinking and
in scientific research. I have chosen the two following cases for
the sake of contrast. In the first, the symptom of intellectual
inhibition is of a comparatively simple structure—the structure
only is to be considered; in the second, the process used is akin
to inspiration.

The first patient, a man in his early forties, has had a fairly
sucecssful professional career. He is a learner, an examination
type, and has endeavored to add to his name a variety of
letters—many more than his father, who had worked successfully in the same field. The rivalry with this beloved father
dominates all the spheres of the patient's activity. His whole
life is a somewhat exaggerated repetition of his father's life,
and his obedience to his father's principles and moral conceptions has taken a turn toward caricature. He distorts any father-
figure he meets in his life by means of the mechanism of projection and he then fights the dummy he has set up. This fight
is clearest in the intellectual field. While his faculty for learning is extreme and his records in cramming have won him
admiration—his memory is extraordinary and literally every
other word he speaks is a quotation—he feels entirely unable
to think for himself and is actually shaken by anxiety when
faced with a new problem. His first impulse is to seek help,
some authority to quote; in terms of instinctual life, some
formula to take in and then to apply. But sometimes, under
special conditions, he tries to fight that authority. Any success
in this fight—his outlook is in many ways a modern one,

153

almost that of a revolutionary—has the greatest emotional value. It is an achievement more desirable than any other. "And I have at last found that out for myself," he will exclaim in deep excitement. It is a victory in a conflict, a victory of activity over passivity, and as such an almost exact repetition of certain of his attempts to overcome the shock of circumcision, experienced in his fifth year, though traces of this attitude were discernible in some much older material, in aggressive impulses connected with anal experiences.

The second case concerns a man in his thirties who, among many other difficulties, shows an almost complete inhibition in working, which forms a severe impediment to his career as a scientific worker. While any kind of routine work is easily achieved, any form of creative activity is associated with extreme difficulties and accompanied by a number of severe physical and mental symptoms. These difficulties are partly determined by an unconscious identification with his father, which follows the line of aggressiveness and guilt. Whereas his grandfather, whose tradition he wishes to continue, had been a famous academic teacher, his father has, owing to an inhibition in his powers of scientific research, failed to reach high academic honors. More interesting, however, than this part of the problem are the patient's attempts to overcome the inhibition. I should like to mention two of them. He can attempt productive work if, by means of alcohol or drugs, he has worked himself up into a state of excitement, in which work is done in a rapture. The second method is more complicated. He manages to find some authority in his own or in a neighboring field of research whom he induces to give him some advice about his work. His reaction to this advice is twofold. He endeavors to prove its futility, or he is afraid of committing a plagiarism. Closer analysis, however, shows that his wish to take away another person's ideas is no stronger than his fear that his own ideas may be used by this same person or by someone else. And furthermore the advice he gets is exactly the sort of advice he wants to get, the sort of advice which he had, in fact, himself suggested. Here the mechanisms of projection and introjection are at work and the process is akin to inspiration, one of the differences being that instead of "an unseen collaborator"—to use Stevenson's words—the collaborator is a person in the outside world. No less than the first method, that of oral gratification, the second method, the "taking advice" and dealing with it, produces states of marked general excitement. In these states the whole pace of his life seems to be accelerated. His attitude is changed. Indeed, one is almost tempted in this connection to use the word "inspired"! As regards the historical background it may be briefly added that analogous tendencies expressed themselves in his latency period when he stole books from his father in order to buy sweets; they were rooted in childhood in a passive oral fantasy of incorporating his father's penis.[5]

In both of these cases a homosexual fantasy forms the background of experiences in the intellectual field, the sexualization being obviously responsible for the failures. The climax in the old fantasy is replaced in the first case by the intellectual fight and the deep satisfaction which eventually ensues, in the second case by the states of excitement. In this second case, however, the aggressive meaning of creative activity leads to the quest for an authority, whose advice frequently represents the patient's own ideas. Here, *si parva licet componere magnis,* lies the analogy with the state of inspiration in the full metaphorical sense.

The sexual character of the concept of fertilization through respiratory functions, which is the nucleus of inspiration in its literal sense, has been discussed by Ernest Jones. He has stressed the fact "that respiratory processes tend to be interpreted in the unconscious in terms of alimentary ones" and "that breath receives much of its importance . . . through the

conception of internal pneuma." He has described how the
conception of the soul derives from that of anal procreation
"which has gradually been purged from all material grossness"
until the "purest and least sexual form of procreation, the
one most befitting the creator himself," has been established.
While this purification, as described by Jones, was mostly concerned with the pregenital implication connected with the
fertilizing power of breath, the various meanings of inspiration
with which we began show how the purification is concerned here with the elimination of the sexual implication. In
the full metaphorical sense inspiration implies a state of a
sometimes scarcely veiled sexual character which is best exemplified by reports of the changes in sex actually occurring with
the shamans of certain Mongolian tribes. The sexual connotation, however, has disappeared in the second stage of the
metaphorical usage. Here inspiration designates a process of
ego activity only, the sudden appearance of ideas. In the third
stage, when we speak, for instance, of the inspiring effect of
leadership, emphasis is laid once again on a libidinal relationship.
But this libidinal relationship concerns the superego. Thus we
may say that the various meanings of the word "inspiration"
seem to be differentiated by a varying degree of desexualization.

This point of view, however, does not concern the various
meanings of the word inspiration only. The states of inspiration
themselves may be more or less sexual in character and where
inspiration is an element in creative activities of any kind a
certain degree of desexualization seems to be a precondition
of success. The spirit of language, however, the connotations
attached to respiratory functions, direct our attention to
another point: to the importance of pregenital elements in
fantasies connected with inspiration. It is my impression that
this is a never-absent feature of these fantasies. Instead of discussing the clinical evidence here, I should like to recall Housman's words: the "natural secretion like turpentine in the fire"

or the "morbid secretion like the pearl in the oyster," the "bubbling up from an abyss," "the pit of the stomach," and "the pint of beer" which initiates the process speak for themselves. The process of inspiration is here clearly expressed in oral, intestinal, and anal terms. This is not astonishing if we think that on the level of pregenital meaning creation itself signifies anal production. But the pregenital elements in the fantasies connected with inspiration stand in a special framework. The fantasies—I can speak only of men—are centered around the father and around the conflict between active and passive tendencies. While in autobiographical descriptions of creative states pregenital connotations are frequently implied or even expressed, as in Housman's words, the relation to the father-figure is better hidden. In Housman's skeptical self-analysis this part of the fantasy seems to have found an expression in the following words: "I have rarely written poetry unless I was rather out of health, and the experience, though pleasurable, was generally agitating and exhausting." This is the description of a process in which passivity is indeed supreme. In terms of our theory we might say: the path leads from anal activity to homosexual passivity and thus another well-known meaning of creation is evoked—that of giving birth to a child.

At this point a number of problems arise which I shall not be able to approach in this connection. I think, however, that at least two of them should be mentioned. How far are pregenital experiences themselves responsible for such fantasies as the one which found its expression in Housman's words, and how far is the pregenital element due to regression? That is to say, how far have they kept their older meaning and how far are they influenced by the fact that the individual has reverted from the genital to an earlier stage? This question is connected with a second one. The process of inspiration being based upon the re-introjection of what was formerly projected, it may be asked how far this process is in itself influenced by earlier experiences of using the same mechanisms, especially as the voice of the unconscious, which is externalized, contains results of former introjections.

It is my impression that in the fantasies connected with inspiration the genital elaboration of pregenital experiences is evident, and that the pregenital layers constitute nothing specific. It is clearly impossible here to discuss this specificity in a strict sense, which would enable us to predict what kind of people are likely to experience inspiration. It is meant for the framework of fantasies and mechanisms connected with inspiration as compared with similar elements in several other somewhat comparable emotional conditions. Such conditions include the various kinds of visionary states, various states of grace and possession, and especially the state of ecstasy. I am inclined to believe that in all these states the fantasies are of the same general nature, especially in so far as the use of projection and introjection is concerned; in all of them they are desexualized and raised to the plane of a mental process. The state nearest to inspiration is ecstasy. "What had been projected as a vision of God is now in ecstasy taken back into the ego, but not as an antithesis between ego and superego or between ego and God: ego and God are one." This description, given by Helene Deutsch, could be applied as such to the first of the steps constituting inspiration in its full metaphorical meaning. We have tried to show that there is another, a second step connected with it: that the driving of the unconscious toward consciousness is experienced as an intrusion from without—an attitude of a passive nature *par excellence*. The decisive difference, however, can be formulated more clearly. In ecstasy the process results in an emotional climax only, in states of inspiration it leads to active elaboration in creation. The process is dominated by the ego and put to its own purposes—for sublimation in creative activity. Thus inspired creation solves an inner contest, sometimes as a compromise between conflicting forces, sometimes as a defense against one particularly dangerous instinct. Where man seems to be at the peak of his activity, in creation, he is still sometimes inclined to bend his head to the Almighty and to be carried back to the period when dependence on objects in the outside world dominated his life.

1939

NOTES

1. For the purpose of this paper a differentiation between externalization and projection may be valuable. If the externalized thought is projected onto some special supernatural being, it may, when communicated to the tribe, bear some features of this being as he is known by tradition. This is the case of prophecy, and this case only should really be called projection.

2. Psychoanalytical experience leads us to confirm this point of view and to stress one part of this relation. We have in our daily work ample opportunity to watch how observations are directed by the mind, that is to say, how human beings notice what they are prepared to see. As Anna Freud once put it, one can almost predict, in the course of an analysis with a woman patient, when she is going to read in a newspaper that an operation has been performed on a hermaphrodite. On another plane, self-observation confirms that even our research work can be hampered or promoted by our dependence on these factors.

3. It is hardly necessary to justify this substitution here. One argument only may be quoted. In mythology, where all inventions and discoveries are either inspired or considered as products of a Promethean impulse, a number of typical legends occur in which the acquisition of new insight or a new conquest in the fight against nature is either ascribed to some father imago (to some great teacher), or else to chance as a *locum tenens*.

4. A closer investigation of the circumstances favoring creative activities seems, for instance, to prove that those habits—they might be called the "working" or "creative" habits of an individual—are no less full of meaning than his sleeping or any other habits.

5. The phase of analysis which dealt with these problems was initiated by a dream in which the conflict with his father was represented as a fight in which books were used as weapons. The oral aggressive impulse persists almost undisturbed in the patient's predilection for eating brains.

▣ THE CHILDHOOD
OF THE ARTIST:
LIBIDINAL PHASE
DEVELOPMENT AND
GIFTEDNESS

Phyllis Greenacre

This presentation may be somewhat premature. The subject is one about which one thinks slowly and hesitantly, perhaps because genius is always somewhat dazzling and mysterious. Whether the term "giftedness," "creativity," or "marked talent" is used, still the idea of genius is close at hand. The differences in definition as well as nuances in their usage reflect somewhat various ideas of the nature of genius. To my way of thinking, creativity is a special capacity which may or may not be associated with great ability; but it is usually only of general significance when it is part of a constellation of special abilities and drives—which make for the creative individual. Creativity does not seem to have a great deal to do with superior intelligence in terms of quotients, even though excellent intelligence may contribute to the productions of the creative person. In this paper I shall use the term the "artist" as a generic one referring to those possessing unusual creative productivity in any field. My presentation is both schematic and hypothetical, without full documentation and supporting evidence even for some fundamental parts of it, except in so far as occasional illustrations may tend to be of this nature. Neither am I reviewing the work of others who have contributed to this subject. There has been a great deal written that I have not yet had a chance even to read, valuable though it is; nor [have I] reread some articles which I am sure have contributed to my ideas. It has been my intention to use the present formulations as a kind of work sheet, or blueprint, of what is to be further investigated and correlated with the work of others.

Before going into the main topic of this paper, I would first like to present a few aspects of the uses and limitations of biography and autobiography in the study of genius. In a naive way it might seem that the study of autobiography supplemented by biography would be the method *par excellence* of understanding the individual genius. What could be more first-hand and authentic than what a man writes about himself? It is, as it were, from the horse's mouth.

This is, of course, an illusion. Every analyst knows that the account of his life which a patient insistently gives at the beginning of his treatment, "for the record" as it were, is not only imprecise but often filled with gross distortions and characterized by startling omissions. It is not only that the patient is not onto himself and aware of his deeper motivations, but that the individual memory is a great remaker of events, modeling and remodeling them throughout life with an extraordinary plasticity to make the cloak of remembrance do duty for one occasion after another, to meet both needs and fashions—with all of the skill and less noise than a good tailor.

A rather striking example of this was the case of a patient who had been through more than one period of analysis without revealing the nature or even the fact of having been involved in a tragic family catastrophe early in childhood. The original stunning pain together with the distress that followed and the neurotic guilt investing it had caused it to be left behind in an unused pocket of memory. It was not forgotten and could not be since it involved the sudden death of more than one member of the immediate family. But the ever-changing and increasing complexity of his life focused vision of himself in a series of changing forms more suitable for the here and now, and practically by-passed memory of this early tragedy. Nor is this patient's autobiographical statement much more distorted than that of most others. Nicolson in the *Development of Creative Biography* remarks, "Creative biography necessitates something more than diagnosis, it necessitates a scientific autopsy; and this sense of a vigorous postmortem is just what the autobiographist has always found it impossible to convey."

It must be recognized that autobiography, whether given verbally in the course of treatment or written for publication, is always produced for an audience, and often for an occasion. The audience always consists of at least two sections: the self and "the others"—whoever they may be. These three factors (occasion, self-estimate, and impression on others) combine to make pressures here, expansions there, possible explanations at one time which in further editions are treated as facts; and so it goes. What is true of the autobiography is also true, perhaps often to a lesser extent, of journals and diaries. But here again, journals which are kept very fully generally have, somehow, phantom figures looking over the shoulders of the writers. Otherwise they tend to deteriorate into becoming mere memoranda. Then there are the letters which famous people have written throughout their lifetimes. They certainly are intensely valuable if they are accessible. They too often partake of the journal quality if they are written after the gifted one has attained some recognition, or at least after he has recognized his own abilities. They generally have the advantage of being addressed individually to the audience and so present varied and sometimes extreme rather than consistent self-moldings. Further there is often more spontaneity and immediacy in their writing. But those seemingly insignificant letters and jottings dealing with unimportant affairs are often most fruitful and revealing and yet are frequently lost or edited out of collections. For example, in the earlier publications of Swift's *Journal to Stella* much of Swift's "little language" was omitted as unbefitting a man of fame even though it gave an understanding of some of the most humanly poignant needs of the great satirist. Consequently in studying any given artist (no matter what his medium), one must draw on all these sources if they are available, and more too.

From my limited experience in studying the lives of artists and saints, I would think that all this is of but limited value unless pondered carefully and correlated with the products of the lifework of the creative person. Here we generally find the less clearly censored dreams of the artist. They too are cut, edited, trimmed down to a beautiful economy if the artist is a good one, and they too are produced for an audience, the collective one of the world at large or even of future generations. But in their emergence they show irrevocably the changing preoccupations, needs for externalization, and the searchings for harmony from the artist's own changing and developing life situations. The true artist may be more faithful with deeper inner integrity in his relation to his collective audience than he is with his personal connections.

If all memory, as we ordinarily use the term, would seem to be but a cloak constantly in process of renovation, sometimes with gross additions of new material—in other words, if all memory has a screening function, how else shall we understand the man within it? Certainly we must examine the cloak and know that it reveals much of the man within and is genuinely a part of him, but neither mistake it for the man within, nor discard it as of no value because it is not he. There are many critics of psychoanalysis and many psychoanalytic patients who protest, "But why should she (or he) put much stock in all this, when there is no clear memory of these things?" There is often a note of triumph in such protests. Or, if our work has been able to go a bit deeper, there may be the addition, "I only feel as though this might have been so, but how can I tell?" If this attitude persists greatly, it has in itself to be analyzed. It generally indicates a rather special need of the patient to see himself as some kind of formal figure on the stage of life, rather than to feel himself as the growing, working, changing individual he is and has been. In my experience, reconstructions, if they are done painstakingly and with an almost sacred regard for the endless forms in which old experiences are emerging, become a working part of the individual, which under optimum conditions are assimilated and used without so much self-awareness. But reconstructions which are forced insistently represent the analyst's image of his patient or of himself, and are worn with increasing distress or discarded by the patient according to the degree of misfit. In studying the psychic life of the artist, it is probably necessary to use the methods of reconstruction of the analyst, in which the artist's production takes the place of many analytic hours. But there are limitations and temptations, for the artist analysand cannot talk back. If all memory is a screening process, so may this be true of official history.

I am indebted to Dr. Ernst Kris for directing me to Misch's *History of Autobiography in Antiquity* and to Dr. David Beres for Nicolson's *Development of English Biography*. But especially invaluable is Dr. Kris's own book, *Psychoanalytic*

Explorations in Art. It is impossible for me to determine how much I have taken over from him in my own terms, for it is not the sort of situation in which I can quote specifically this and that passage, but rather, like a good analysis, it has worked upon me against my own considerable resistances, in ways that I have assimilated without being clearly aware of how and when. In the chapter on "The Image of the Artist— A Study of the Role of Tradition in Ancient Biographies," Kris presents in a much more specific and detailed form the story of the distortions of biographies of Italian Renaissance painters to fit a family romance pattern in which the artist is biographized as a shepherd boy whose talent is accidentally discovered by an older already renowned artist, who becomes his genius father and patron. Kris points out that this was given a specific form in commentators on Dante's *Divine Comedy* who made the construction from a scant reference of Dante's and gave rise to the tradition that Giotto was a shepherd boy who was so discovered by Cimabue, the then-established master, whom Giotto subsequently surpassed. Kris points out that there is little factual evidence for this story, but that it was the crystallization of a tradition which became fixed for some time as the appropriate biographical account of painters of genius. Its connection with the Christ story is obvious. It seems, however, that the family romance problem is inherent in unusually deep imprint in the lives of artists. We no longer demand that the official biography shall be literally cast along these lines. But reading the lives of various writers has led me to think that the family romance constellation has an intrinsically strong place in their psychology and probably in that of the creative person in any field.

Before deserting the subject of the biography or even autobiography of the artist, we might emphasize certain changes in what might be called "biographical perspective" in the fairly recent past. I am not a sufficiently serious student of history,

history of literature, or history of the development of science to present this in any accurate detail. It is apparent to the naked eye, such as mine, however, that a change in the accepted demand of biography appeared in English literature after the First World War and was clearly announced in the biographies of Lytton Strachey in the early twenties. This began to be called, in this country at any rate, the debunking method of biography. It sometimes became as fanciful and as faulty as the bad historical novel has become, and represented the hauling down of heroes. It sometimes contained, however, a new growing respect for life as it is, and not as it is glorified to appear. Something similar had already been appearing in a gradual way in changes in English literature. Only in the first half of the nineteenth century could a heroine in an English novel be homely—a feat scarcely yet achieved by the American cinema. It is conspicuous that since the beginning of the twentieth century there has been an increase in interest in the childhood of great people. This interest is reflected in many fields and is certainly apparent in changes in education, in literature, in social legislation, as well as in many other ways. In my own mind I always think of the possible influence in this country as well as in England of the novels of Charles Dickens nearly half a century before such interest crept definitely into biography and autobiography. Certainly this interest in childhood antedated psychoanalysis, which gave it, however, new depths and perspectives with an enormous interest in artistic productions as well as in the artist's estimate of himself. Having recently read such autobiographical accounts of present-day writers as Sean O'Casey, Herbert Read, Richard Church, Osbert Sitwell, Stephen Spender, C. S. Lewis, Christopher Isherwood, and a few others, I have been impressed with the willingness of many writers of today to reveal much of their early emotional life and problems, and in a few instances to view themselves self-consciously much in terms of analytic

167

patients or as they conceive analytic patients to be. All this deserves more than this extremely hasty account, but will have to wait for more careful study in the future.

This second section of the paper consists of a series of tentative formulations and questions regarding the effect of marked talent or potential talent or giftedness on the early childhood of the artist. I have used the term "talent" rather than the more exalted one of "genius," although I believe that the same questions and problems would be true in both conditions, which may differ only in degree. I am aware again that some would consider talent and genius of quite different quality and that talent is often used to mean simple unusual brightness or special skill, without regard for the element of originality. In this present paper, however, I shall not differentiate talent from genius except in the matter of degree. Talent is defined by the Oxford Dictionary as "mental endowment, natural ability," from the parable of the talents (Matt. 25:14-30) and further as "power or ability of mind or body viewed as something divinely entrusted to a person for use and improvement"; while the term genius has much more the connotation of spirit or the visitation of the God-power himself, alternately described as extraordinary capacity for imaginative creation, original thought, invention, or discovery. In the sense in which I am using the term talent, it is necessary to differentiate it from brightness or appearance of brightness whose development is the result largely of enforced practice or drill.

What then are the basic characteristics of creative talent? Are they inborn? Both questions seem difficult to answer. From the subjective accounts of creatively talented people writing of their own work and lives, and especially from some descriptions of the creative process itself by those gifted ones who were experiencing it, it seems possible to describe the basic

168

characteristics under four headings: first, greater sensitivity to sensory stimulation; second, unusual capacity for awareness of relations between various stimuli; third, predisposition to an empathy of wider range and deeper vibration than usual; and fourth, intactness of sufficient sensorimotor equipment to allow the building up of projective motor discharges for expressive functions. The unusual capacity for awareness of relations between various stimuli must involve sensibility of subtle similarities and differences, an earlier and greater reactivity to form and rhythm—thus a greater sense of actual or potential organization, perhaps a greater sense of the gestalt. It has been said that the creatively talented person sees three dots at once, not as three separate points, but as constituting different line and triangle forms. The increased empathy associated with creative talent would seemingly depend on the sensory responsiveness to the individual's own body state as well as to the external object, and appears as a peculiar degree of empathic animation of inanimate objects as well as a heightened responsiveness and anthropomorphosizing of living objects. The difference between empathy and sympathy is here especially conspicuous. Such animation of the inanimate and anthropomorphosizing ordinarily is lost after early childhood, but in gifted individuals remains active either in its own right or appears in the form of the ease and wealth of symbolization.

Next as to the question of whether talents are inborn, this may be further subdivided into questions whether they are inherited according to definite biological laws, or whether they are otherwise congenital, i.e., potentially present at birth but due rather to a sport appearance. Obviously genius or marked talent has, through the ages, been thought to be the gift of the gods, as the very definition of the word implies. Galton's early study of *Hereditary Genius*, first published in 1869 and revised in 1892, strongly supported the idea of inherited genius. When one reads this today, however, it is singularly unconvincing in certain respects. There is doubtless much to be learned from biologists on this point. But I know of no decisive study.

It is also apparent that it is difficult, if not impossible, to differentiate potentially talented infants from less gifted ones. Not only is there the problem of how much any difference is already operative to a degree to show in behavioral responses in infancy, but further that temporary variations of general bodily conditions or of external environmental ones may obscure or heighten the degree of responsiveness of a more ordinarily endowed infant, as well as that of the gifted one at a time when inherent differences are not yet decisively projected in performance. Especially may it be true that a potentially gifted infant with oversensitivity in sensory responsiveness, either in general or in some special sense, may be at first more than usually overwhelmed by the onrush of stimulation and in the extreme react less rather than more. In all of this, it seems one must be aware of the limitations of direct observation even though study of such observations as part of the development of life studies may ultimately lead to the most valuable results.

There are also dangers in overemphasizing heredity. Identification plays a very important role in the selection and zeal for a field of development of talent. Particularly is one aware of the complete disregard of or ignorance of such possibilities in a study like Galton's, important as that was for its time. The problem of identification simulating inheritance is probably as great in the development of talent as it is in the appearance of certain neuroses in successive generations. In the latter case it may appear as though the neurosis were inherited when more thorough scrutiny shows clearly that it is passed on by contact, direct and indirect, through subtle processes of identification. (The influence of identification even with legendary parental figures is seen strikingly in the case of the tragic poet, Thomas Chatterton, who wrote phenomenally good poetry when under the influence of identification with a fifteenth century "father," but otherwise, under his own aegis, showed much less talent.) It is also particularly tempting to ascribe genius to heredity when it appears in a member of a family possessing other members who are unusually bright. Undoubtedly intellectual brightness, e.g., involving excellent memory and quickness of response, is a help to greater productiveness and enhances creative imagination but cannot substitute for it. Observation of many of the quiz shows of current television programs is sufficient to indicate the striking difference between the accomplishments of unusual memory (piling up impressive stores of factual information, possibly of neurotic defense value) and the flowering of really creative imagination.

Further it may be useful here to consider certain questions regarding the development of the child prodigy and even those extraordinary cases of pseudo-prodigy or skill development against a background of generally undistinguished or even inferior intelligence—the peculiar prodigy known as the idiot savant. This condition sometimes occurs in childhood, less frequently in adult life. There are some people of genius who have shown a prodigious development early and whose mature genius appears as a fairly continuous outgrowth from the promises of childhood. There are also a number of others whose genius does not become evident until adolescence or young manhood; and still an appreciable few whose genius only flowers in middle age or later. Conversely it is true that some spectacular prodigies peter out and develop into humdrum, rather undifferentiated individuals doing routine work. Others become bright and effective individuals but not seemingly possessed of remarkable talent or genius.

It appears that child prodigies may be divided into three groups. First are those in whom the precocious development appears as a spontaneous, rapid unfolding of the inner demanding pressure for unusual growth in some way inherent in the child himself. Second are those in whom the prodigy performance is mainly the result of demands of adults, usually the parents who push the child, using him as an extension of themselves in an attempt to realize some expansive ambitions in which they have felt themselves frustrated. One sees this not uncommonly in the field of athletic prowess and physical skill as well as in intellectual and artistic endeavors. A very restrained but moving account of the problems engendered or accentuated in such a child is given in the autobiographical account of Norbert Wiener, indubitably an extraordinarily brilliant boy but so pushed by an ambitious father as to limit his spontaneity and his confidence in spite of his considerable attainment. Third are those in whom the remarkable performance is the result of neurotic conflict with the development of special achievement usually on a somewhat compulsive basis as part of an effort to overcome or counteract a masturbation addiction which is heavily charged with anal problems. From a recent review of some of the clinical reports on lightning calculators as this condition developed in imbecilic as well as in well-endowed individuals, it seemed rather indicated that the apparent facility at calculation resulted from an extension of counting compulsions. This is of some interest since the propulsive force of fantasies first associated with and then detached from masturbation appears to be of considerable importance in gifted individuals as well as in these retarded ones. But skill on a compulsive basis as a substitute for masturbation is limited by the span of the memory and the continuation of practice; whereas skill in a gifted individual is but part of the unfolding of the imagination which may originally gain impetus in connection with masturbatory activity but becomes liberated from it.

It is striking that some of these skilled but untalented individuals appear to be sensitive to gestalt configurations of numbers. Further scrutiny of the accounts of their performances suggests, however, that such awareness of patterned relationship of figures and groups of figures is not flexible or general, but restricted to a set of ritualistic performances, possibly derived from some elements in the situation in which the counting calculation was originally developed. It partakes rather of a rigid and empty, though superficially spectacular, mnemonic scheme of narrow applicability.

In discussing the relationship between potential talent and libidinal phase development, I would wish to make clear that while recognizing the difficulties in making direct observations on infants and in determining the presence of potential genius at birth, I am myself largely convinced that genius is a "gift of the gods," and is already laid down at birth, probably as a sport development which finds especially favorable soil for its evolution in families where there is also a good inheritance of intellect and a favorable background for identification.

If we think then of the potentially gifted infant as possessing a conspicuously greater than average sensitivity to sensory stimulation, this might mean both an intensification of the experience and also a widening of it to include not only the primary object which is focused on but more peripheral objects which are related in some degree or fashion to the primary one in their ability to arouse somewhat similar sensory responses. To illustrate this with a hypothetical example: we might conceive that the potentially gifted infant would react to the mother's breast with an intensity of the impression of warmth, smell, moisture, the feel of the texture of the skin, and the vision of the roundness of form, according to the time and situation of the experience—but more than might be true in the less potentially gifted infant. Such an infant would react also more widely and more intensely to any similar smells, touch or taste sensations, or visions of rounded form which might come its way. Thus we can conceive of the fact that for the potentially gifted infant the primary object which stimulates certain sensory responses to it is invested with a greater field of related experiences than would be true for the infant of lesser endowment. As part of this reaction, too, there would inevitably be a greater vibration and need for harmonizing the inner object relationships (as the perception of the object reacts on and combines with other body sensations) and the world of sensory impingement. In an effort to clarify this in my mind, I have adopted the phrase "collective alternates" to describe this range of extended experience which may surround or become attached to the main focus of object relationships. I am not sure that this is a good term, but I have not been able to think of a better one and for the sake of economy shall continue to use it in the present discussion.

In this connection it seems to me that this may be the beginning of the love affair with the world which seems to be an obligatory condition in the development of great talent or genius. From the study of lives of artists and from such analytic experience as I have had with them, it seems that the artist invariably has some kind of genuine collective love affair. "Writing is an act of love" says an epigrammist. "If it isn't that, it is handwriting" (Cocteau). I believe that this collective love affair has been too often considered largely as the narcissism of the artist, whereas it partakes more of an object relationship, though a collective one, than has been considered. It seems unlikely that the artistic performance or creative product is ever undertaken purely for the gratification of the self, but rather that there is always some fantasy of a collective audience or recipient, whether this is a real audience, as for the stage, or the unseen audience of the writer or painter; whether this be contemporary or extend into the limitless future. The artistic product has rather universally the character of a love gift, to be brought as near perfection as possible and to be presented with pride and misgiving.

Such love affairs with the world occupy varying relationships with individual love relationships, sometimes one being at the expense of the other; at other times, or in other individuals appearing as quite separate or as complementary attachments. But generally the more powerfully demanding one is that of the world. Further it is possible that in the libidinal phases of development of the infantile years, the presence of such collective alternate relationships permits diminution of the effect of critical situations involving the individual object relationships— critical situations which would otherwise tend to limit or temper the dominance of any given phase in the process of or at the height of maturing. Again to illustrate this with a hypothetical example: such a gifted child, on being forced to exert control of his bowels, may the more readily turn to play with mud or fecal substitutes, which he begins to fashion according to his current imaginative play wishes toward his own bowel movements. He will do this more readily and more extensively than the less lifted child, and will submit to bowel training, which at the same time may have less meaning to him than it would to the more average child. This has some bearing on problems of sublimation.

Especially is this true in the oedipal phase which may normally, in the male child at least, end relatively abruptly—to be reinvoked in a new version at puberty and thereafter. In the gifted one, however, the individual object may be only apparently relinquished, to appear rather in a glorified collective form which becomes the object of the love for a time. The ideals seem to be extended even more than the prohibitive conscience is developed, as the oedipal wishes are expanded, apparently desexualized by their deflection from a personal genital aim, but not renounced. The castration fears remain active and may invade the functioning toward the collective alternates, but their force is usually somewhat less focused. It is usually intensely strong and vivid, however, in the individual object relationship, where it does not produce an abandonment of the oedipal object but only a by-passing of this in favor of the larger, collective, more powerful one. It seems that gifted children may solve their oedipal problems less decisively than more average children do. The apparent desexualization of the love object may be due as much in the post-oedipal phase to the biological lessening of sexual pressure at this time as to the reaction of the castration fear which is further overcome by heightened identification with collective power.

Indeed the conditions of the latency period generally appear as a paradigm of the development of talent. It is conspicuous then that under the lessening of sexual pressure and the relinquishment of the oedipal aims, a period of actual heightened physical growth sets in normally in which aggressive drives are used much in the service of mastery, of learning, exploring, and experimenting. Even in non-gifted children the latency period may be a time of great artistic interest and development. Especially if the incomplete closure of the oedipal phase has permitted the extension of some sexual interest, the explorations and drives toward creative productions seem propelled and colored by the conflict. Under such circumstances there may be the appearance of seeming talent, and the expectation arises in others that the child will mature as an artist. Commonly, however, except in the presence of inherent gift, this flowering of the latency period goes into eclipse with the onset of puberty and reappears scantily, if at all, as "interests" and hobbies thereafter. In such latency development of artistic interest, the content of the productions is sometimes discernible as derivatives of masturbation fantasies, either extended from or detached from masturbation itself and presented in projected and disguised forms.

In the libidinal phase development of the child of potentially great talent or genius, there is then an even less decisive than ordinary progression of the phases which overlap and communicate with one another in a way which more closely resembles the libidinal organization of the perverse individual than

176

that of the neurotic. At the same time it is coupled with an intensity of all experience, which may be disconcerting as it is revived in later life. Talented people are not immune from neurotic and psychotic developments under all conditions, but neither is there an intrinsic connection between talent and neurosis, except in so far as this kind of incomplete organization of libidinal structure may predispose to intense episodes of dissociation, which are, however, of less ominous prognostic significance than would be true in the less gifted person.

In the perverse individual the overlapping, fusion, or at best too great communication between different phase drives results in too easy substitution of one for another or sometimes in chaotic disorganization. Problems resulting from these states are frequently played out on his own body. In the talented person or one of genius such confusion may be obviated by the discharge through channels of developed or developing talent. In this situation there may be a full play at different times of the different preoedipal drives, continued even with or accessory to an oedipal re-enactment in the formation of the love gift of the creative product. In studying the creative process, however, as it is described by various people of genius, one is struck by the imprint of the pregenital patterns.

The question of the choice of form of creativity—the area of expression of talent—also demands consideration: the problem of why there is the universal genius such as Leonardo or the more frequent development of talent in one or at most two directions. Indeed in slightly gifted people the stimulation to work in more than one direction sometimes seems to produce distraction and limitation of development. It is possible that the universal genius may have been more frequent in past centuries and during times when the mass of technical knowledge was not so great. Certainly too the direction of development of creativity may conceivably be influenced by the needs of the surrounding world and the way in which they are indirectly transmitted to the developing child. It is also conceivable that the direction of expression of genius may be determined by special gifts, transmitted by inheritance or in some way determined before birth in which some sensorimotor functional constellation is especially superior and becomes the dominant channel of reception and production. In general, however, we are more impressed with the probability that a potential genius has polymorphous possibilities, some of which may be inhibited by special circumstances of early development; but more conspicuously that direction of development of geniuses or talent is largely determined by identifications.

The experience of awe in childhood, the forerunner of the mystical experience, is described with special intensity by creatively gifted ones. That this belongs to the two periods of special sensations of exhilaration and upsurges of intense animation, characteristic of the latter part of the second year and to the fourth-fifth year (the phallic phase), has seemed to me evident in many clinical studies of less gifted individuals, as well as in the autobiographical statements of artists. It may be that the identification then with a father—or with a specially powerful god-like father—begins at this time and is felt rather regularly due to the combination of the sharpness of the body sensation with the intensity of the sensory sensitivity to the outer world. Whether this image of the father is then retained as a god or put in other terms remains largely determined by the tradition of the time and place. Kris, in discussing this same problem, remarks, "A young sculptor in whose life the idea of being 'discovered' could play a considerable role, associated the fantasy of the sudden unfolding of his talent with the idea, disclosed in his dreams, of being given a real, i.e., a fully grown, penis by the father image of his discoverer. The matrix from which this fantasy evolved was the old competition with the patient's real father who had been successful in the same branch of art."

178

It would appear to me that this description takes very much into account the phenomenon which I have described as penis awe, dependent in most individuals on the actual seeing of the adult tumescent penis at a time when the child himself is in a particularly sensitive state. It is possible that in children of potential genius this inner state of awareness of tumescent feeling may be especially strongly pervasive. Combining with the sensitive perception of external objects, it may give rise to sensations of invigoration, inspiration, and awe. These depend not so much on the actual sight of the penis as on a communion with outer forms which reflect inner feelings in a way which I have tried to describe under the title collective alternates. It seems to me also that under such conditions the development of the family romance in especially strong form is inevitable. Such a child must develop an early attitude of glorification of the parents in accordance with the peculiar vibrancy and capacity for near ecstasy derived from his own body states. Fortunate is such a child if his own father fulfills the need for the model with which then to identify. It is my suspicion, however, that in some instances where this is not true, the child carries the ideal with him as though it were the real father, and that subsequent identification may be made and the development of direction of talent determined in part at least by the chance encounter with some individual or even some experience which strikes a decisive harmonizing note with a part of the hidden image of the father, belonging to the original experience of infantile inspiration. I am not sure that with children of potential genius the contact with an actual individual may be required for the crystallization of the identification with the idealized image.

Certainly the family romance in exaggerated form is present in many writers, and may be ubiquitous in artists of all sorts. It is readily decipherable in many of the nom de plumes of writers as well as in the search for and expectation of finding the patron, which seems part of the apparent naive dependency and unworldliness of many gifted people.

All of this leads to questions of the relation of creativity to the process of sublimation and allied problems in less talented people. I see these questions in slightly different perspectives than those presented by Hartmann and Kris. I would not limit the term aggression to hostile aggression—certainly not to the expression of a force always hostile in its aims. An army which enters a territory to improve it and make new constructions is still an aggressive force and its energy may be turned with varying degrees of rapidity from benevolent to hostile aims. Hostility seems further to have some implication of motivation. I would think of the aggressions of life as shows of force in whatever direction. The expansive aggression of growth of one organism may be destructive to another without being hostile.

During the first months of life there is not a clear differentiation of the sexual drives from the general energetic aggressive ones. This condition gradually changes during the first two to three years. A great deal of the energy endowment of the young infant is still used in the process of growth—in the actual increase in the size of the infant and in the unfolding of its functioning. This utilization in growth has been even more extreme in the prenatal period when the increase in size and organization from a single fertilized cell to the fantastically complicated and developed infant at birth is a demonstration of a force which would really overwhelm the universe very shortly if it were not slowed down. Such slowing down in rate of physical development does occur progressively until mature body size is reached in late adolescence. That the process of growth involves aggressive force was brought vividly home to me by the remark of my friend, Dr. Susanna Haigh, who said: "When I see the crocuses and the snowdrops pushing their way through the frozen earth at the end of winter, I am appalled at the fierceness of the tender shoots. It would take a swing of a pickaxe to do as good a job." Incidentally, the use of the word "shoots" for these early growths is a significant recognition of their force. This is the fierceness of expanding development and not of hostility. It is in this process of growth and its slowing down lest it explode the organism that I would see the basis of the death instinct; granted that this evolution from the beginning of life to death is at a different level than we conceive of instincts biologically. It more nearly approaches a cosmic rhythm, which affects inanimate as well as animate organizations. Personally I can no more conceive of life without an intrinsic movement toward death—the death instinct, so called—than I can conceive of perpetual motion.

But to get back to the human species, the baby of five to six months extending its legs and pushing with its feet against the lap of the mother does so from the aggression of developmental force, not from the aggression of hostility. Later on, however, derivatives of this same force may be used in hostile attacks against the mother or others who stand in his way or interfere with the attainment of some goal or desire. Hostile aggression implies a sufficient degree of individuation for there to be a sense of the self and the other(s) against whom activity is directed.

Further in this early little-differentiated stage of the drive development, the libidinal aspects of activity must consist in the state of gratification and comfort (or lack of it) achieved in the course of any activity, whether this is accomplished as a result of the patterned inherited instinctual pressure or in a more diffuse pleasure when performance itself fulfills the needs of expanding growth. To attempt an illustration: the gratification to the infant in nursing may not only be the attainment of a sufficient supply of warm milk for the satisfaction of hunger (and so indirectly for the further growth of the body), nor the passive comfort of warmth of contact with the mother's body, but it probably contains also the satisfaction of the use of the special neuromuscular equipment engaged in sucking, i.e., the satisfaction of the discharge of a developmental tension.

I would understand the unfolding growth pressures as they become organized, partly through maturation and partly through experience, and are increasingly capable of working in some sort of relative harmony as forming the somatic nucleus of the beginning development of the primary autonomous ego. There follows then a further development of libidinal (sexual) drives and the capacity of hostile aggressive ones in the service of self-defense or positive attack. The maturing of the central nervous system means the development of the psychophysical equipment for the more economical control and direction of the forces of the body. I would conceive of there being possible a considerable interchange between the expression of aggression in autonomous growth and that which is object- or goal-directed in necessary co-operation with growth processes, but acts directly and sometimes destructively on the environment for the satisfaction of its own needs.

This may be of some importance in understanding special conditions of early ego development and of sublimation in creative people. These may in turn contribute something to the understanding of sublimation in more ordinarily endowed ones. It is also possible that in very gifted people a process comparable to sublimation in those of more average endowment does not occur, inasmuch as they possess much more mobility of libidinal energy, and change of aim and object is achieved with greater flexibility, although often accompanied by outer displays of disturbance. I want to make clear, however, that I am not here attempting any comprehensive statement but only making a few tentative suggestions regarding some problems which need much more careful study.

If the conception of libidinal phase development (under condition of potential creative giftedness) which has been presented has any merit, it may be considered further that this early sensory oversensitivity together with the greater reactivity to rhythm and gestalt relationships of form would bring the infant into a wider range of awareness of his own body and of the surroundings as well. How early and in what way this might operate would of course depend on other early circumstances as well, including special birth conditions, the presence of any defects in development, and the nature and immediacy of the relationship to the mother. It may also be that such an intensification and extension of the field of reactivity would form the *Anlage* for the development of a greater richness of capacity for symbolization, which is so characteristic of creative people, and for the continued exigent demands of the primary process later in life.

Under most conditions such an infant would probably develop an intense and demanding relationship to the mother and to other early personal objects. The reactivity to the peripheral field might at first be largely extensions of these. Subsequently (I would conceive it roughly as from the latter half of the first year on) a powerful libidinal investment in the areas of the collective alternates, either in general or in some chosen part, might arise coexistent with that to the personal objects. The relationship between the forces of the individual personal object cathexes and those of the collective alternate ones would appear to exist in varying balances depending on a complexity of factors which cannot now be gone into.

What I would want to emphasize, however, is that this balance would influence very much the outline and organization of the incipient ego development, especially the growth of any self-image or self-representation, and even of perceptions of the self. It is conceivable that under what are generally considered favorable conditions of infancy, the primary (personal) self-representation would be at first the dominant and might always remain the firmer or more solid one. But in the course of time there may precipitate some rival or accessory self-image, again partly determined by the contact with some accessory adult idealized figure, who condenses and consolidates some area of the collective alternates through furnishing special sources of identification. Fortunate is that creative child or youth who has available within his own family individuals suitable for these identifications and reinforcements of his own creative needs.

Indeed, I do not believe that this is a mere whimsy of mine. It is evident in studying the lives of markedly creative people that such splits in the self-presentation, going over into even a split in the sense of identity, do occur and relatively frequently—sometimes developing along parallel lines and sometimes alternating, one emerging from cover of the other. This division into the two or more selves may be experienced in childhood with some distress and with the wish to deny the creative self in favor of the social stereotype, which exerts so much constricting pressure during the school years. The creative self is then felt as freakish, abnormal, and to be fought. Under many circumstances, this struggle continues into adult life, when the more conventional self may be more or less guardian or enemy of the creative self. In the latter instance one may see the literal escape from one to the other. All this, it would appear, must also contribute to the ubiquitous and specially strong family romance among creative people.

Under conditions of frustration and disappointment in the personal object the creative individual may turn to the collective one(s); or the movement may be in the opposite direction. Under still other circumstances frustration in one area may lead to reciprocal inhibition in the other. These are matters determined by—among other factors—the degree and fashion in which the collectively determined creative function has been used too much in the service of the personal defense mechanisms, i.e., has been subjected to the burden of displacements, the effect of which depends on the amount, form, and location of the libidinization. In the extremely gifted individual, however, there may be a sufficient margin in the development of the artist-self to overcome all but the most sweeping displacements of this kind. It also means that among some creative people, the rhythm of personal disappointment giving rise to renewed efforts of realization through artistic endeavors has become established early and sets a pattern which causes them to fear even the illusion of a well-developed personal life, lest it deprive them of the impetus for creative production.

At this point I would want to make clear that my own conviction is that creative activity is highly libidinized and that without this libidinal charge it could come to naught. I would even suspect that it may carry the whole gamut of mixed libidinal phase pressures, genital and pregenital, more diffused and with wider and deeper range than is true in the less gifted person, but discernible in the form and nature of the creative process and in the artist's relation to his own creative product. It may be that the capacity to turn emotional drive to artistic creation is determined not only by the amount of gift endowment, but as part of this by the ease, mobility, and plasticity of the communication between the individual (personal) emotional interests and those of a general outer world, or collective significance. Further, the creative activity of the artist seems to me also highly aggressive, but with aggression allocated to special growth developments, to extents probably much greater but not wholly different from the situation of sublimation in those of lesser talent. The problem of ego-syntonicity in the artist is further complicated by the degree of acceptance or denial of the creative talent by the total individual and not merely by some competent part of the self.

What I have said here may not differ greatly in some essentials from others' views, even though terms may have been used somewhat differently. My formulation indicates, however, why I find the term *neutralization* so difficult in this connection. To me *neutralization*, borrowed presumably from chemistry, has the natural connotation of something which has been rendered inert, or at least temporarily ineffective. I would think of the need for a specific process to produce neutralization and a somewhat similar but reversed one again to produce deneutralization before a new direction of force or activity might arise. It is not that borrowing a chemical term is in itself objectionable. "Sublimation" itself and "valence" are such borrowed terms. But sublimation seems a more apt and condensed metaphor, for it implies change in physical form—through diffusion as a gas and reprecipitation as a solid—without change of chemical structure. This is, however, accomplished by changes in temperature. Sublimation also has the connotation inevitably— though without chemical foundation—of conversion into a higher form. With "neutralization" the comparison fits less well. If by neutralization one meant a stage of busy and productive peace such as neutral nations are supposed to have, then the metaphor would seem more appropriate. Parenthetically I have thought the limitation of the term "aggression" to mean "hostility" may have been reinforced in recent years by the emphasis on the culpability of the aggressor nations.

There is one way, however, in which the energy passing from individual to the collective objects might seem to me to approach something like a neutral state. That is in relation to specific masculine or feminine differentiated direction. In other words, I would think of some degree of loss or diminution of sexual polarity; love of mankind, fervid but both diffuse and intense, expressed very much in the creative love gift, may take the place of or be in communication with the love of a man or of a woman. Perhaps this is the more possible in those gifted ones, the artists, who by the very nature of their early libidinal phase development must have not only a higher capacity for bisexuality, but a greater fluidity in changes of emphasis between the various libidinal phase drives. The reaction of the

186

artist to the collective object(s) also involves utilization of the most primitive but acute empathic responses to an extent greater than is true in relation to the personal object. It is the force of the amalgamation of this dominant primitive empathy with the summation of experiences of the total span of life, which acts then in a depolarized sexual way in the struggle for harmony of which the creative product, the love gift, is the outcome. This struggle for harmony takes the place of some (much or little) of what might otherwise go into the personal love relationships of a polarized sexual nature. When the polarity of the personal sexual investment is not appreciably diminished and displacement has occurred too massively, then the collective love affair also assumes (by this direct displacement or by the rigidity of reaction formation) too much of the personal conflict. It is then subject to the same hazards, usually derived from the castration conflict, which have existed in the personal sphere. The site and nature of the displacement will further determine the character of the symptomatic invasion of the creative activity.

One may examine these matters sometimes in the situations of slightly or only moderately gifted people in whom, through early overtraumatization, a sensitivity and flux of libidinal phase development has occurred. Here one sees a much simpler situation, complex though it is. Though the analysis of such patients is extremely difficult and arduous, one sees the gradual liberation of the bound energy to produce a greater possibility of dominantly genital-sexual love, but the constitution remains susceptible and the personal sexual love relationship may be sustained only in so far as it may be supplemented by libidinized interests of a nonpolarized type. That such a person may not become a good creative artist depends rather on the mediocrity or at least lack of superiority of the basic endowment; and on the fact that his sensitivity, the result of unfortunate early conditions rather than of special gifts of nature,

187

has not had the same range of reactivity, nor produced the same compelling need for seeking harmony. I must reiterate, however, that I have not carried these ideas into repeated and carefully checked extensive application to clinical cases, nor tested them out in the study of famous people. In any event, they may need both correction and refinement.

Some few rather less important observations may be discussed before closing this paper, certain special problems and difficulties of people of marked talent. If the talent is very great, there is indeed a sense of pressure, an obligatory quality to the expansion of development. If, while this is still in a state of potentiality, for any reason channels of outlet are blocked, states of frustration and blind frenzy with very slight provocation may arise. The best description I know of this is in Helen Keller's autobiography, in which she gives a picture of her inner explosiveness before her need to communicate could be channeled expressively after the illness which cut off both sight and hearing.

It was probably an intuitive awareness of this obligatory creative pressure as well as his enthusiasm for a biological genetic classification of people that led Galton to conclude that genius always asserts itself: that it will not remain hidden. Indeed, the compelling drive of creativeness, sometimes contrary to the conscious wishes of its possessor, may give the creative activity the semblance of a special kind of addiction for which there is no cure. Galton considered that three qualities of "ability—combined with zeal, and the capacity for hard labor" are essential to genius and are inherited. Again he says, "If a man is gifted with vast intellectual ability, eagerness to work, and the power of working, I cannot comprehend how such a man should be repressed." Once more he took an emphatic stand: "People seem to have an idea that the way to eminence is one of great self-denial from which there are hourly temptations to diverge: in which a man can be kept in

188

his boyhood only by a schoolmaster's severity or a parent's incessant watchfulness and in after life by the attractions of fortunate friendships and favorable circumstances. This is true enough of the great majority of men, but it is simply not true of the generality of those who have gained great reputations. Such men biographies show to have been haunted and driven by an incessant craving for intellectual work. If forcibly withdrawn from the path that leads toward eminence, they will find their way back to it as surely as the lover finds his mistress. They do not work for the sake of eminence, but to satisfy a natural craving for brain work, just as athletes cannot endure repose on account of their muscular irritability, which insists upon exercise. It is very unlikely that any conjunction of circumstances should supply a stimulation to brain work commensurate with what these men carry in their own constitutions. . . . [The natural disposition of genius] keeps a man ever employed—now wrestling with his difficulties, now brooding over his immature ideas, and renders him a quick and eager listener to innumerable almost inaudible teachings, that others less keenly on the watch are sure to miss."

Thus Galton makes quite clear his appreciation of the difference between superior skill attained through demanded practice and that achievement which derives chiefly from the inner pressure of essential endowment. While his insistence on the constitutional elements in genius, or as he sometimes refers to it as "great eminence," led him to emphasize inheritance in ways which we might now question, he brings out some interesting peripheral observations and assumptions. In accordance with his belief in the inheritance of genius and its appearance, he may rather have ignored the instances in which genius became manifest and obligatory late in life. From the analyst's angle, the study of such men would be most illuminating.

I would interpolate a few of Galton's observations—aside from his emphasis on inheritance—because they are interesting

189

and because they show that, in spite of his conscious focusing on inheritance and insistence that it alone was responsible for the appearance of genius, he inevitably came upon other determining factors. Although he concluded generally that the "female influence is inferior to that of the male in conveying ability," he realized that this might not be entirely due to hereditary factors, and added cautiously at a later time, "I think there is reason to believe the influence of females but little inferior to that of males in transmitting judicial ability," and that such influence might not be wholly due to inheritance is tacitly admitted in his discussion of men of science. Here he states that the fathers of the ablest men in science have frequently been unscientific; and elsewhere states, "It therefore appears very important to success in science that a man should have an able mother. I believe the reason to be that a child so circumstanced has the good fortune to be delivered from the ordinary narrowing, partisan influence of home education . . ." and again indicates that the sons of the most gifted men in science have only become themselves distinguished in science if they have also truth-loving mothers.

Another interesting conclusion arrived at by Galton was that in general men of genius were more often of good physical constitution than otherwise and added, "I do not deny that many men of extraordinary mental gifts have had wretched constitutions, but deny them to be an essential or even a usual accompaniment." From studying the mortality of his men of genius, he concluded "that among the gifted men, there is a small group who have weak and excitable constitutions, who are destined to early death, but that the remainder consists of men likely to enjoy a vigorous old age." This was true in the group of artists and distinctly so in that of poets, but it came out in most startling definition in the cases of men noted for their remarkable precocity. The mortality curve was only normal in those who did not appear to have been eminently precocious. Scientific men lived the longest and the number of early deaths among them was decidedly less than in any other groups. All this is interesting and provocative and deserves much more careful study. I have quoted Galton's work, for though first published nearly a century ago, it was one of the most comprehensive studies of men of genius ever attempted. Incidentally, in my hesitation to psychoanalyze the dead artist, I found some amused comfort in the discovery that in recent years the psychologist, Terman, did postmortem tests on Galton and decided that in his childhood his I.Q. had been 200.

1956

□ THE TOTAL PERSONALITY

IN CREATIVE THERAPY

Ernest Zierer

Diagnosis and therapy are intrinsically interwoven in creative therapy since both are based on the premise of the personality as a totality. Fenichel's words apply to creative therapy: "It attempts more than mere description. It explains mental phenomena as the result of the interaction and counteraction of forces, that is, in a dynamic way."

Creativeness is conceived of as the integrative capacity of the ego as expressed through the medium of art. Art activity is postulated as the direct expression of the conscious, the preconscious, and the unconscious. In this paper the total personality will be approached by way of the unconscious drives as manifested directly and immediately in painting.

Creative therapy uses a non-associative or non-ideational approach and utilizes painting activity literally as a non-verbal mode of expression of all levels of the personality. Since associations are not encouraged and interpretations are not given, the subject matter (content and form) is in this sense neglected. However, beyond content and form (and thereby including it) a painting is also the immediate expression of the individual's instinctual drive. Creative therapy tries to gain insight into these unconscious instinctual forces by methodically provoked unconscious reactions.

These unconscious reactions are provoked, chiefly, by what the writer calls the "push-tests." The technique of push-tests is of necessity different from the technique used in psychoanalysis. But the ultimate goal is the same: to reveal and to reintegrate the total personality. The push-tests have various therapeutic and diagnostic aims. In this paper, however, only the dynamics of developmental reactions are considered for the characterization of the total personality.

Every individual is exposed to certain developmental situations. The push-tests confront the patients with these various situations and provoke their repetition and emotional revival. "Developmental situations," however, do not refer here to specific and in this sense to individual situations, experiences, or traumata. Developmental situations refer instead to the developmental phylogenetic and ontogenetic "traumata" entailed by the succession of the oral, anal, and phallic organizations. In other words: not the specific "incident" of a situation or trauma is dealt with in the reactivation process of the push-tests, but, instead, the trauma of specific "developmentally" determined infantile ego states is being reactivated. The push-tests or obstacle-tests are experimentally provoked developmental situations and the so-called push-colors or obstacle-colors are deliberate interferences with the patient's habitual reaction pattern.

It will suffice to mention three push-tests. This limitation is determined by lack of space and their selection is determined by their relation to the three phases of infantile development.

The push-tests confront the patients with various developmental situations and provoke their repetition and emotional revival. The description of this provocation is simple, since, in terms of creative therapy, provocation is necessarily limited to color arrangements. These color arrangements might seem irrelevant or arbitrary; the emotional reaction, however, is relevant and cogent. The therapeutic and diagnostic as well as the dynamic significance of these color arrangements will be discussed later.

The first push-test. When the patient is prepared to start his third oil-painting, he is also ready for interference. The therapist places three color patches on the blank paper. The choice of the push-colors is not arbitrary, but determined by the patient's previous paintings. The patient is then asked to paint whatever he wants to, but is told not to paint over the push-colors.

The second push-test. Here the therapist does not interfere until the pencil sketch for the painting is finished. The push-colors are not placed on the canvas until the patient has planned his painting. The patient is then asked to continue the painting in oil and again without painting over the push-colors.

The third push-test. After the patient has finished the pencil drawing, that is, the plan for another painting, he is asked to start to paint in oil. However, when about a quarter of the canvas is painted, the therapist interrupts the patient and inserts the push-colors in an unpainted area of the drawing. Again the patient is requested not to paint over the push-colors while he completes his painting.

These three push-tests or obstacle-tests show three different types of interference and by that they create three different and clearly defined development situations (oral, anal, and phallic). In the beginning of his development the infant experiences, first of all, himself. His narcissistic omnipotence, however, does not free the infant from the necessity to cope with the object world. Actually the object world starts to intrude upon the infant from the time he draws his first breath so that he is soon forced to give up his feeling of "unconditional omnipotence." In the words of Freud the infant is constantly interfered with by objects and beings who do not obey his will and also by the increasing complexity of his own wishes, so that the "omnipotence" of human beings comes to depend on more and more "conditions." In terms of creative therapy the infant's narcissistic omnipotence meets with an increased number of obstacles. The reality principle demands of the child a progressive libidinal attachment to the object world—or, as creative therapy defines it, its integration. The experimental situation as created by the therapist in the first push-test is the revival of the first discovery of the child that he is not alone in the world. Before he starts to act he meets with obstacles in life with his environment, in creative therapy with the push-colors.

In the second push-test the therapist does not place the push-colors on the blank canvas. He puts down the push-colors after the patient has completed his pencil drawing; that is, the push-colors as obstacles emerge only after the patient has defined his plan for the painting. Again this is a repetition of a developmental situation. The child's modest attempts to decide for himself, to plan, are also frequently and necessarily interfered with.

In the third push-test the patient is confronted with the obstacle-colors after he has carried out part of his plan, i.e., integrated one fourth of his painting. Integration is explained elsewhere as psychic energy, as the premise for object relation. In push 1 and 2 the patient meets with interference before he is asked to integrate, i.e., to express his object relation. In push 3, for the first time the patient is faced with obstacles after he has succeeded in integrating part of his painting. In this developmental situation, which might be compared to the phallic phase, object relation is successfully expressed within certain limits when once more obstacle-colors necessitate a reorientation and stimulate a more complete object relation. The first two push-tests revive developmental situations in which the infant's omnipotence and mastery are challenged while the third push-test reactivates a phase in which the child's object relations are threatened and, simultaneously, broadened.

The push-colors represent various types of obstacles. These obstacles in turn provoke aggression in the patient, and in provoking aggression they stimulate the release of repressed integrative capacity. Aggression is instinctual energy which strives for an outlet, but not necessarily an acting out. In creative therapy acting out is barred by the therapist's request to integrate the push-colors, i.e., to transform destructive aggression into constructive energy. What is more, the choice of the colors is such that they serve as a "push" toward the reintegration of the past developmental situation on a present-day adult level. The principle of the push technique is similar to that of the association technique. Both the associative and the creative push stimulate the re-experience of past events and both techniques provoke the release and the reinvestment of repressed instinctual energy.

As mentioned before, in the first push-test the interference by obstacle-colors revived a developmental situation on the earliest, i.e., on the oral, level. There the blank "unlimited" paper stimulates the patient's imagination and fantasy; it also provokes a feeling of absolute freedom and, in this sense, of omnipotence. Soon, however, the therapist's interference limits the play of unrestricted fantasy. The patient finds himself confronted by the obstacle-colors. A new condition is created in which awareness of the interfering object world is experienced as a first "reality situation." Simultaneously fantasy and imagination are challenged to cope with this obstacle, i.e., to integrate it. We may say that by the successful integration of the push-colors the obstacles are incorporated into the remaining picture. We concur with Fenichel who states that "the aim of incorporation of objects does not necessarily reflect a subjective destructive tendency toward the object."

In the following phase the infant has to learn to give up to a great extent his fantasied omnipotence; he has to learn to postpone or to renounce a direct instinctual gratification out of consideration for the environment. In exchange the infant acquires some active mastery of the object world and of his own instinctual demands. Fantasy and imagination as the source of immediate and unconditioned wish fulfillment are gradually relinquished and replaced by a feeling of mastery and by the gratification in planning and deciding.

In the second push-test the patient is asked to do a pencil sketch, i.e., he is stimulated to decide and to plan beforehand. The outline sketch is the pictorial equivalent of the anal tendency toward orderliness, parsimony, and stubbornness. Lack of space does not permit elaboration of this parallel. It must suffice to point out that the outlining of objects limits imagination, but on the other hand literally leaves enough space for fantasy to experience the outline as a magic circle within which the creator of the "sign" is all-powerful. In this sense the outline drawing is also a pictorial equivalent of the magic of thoughts, gestures, and words. On an adult level the outline sketch (as any other system) is the result of scientific planning.

In this second push-test the obstacle-colors placed within the outline sketch reactivate a developmental situation on the anal level. The patient is confronted with the recognition that reality often interferes with the execution of his plans. But again the patient is stimulated to overcome these obstacles, to integrate the push-colors. New obstacles arise in the phallic phase. This developmental situation is emotionally revived in the third push-test. A comparative description of this situation can be omitted since the comments on the first two push-tests indicate that all push-tests are dynamically conditioned by the evolutionary development.

There is, of course, only a limited number of obstacle-tests or push-tests but there is an unlimited number of push-colors and countless ways to react to them. As mentioned before, the push-colors are not arbitrarily selected but are determined by the patient's first paintings and by the "potentiality tests." The unlimited number of push-colors therefore corresponds to the individually different "integrative potential" which in turn is determined by the individual's inherent capacities and by his environmental experiences. The limited number of push-tests corresponds to the limited number of developmental situations or developmental obstacles. The patient's reactions again to both the obstacle situations and to the specific obstacle-colors indicate his actual present capacity (or actual integrative ego-strength) to cope with a specific reactivated developmental situation.

The transition from one phase to another (and within one phase from one stage to another) is necessarily painful; it represents a developmental hazard, an obstacle, and in this sense a traumatic experience. The so-called normal adult has succeeded in overcoming the developmental vicissitudes. The neurotic and the psychotic have failed somewhere along the line.

The revival of developmental situations is, I repeat, a diagnostic test and a therapeutic procedure. The patient's reactions indicate what specific developmental situation he has failed in originally and disclose also the patient's actual ego-strength to cope with these reactivated situations on an adult level. Simultaneously the push-colors—which correspond not with the actual but with the potential integrative capacity—stimulate the redevelopment of repressed integrative capacity and thus enable the patient gradually to modify his habitual reaction pattern.

Lack of space does not permit more than this indication of the obstacle-and-push technique. It is sufficient to keep in mind that the developmental situations are intended to represent oral, anal, and phallic obstacles in our developmental struggle. The patient is expected to identify and to experience (emotionally) the push-tests as obstacles in his habitual, developmental reaction pattern. He is provoked to do so in response to the therapist's interference. This interference again—because of the specific arrangements of the push experiments—assumes the character of a psychological shock.

Every push experiment causes psychological shock, similar to emotional shocks provoked by interpretations, comments, dreams, and associations in the course of psychoanalysis. Irrespective of whether or not we assume that shock is nature's first and most significant emotion or whether we consider it characteristic only of traumatic situations, shock is an emotional force in development; it is emotional energy, too, in a way. Shock releases certain developmental changes by intensification of actions and/or by provocation of reactions. Shock through push-tests provokes and intensifies the patient's aggression. This aggressive reaction is, however, rarely acted out since the patient is prepared to act in and through painting by "color integration."

Color integration is explained to the patient before he starts creative therapy. Color integration is demonstrated as a pure emotional process, as an unconsciously determined interrelation of elements. It is emphasized that color or element integration is not synonymous with gestalt integration and is not based on the individual's intellectual or aesthetic approach to the subject matter, and obviously not on form, content, composition, color harmony, etc. Instead, element integration is repeatedly pointed out to the patient as the unconscious expression of the personality's emotional integration. Element integration is explained as the expression of psychic energy. The patient realizes that he is not asked merely to integrate a painting, but that in doing so his (repressed) integrative capacity as such will be mobilized. The patient is made aware that in this sense color integration is the expression of his ego-strength. Later the patient learns to grasp that element integration can be carried through on a higher or lower level, i.e., the patient learns to experience that integration discloses ego-strength on different levels. The very young child, for instance, is unable as yet to integrate the object world, i.e., to invest reality with feeling and significance. The psychotic has regressed to a level where the environment becomes meaningless in spite of its objective existence. The neurotic again has repressed his capacity to relate with reality and in this sense to form true object relations. The patient learns ultimately to utilize his integrative ego-strength (limited as it may be as in the case of schizophrenics) and to develop his actual integrative capacity to its highest potential level.

In this writing no explanation of element integration is intended. Element integration has been referred to only to indicate that the developmental character of the push-tests is, by no means, separable from the emotional problem of integrative ego-strength.

As mentioned before, there is a complete series of various push-tests, which by their selection and developmental totality aim at the reintegration of the patient's total personality on its own integrative level. The unconscious reaction to each developmental situation is determined by the patient's integrative ability to cope with the therapeutic situation on an adult level. How far he succeeds in his attempt to reintegrate his reaction pattern—better in one push-test, less successful in another, or differently at different times—is expressed by the integrative levels. A graph, the integration curve, registers the reactions of the patients and indicates thereby progress or stalemate in therapy.

We subscribe to the definition "that personality is largely the resultant of the interaction of the instincts and the environment." Both instincts and environmental influences are expressed immediately in a painting, and naturally they are expressed simultaneously. For the sake of brevity no explanation could be given of how the environment is manifested in a painting, nor could it be indicated what exactly replaces the significance of content and form. More specifically no indication could be given of as to what degree and by what means individual experiences and traumata are taken into consideration.

In this paper the reactivation of evolutionary development was referred to as a revival of the trauma of development. In other words the phylogenetic and ontogenetic succession of the oral, anal, and phallic organizations was conceived as a succession of traumatic situations. It was proposed that the patient's reactions to the revival of developmental situations— as re-enacted in the push- or obstacle-tests—indicate his ego-strength. The painting was considered as a screen on which the unconscious became conscious and which reflected the patient's total personality directly and immediately. Every essential disturbance of the personality can be traced back to a disturbance in the patient's evolutionary development (regression or arrest of the evolutionary drive). Simultaneously, this disturbance presupposes, and shows repression or insufficiency of, the patient's integrative capacity, the weakening or the weakness of his ego.

Development cannot be turned back for therapeutic reasons and its mere revival is therapeutically meaningless. Indeed, the reactivation of developmental situations alone would reactivate only the patient's habitual reaction pattern. For this reason the double function of the interfering colors was emphasized by their description as both obstacle- and push-colors. We find a similar situation in psychoanalysis. Catharsis in its narrow original sense is no longer considered as the sum total of the therapeutic approach. Although psychoanalysis continues to reactivate traumatic memories and complexes, the emphasis is on insight and the realization of the transference of the past experiences to present-day situations. Concurrently with the revival of repressed emotions, repressed energy is released and by that a strengthening of the personality is achieved. With the reactivation of the developmental situations, past developmental obstacles are revived on a present-day level. Simultaneously the push-colors release and stimulate repressed integrative energy which enables the patient to reintegrate these past obstacles. Reintegration of the past in the present re-establishes once more developmental totality. The therapeutic aim therefore is to reintegrate the evolutionary drive through full utilization of the potential integrative ego-strength.

In this paper, the dynamic interaction of only two constituents of the total personality was discussed: the evolutionary drive (as reactivated in the developmental situations) and the integrative drive (as an expression of ego-strength). The third constituent of the total personality finds its expression in creative therapy in the manifestations of the bipolarity drive; and it goes without saying that in the patient's reactions to the developmental situations his bipolar or ambivalent tendencies also become evident, either as compatible or as incompatible opposites or as bipolar tendencies which are accessible to compromise (normal, psychotic, and neurotic reactions respectively).

We may propose therefore that the patient's unconscious reaction pattern as provoked by the push-tests and his varying integrative responses are expressive of his total personality. It should be emphasized that a single painting is never considered as a diagnostic criterion; the diagnostic and prognostic data are derived from the developmental interrelation of quite a number of paintings. Every change in the patient's reaction pattern is observed for therapeutic as well as diagnostic reasons. The integrative responses may be excellent to any one or to some of the various push-tests; they may be poor or indifferent to others. These differences in the integrative responses indicate the personality's conflict. The specific conflicts are further explored by the self-push tests, the repetition of push-tests, and various other tests and projects.

During the past eight years, the creative therapy findings concerning the developmental situations were compared with the clinical observations presented by the staff psychiatrists in weekly conferences held at the Hillside Hospital, Glen Oaks, New York. This comparison of the conclusions derived in creative therapy with clinical material indicated a striking correlation in most cases between the concept of developmental situations and the psychoanalytic concept of ego development.

In a number of cases the findings in creative therapy actually anticipated the clinical manifestations. Wherever it was possible, a follow-up study was made which confirmed the conclusions drawn from these total personality tests to such an extent that it is felt justified to claim an essential validity of these concepts.

In a detailed study of five patients which was chosen from a much larger body of material, Kleinschmidt and Miller stated: "All these patients worked in the creative therapy department. Right from the beginning—that is to say, at a time when clinical criteria as well as psychometric tests did not reveal definite signs of schizophrenia—they showed in tests developed by Zierer an integration curve typical of schizophrenics, and the breaking down of their ability for abstract thinking and conceptual thinking."

In the case of non-hospitalized patients, detailed reports were sent routinely to the treating psychoanalysts. The creative therapy and analytic findings showed a most gratifying concurrence. It should be stressed in this connection that no transference differences were encountered in the course of the joint application of creative therapy and psychoanalysis or analytically oriented psychotherapy.

With regard to the statistical reliability, it must be emphasized that diagnosis in creative therapy is not based on any single test but on the combined findings of body-space, bi-polarity, and push-test aggression and conflict tests, personality-structure test, and the integration curve. However, a statistical evaluation of two thousand patients tested showed that our diagnostic conclusions drawn from the body-space test alone conformed in eighty-six per cent of the cases with the clinical discharge diagnosis at the Hillside Hospital. Only after this test has been given does the patient start on his push-tests and bi-polarity tests. It then becomes possible to draw a graph of the patient's integrative capacity and to conform or correct the initial diagnostic impression.

1952

▣ COMMUNICATION IN PSYCHOANALYSIS AND IN THE CREATIVE PROCESS: A PARALLEL

David Beres

This inquiry is an attempt to place in sharper focus the question: how are changes effected in psychoanalysis which lead to the acceptance of insight into unconscious processes? What fosters the acceptance by the patient of the interpretations and constructions which appear in the course of the analysis? Later developments in psychoanalytic thought have modified the sanguine comment Freud made in 1910 that "the mechanism of our curative method is indeed quite easy to understand; we give the patient the conscious idea of what he may expect to find (*bewusste Erwartungsvorstellung*), and the similarity of this with the repressed unconscious one leads him to come upon the latter himself." In a later paper Freud said: "Instead of inquiring *how* analysis effects a cure (a point which in my opinion has been sufficiently elucidated) we should ask what are the obstacles which this cure encounters." Also, in 1937,

Freud, speaking of "the way in which our conjecture is transformed into the patient's conviction," said that "it is hardly worthwhile describing how this occurs in the process of analysis. . . ." All this may be true at the level of pragmatic experience, but if one seeks an answer in deeper terms of process, the problem is still an open one. It is to one aspect of this problem that I propose to direct my scrutiny. I shall limit myself specifically to indicating a parallel between psychoanalysis and the creative process and describing the role of communication in both. I shall then attempt to demonstrate the part that communication has in leading to insight and conviction. I should not mislead the reader to expect in this tentative discussion an answer to so complex a problem, but I hope to make the question, at least, more clear.

Freud in 1912 described a communication which exists between the unconscious of the patient and the analyst and said, ". . . he [the analyst] must bend his own unconscious like a receptive organ towards the emerging unconscious of the patient, be as the receiver of the telephone to the disc." Communication in the psychoanalytic milieu is between the analysand and the analyst. What is communicated is a creation of the analysand, who becomes in a sense a creative artist. The analyst is the audience to whom the creation is communicated, but his role in the process is not, as I shall show, a purely passive one.

When we turn to artistic creation we find that many writers on aesthetics and literary criticism consider communication to be an essential component of the creative act. For instance Lascelles Abercrombie in *The Theory of Poetry* says, ". . . it is . . . the essential thing in poetry, that imagination should thereby [by technique] escape from the self-consciousness of the poet and become the property of the whole world," and again, "The theory of poetry, then, must take account not only of the quality of certain remarkable kinds of experience, but also of the no less remarkable art by which the poet has communicated his experience and enabled it to become ours as well."

Wordsworth is equally explicit. In his preface to the second edition of *Lyrical Ballads* he asks: "What is a Poet? To whom does he address himself? And what language is to be expected from him?" And he answers: "He is a man speaking to men." Coleridge too defines poetry as "the communication of thoughts and feelings so as to produce excitement by sympathy, for the purpose of immediate pleasure. . . ."

With the two assumptions, that the psychoanalytic process includes creative activity and that an important component is communication, a parallel is set up between psychoanalysis and the creative process. That this must be a thesis by analogy is unfortunately determined by the subject matter. But it is not necessary to apologize for analogic thought, which has indeed an honored place in the development of ideas, if it is used with caution and an awareness of its limitations. It will be necessary to point up not only the parallels between psychoanalysis and the creative process but also the differences.

The production of the analysand appears in an atmosphere of regression. The secondary process is abrogated—to the extent that the resistances can be overcome—and the result is a fantasy, dream, thought, or image characterized by symbolism, condensation, and displacement, the hallmarks of the primary process. There is to a greater or lesser degree a breakdown of defenses, the overcoming of repression.

This regression takes place in the controlled environment of the psychoanalytic interview where the analyst by his presence and his attitude makes possible in the analysand an increased tolerance of id impulses. Kris describes the capacity of the ego to regulate regression in certain normal situations such as sleep, dreaming, wit, and orgasm, as well as in creative activity. He points out that the organizing function of the ego includes the capacity of voluntary and temporary withdrawal of cathexis, in order to regain improved control. In these states the processes of the ego are temporarily largely in the service of the id drives, functioning according to the primary process with mobile unbound energies.

This step in the analysis comprises the relaxation of ego control and the release, though in distorted forms, of id impulses. It is essentially a passive phase and corresponds to the inspirational phase of the creative act, the phase of the "untamed" creation. There remains both for the psychoanalytic process and the creative act additional work in which the passivity is replaced by activity—for the former, working through and for the latter, preconscious elaboration.

Coleridge, in his figure of the Eolian Harp, created an image which continues to serve in the literature of criticism as a symbol of the passive phase:

> And that simplest Lute,
> Placed length-ways in the clasping casement, hark!
> How by the desultory breeze caress'd,
>
> Full many a thought uncall'd and undetain'd
> And many idle flitting phantasies,
> Traverse my indolent and passive brain,
> As wild and various as the random gales
> That swell and flutter on this subject Lute!

Although communication at this phase is not a prominent feature in the artist, one may only speculate that he is already addressing himself unconsciously to a fantasied audience or even that he anticipates consciously that his creation will, in time, reach other ears. The analysand, however, even in this phase requires the reassuring presence of the analyst to permit the externalization of the derivatives of his unconscious. It is an established psychoanalytic dictum that whatever the analysand says or does in the analytic session has reference to the analyst and even with these unformed productions the analysand is in communication with the analyst, whether on a verbal or a nonverbal level.

The analysand may be in a state of abreaction, of discharge of dammed-up energies; the artist may be in the chaotic ecstatic "madness" with which Plato compared the inspirational activity of the artist. But in both instances at this stage we have neither psychoanalysis nor art—we have at best the preparation for the one or the other.

The next phase was described by Coleridge, who has been called "the first really great modern critic" and whom I quote as the spokesman for the artist because he continues to influence critical thought even to the present. Coleridge did not accept the concept so widely held up to that time that the mind was a passive recipient of sensory impressions and that the function of the artist was to imitate either nature herself or a Platonic ideal. He saw in the imagination an active creative force and he distinguished between fancy and imagination, the former corresponding closely to what in psychoanalytic terminology is the imagery of the primary process, the latter suggesting the secondary process. Imagination, he said, "dissolves, diffuses, dissipates, in order to re-create; or where this process is rendered impossible, yet still at all events its struggles to idealize and to unify." Fancy, by contrast, "is indeed no other than a mode of memory emancipated from the order of time and space." He introduces into his concept of imagination what corresponds to the synthetic function in psychoanalysis, in language that is startling in its similarity to the language of psychoanalysis. In another passage, Coleridge adds to his description: "The poet, described in *ideal* perfection, brings the whole soul of man into activity, with the subordination of its faculties to each other, according to their relative worth and dignity. He diffuses a tone and spirit of unity, that

211

blends, and (as it were) *fuses*, each into each, by that synthetic and magical power, to which we have exclusively appropriated the name of imagination."

Hanns Sachs in *The Creative Unconscious* says of the artistic creation: "The chaos is left behind and we are no longer under its influence; an id-content is changed into an enrichment of our ego." How striking is this passage when compared to that of Coleridge: "Idly talk they who speak of poets as mere indulgers of fancy, imagination, superstition, etc. They are the bridlers by delight, the purifiers; they that combine all these with reason and order—the true protoplasts— gods of love who tame the chaos." The analysand also must shape the images of his fantasy or dream—he also must "tame the chaos."

But for this synthetic activity to be carried on a new factor enters both in the creative process and in psychoanalysis. Sterba describes it in analytic therapy as a dissociation within the ego which permits one part of the ego to stand off as an observer in the neurotic struggle between the rest of the ego and the id. Freud described the "condition of calm self-observation" necessary for free association; and Wordsworth, when he defined poetry as "emotion recollected in tranquillity," referred to a similar phenomenon—the *distance* which must exist between the experience and its contemplation or analysis. Without this distance there is only the momentary relief of discharge of energies, the irruption of instinctual impulses— there is not the insight, the imaginative awareness which constitutes the true content of the aesthetic experience or the analytic revelation. But Wordsworth recognized clearly that there was more to poetic experience than the *recollection* of emotion, that the emotion had to be re-created and relived. He states this in the quotation to which I have referred and which I quote more fully: "I have said that poetry is the spontaneous overflow of powerful feelings: it takes its origin from emotion recollected in tranquillity; the emotion is contemplated till, by a species of re-action, the tranquillity gradually disappears, and an emotion, kindred to that which was before the subject of contemplation, is gradually produced, and does itself actually exist in the mind." Only then does the work of the poet take form. Wordsworth says, "In this mood successful composition generally begins, and in a mood similar to this it is carried on."

So too in psychoanalysis the "calm self-observation" must be followed by an emotional experience, the working-through process. But what the artist can do with his own creative genius, the analysand can accomplish only with the help of the analyst in a mutual communicative experience.

It must not be assumed that either in psychoanalysis or in the creative process there is an orderly progression from one phase to the next—from initial chaos to organization into fantasies or thoughts, to the experiencing of emotions. There is rather an intermingling of all these processes at all times and there is also communication of the productions at various stages as a leaven to the interchange between artist and audience, or between analysand and analyst.

The analysand discovers in the course of his analysis memories, fantasies, and the nature of his inner self that had previously not been in his awareness. Freud demonstrated that it is possible for a memory or thought to exist in consciousness and at the same time to exist in an unconscious version that is separated from the other through the effects of the unresolved defenses. Such a condition may result from an interpretation offered by the analyst before the resistances have been analyzed. The distinction between the two kinds of knowing is that one is purely intellectual whereas the other includes an affective component. A memory or fantasy which is brought to the attention of the person as an intellectual insight does not have the quality of inner conviction that comes with the emotional reliving of the experience. Lewin describes the sense of conviction that is experienced when an infantile event is remembered with all its feeling tone and he relates this conviction to the recovery of the sense of partial omniscience of the child at the breast, an experience that contains "a feeling which in the beginning was part of narcissistic omniscience, of complete trust in the infallibility and adequacy of immediate perception."

How then in the analysis is the intellectual concept changed into an inner conviction? By what means does the unacceptable idea become acceptable? How does disbelief and skepticism change to belief and knowledge? And most specifically, what is the role of communication in this transition?

In *The Interpretation of Dreams* Freud had already posed the problem of the transition from the unconscious system to the conscious system. The role of communication appears in his statement that one learns of unconscious processes when they have produced an effect on consciousness that admits of communication or observation. The importance of verbalization in the transition to the preconscious state was also brought out at that time, though later Freud modified this and implied that the preconscious condition is not altogether dependent on connection with memory traces of speech. Kris, in an exhaustive study of preconscious mental processes, describes the transition of thought processes from one topographical level to the other in terms of the vicissitudes of cathexis in the different systems. He states that unconscious material becomes preconscious "when id derivatives are cathected with ego energy and become part of preconscious mental processes at a considerable distance from the original impulse." One factor that facilitates this transition is indicated by Kris as a change in the distribution of counter-cathexis by the reduction of the level of conflict and the greater acceptability of id impulses.

In the psychoanalytic situation this tolerance of id deriva-

214

tives is effected through the transference, through identification with the analyst and through changes in the superego. Freud described the parallel function of the poet in overcoming the repulsion of the unconscious basis of his production by the use of his skill. He says: "The writer softens the egotistical character of the daydream by changes and disguises, and he bribes us by the offer of a purely formal, that is, aesthetic, pleasure in the presentation of his fantasies." There is in the analytic situation and in the aesthetic experience a comparable atmosphere of ego regression and permissiveness. In both the primary process becomes more evident, contradictions are tolerated, forbidden basic needs are expressed and fundamental issues are raised. These are what Freud called the "primal fantasies" and they form the content of myth and folklore of all peoples.

The productions of the analysand, the themes of the artist, and the myths of all people have a similar content. Wordsworth considered the interest of the poet: "Among the qualities . . . principally conducing to form a poet, is implied nothing differing in kind from other men, but only in degree. . . . The poet is chiefly distinguished from other men by a greater promptness to think and feel without immediate external excitement, and a greater power in expressing such thoughts and feelings as are produced in him in that manner. But these passions and thoughts and feelings are the general passions and thoughts and feelings of men. And with what are they connected? Undoubtedly with our moral sentiments and animal sensations, and with the causes which excite these; with the operation of the elements, and the appearances of this visible universe; with storm and sunshine, with the revolutions of the seasons, with cold and heat, with loss of friends and kindred, with injuries and resentments, gratitude and hope, with fear and sorrow."

The themes which appear in the analytic session are those of the mythmakers and poets: of birth, death, love, hate, incest,

215

sex, perversion, parricide, matricide, destruction, violence, castration, hunger, greed, jealousy, ambition, dependence. They are themes of the forbidden, the unattainable, the repressed—and the techniques of the artist are required to present them to consciousness, even in their disguised forms. In the artistic act and in the analytic situation the forbidden and the repressed are re-created.

What is the special role of communication in this complex process? The analysand and the artist approach their productions with guilt and anxiety. The sharing of the fantasy relieves the guilt and this calls for communication. It is to be seen in the communal daydreams of children which are, as Sachs pointed out, the forerunners of artistic communication. Also the borrowed fantasy allows an individual to tolerate an id impulse because it removes the sense of responsibility and gives absolution from the feeling of guilt.

Sharpe speaks of the magical reassurance of art and sees in it the beginning back of life—an act of reparation, atonement, and nullification of anxiety. The need to share the guilt and anxiety motivates the act of communication, and that in turn yields pleasure in the act of creation. Anna Freud describes a girl who transformed a masturbation beating fantasy accompanied by guilt and anxiety into a daydream which was, in effect, an acceptable artistic creation that served the functions of communication and pleasure out of the creative art. Wordsworth also describes the pleasure of creation. He speaks of "the sense of difficulty overcome" and "a complex feeling of delight, which is of the most important use in tempering the painful feeling always found intermingled with powerful descriptions of the deeper passions." This is the "functional pleasure" familiar to psychoanalysis.

The act of creation thus implies a need to externalize, to objectify, and to communicate, both in the artist and in the analysand. Shawcross in his introduction to the *Biographia*

Literaria says pointedly: "If there is one motive common to all genuine poetic impulse, it is surely the desire to objectify, and in this object to know and love, all that in the individual experience has seemed worthy of detachment from the fleeting personal life."

In psychoanalytic writings the need to communicate has been described in various clinical situations. The drive to confess under the pressure of guilt feelings is a familiar phenomenon. Hoffer, in a study of the diaries of adolescent schizophrenics, describes the urge of normal as well as abnormal adolescents to write down their thoughts, and also the restitutional function of the writing in the latter. In her description of the child's urge to communicate, Dorothy Burlingham examines the libidinal relationship of the child to the recipient of his communication or confession. The libidinal relationship which characterizes the transference in the analytic situation is of a similar nature.

Communication does not of itself effect the dynamic changes that mark the creative process or the psychoanalytic conviction, but it is a necessary part of the total process in each instance. Abercrombie makes this clear in relation to the poet. He says: "A man is not to be accounted a poet simply for being sensitive or excitable. A sunset may mean wonders to him; an old story may have fired his fancy into a rapture. But he is not a poet unless his wonders and raptures have ceased to be private to himself, and have become available to everyone." But communication in art is not the transmission of an intellectual thought alone—it is the transmission of an emotional experience, the re-creation by the audience of the emotion that motivated the artist. This is expressed by A. E. Housman who says: "And I think that to transfuse emotion—not to transmit thought but to set up in the reader's sense a vibration corresponding to what was felt by the writer—is the peculiar function of poetry." Similarly, Abercrombie says: "Language in

217

poetry is a transmission of energy rather than of substance. It sets the reader's mind working and directs the tendency of the work." Kaplan and Kris also note that "communication lies not so much in the prior intent of the artist as in the consequent re-creation by the audience of his work of art."

What is the corresponding situation in the psychoanalytic process? Verbalization and objectification are, as has been noted, basic components of the analytic process. Nunberg emphasizes the therapeutic value of verbalization: the discharge of affect in speech, the magical effect of the spoken word, and the cathartic effect of the act of becoming conscious. Beyond the magical power of words in the discharge of energy there is the realistic use of verbalization in the creation of the image and the symbol, and finally its use in communication.

It is necessary to go beyond simple discharge to effect dynamic changes in the ego that have lasting therapeutic effects and in this regard psychoanalysis goes beyond art in its use of communication. Hartmann points up the specific role of speech in the analytic situation, which, he says, "contributes toward fixing the previously unconscious element in the preconscious or conscious mind of the patient." He compares the function of the fixing of verbal symbols in the development of concept formation and objectivation in the child with a similar function in the analytic situation for the facilitation in the patient of the grasp of physical and psychic reality. The patient as well as the artist requires an audience for the expression of his fantasies, for his synthesis of them, and finally for his conviction of the truth behind them.

The analytic situation favors communication. Consider, for instance, the phenomenon of dreaming. The function of the dream is to preserve sleep, and it is of no consequence to the dreamer that he remember his dream. Where the dreamer, not in analysis, is impelled to record his dreams, as may occur with troubled adolescents or with poets, it is evidence that the disturber of sleep continues its action into the period of wake-fulness. Ferenczi, in his short note on the question, "To Whom Does One Relate One's Dreams?" states that it is to the very person to whom the content relates, and Wangh, in his study of Shakespeare's play, demonstrates a similar mechanism in Iago's recital of his dream to Othello. Kanzer makes communication an inherent component of dream activity and postulates that "the dream serves a communicative function—directly in terms of introjected objects, and indirectly in relation to the external world." He believes that analytic therapy finds the analyst drawn into the intrapsychic as well as external communicative system of the dreamer. Lewin also suggests an "occult transference figure" in the case of the solitary associater, the self-analyst.

In analysis the remembering of dreams and their communication to the analyst becomes a matter of great importance. Whether the remembering and communication go on to understanding is another matter. There is a continuous struggle between the drive to expression and the forces of resistance and in this struggle the analyst has an active role.

What happens to the analyst as the listener to the communications of the analysand? I have already quoted Freud's well-known passage in which he describes the analyst's use of his own unconscious as a receptive organ toward the emerging unconscious of the patient. Freud continues: "As the receiver transmutes the electric vibrations induced by the sound-waves back again into sound-waves, so is the physician's unconscious mind able to reconstruct the patient's unconscious, which has directed his associations, from the communications derived from it."

The analyst is thus not a purely passive participant in this communicative relationship. In this he is indeed as the audience of the artistic creation. The analyst must be free to respond to the productions of the patient, to create in his own mind the images and feelings which correspond to those of the patient. Eissler, in a paper on the psychoanalysis of schizophrenia, de-

219

scribes "the stirring agitation of artistic experience in the therapist" and he adds, "Many of these patients will respond favorably if approached in the way one approaches works of art from which one expects artistic exaltation."

But the analyst has a further function. He must maintain the distance, the tranquillity of Wordsworth, and then by his interpretations recommunicate to the patient the significance of the latter's productions, especially as they may be manifested in the transference. He collaborates in the creative process by supplying the skill of the poet to bring to the surface emotions and images (which are id derivatives) but to keep them controlled within the demands of the ego. But he must do this with skill and sensitivity so as not to destroy the awakening imaginative powers of the patient, which must remain as the patient's own. To this end the analyst must in his own analysis have lived through a creative experience and recognized the value of maintaining the individuality of the analysand.

The interpretations of the analyst, communicated to the analysand, reinforce the synthetic function of the ego in the latter, already in operation through the process of free association. Kris especially has described this process in relation to preconscious mental activity leading to recognition and recall. Kris points out that the interpretation of the analyst is in effect a perception that brings recognition further along toward recall.

The analyst's role is not simply to translate to the patient the meanings of the derivatives of the unconscious. Rather the role of the analyst is to free the patient's imagination so that he may re-create the fantasies of his childhood and communicate them to himself and to the analyst. It is the re-creation, the process of reconstruction that is the primary feature—the communication, both from analysand to analyst and from analyst to analysand, is only a facilitating factor, though an essential one.

The patient then re-experiences his emotions, recollects, reconstructs, and relives; and in this accomplishes the conviction that marks the true insight of the analytic experience. This is indeed the equivalent of the aesthetic experience which provides, in Coleridge's words, "the willing suspension of disbelief" that leads to the sense of conviction.

Freud notes that reconstruction in analysis produces in the patient "an assured conviction of the truth of the construction which achieves the same therapeutic result as a recaptured memory." He says that it is the task of the analyst "to make out what has been forgotten from the traces which it has left behind, or more correctly, to *construct* it." Lewin describes the sense of certainty that comes with "what one knows because it is primal, immediate, and unquestioned experience. It was not learned by seeing or by hearsay, but represents the primitive narcissistic trust in sensory experience."

Art too is experience. As Abercrombie says, "We can see every poem as the capture and the preservation of some perfection of experience." Both in psychoanalysis and in art there is a searching for the specific and the immediate, and with their discovery there is the response, so difficult to define, comprising the emotions of aesthetic pleasure and self-awareness.

Here one is forced to ask, why then does art not cure? There is no simple answer, but a point of departure is that psychoanalysis goes beyond art in that it involves conscious awareness as well as experience. In this regard the parallel between psychoanalysis and the creative process no longer holds. The unconscious is expressed in art—it is felt but it is not understood. The artist avoids direct conflict, especially with his superego. The analysis must resolve this conflict. It is not enough to say with Wordsworth:

> To me alone there came a thought of grief:
> A timely utterance gave that thought relief,
> And I again am strong.

It is, in fact, necessary for aesthetic pleasure that the unconscious meaning of the artistic creation remain unspoken

(Freud). The artist evokes emotion and gives pleasure; he does not need to go beyond this to the translation of his imagery into the language of the secondary process. Art does not aim to cure: it arises out of conflict, not out of neurosis. Psychoanalysis must take an additional step beyond the aesthetic experience; its aim is to make conscious what was unconscious. What I contend is that without the equivalent of the aesthetic experience in the psychoanalytic process, the transition from the unconscious state to consciousness will carry no conviction. For this to be accomplished, communication is essential.

I hope that I have made it clear that I do not in this venture into the realms of aesthetic theory and criticism mean to imply that communication is the key to the psychoanalytic process, any more than it is the key to art. Communication is one facet of these complex human activities and that I have chosen to discuss it does not deny the equal or even greater importance of other factors.

Communication is a complex phenomenon that appears in different forms wherever there is social structure whether in human or animal society. In human beings communication is supplemented by language and speech and becomes the more subtle and delicate an instrument. In art communication achieves its most human expression, the transmission of emotion, and this quality is shared in psychoanalysis. Communication in art and in psychoanalysis is an essential component of the creative process that comprises both. In the psychoanalytic interview specifically, communication between analysand and analyst plays a major role in breaking down the patient's resistances and preparing him for the insight and emotional experience that lead to conviction.

1955

▣ NEW VIEWS OF ART

AND THE CREATIVE PROCESS

IN PSYCHOANALYTIC

EGO PSYCHOLOGY

Louis Fraiberg

If we recall Philip Wheelwright's definition of the Metaphoric Imagination as that which "fuses heterogeneous elements into some kind of unity" and Lionel Trilling's remark that the mind is "exactly a poetry-making organ," then we see two of the chief ways in which psychoanalytic ego psychology can be useful in the study of literature. For psychoanalysis has developed in the past forty years to the stage where even cultural lag is no longer an excuse for pretending that it can be regarded as merely the key to a cipher. With the new emphases it was given by Freud shortly after World War I, it has become an instrument capable of examining intellectual problems of considerable complexity, and as it proceeds in its study of the ego, it becomes increasingly complex itself. Instead of explaining as symbols single components of psychic processes or simple combinations of them (the common misunderstanding of its function), it is more and more seeing whole constellations of psychic life and their total effects. It is now becoming possible for psychoanalysts and others to study such problems as those of the artist and his materials in ways whose subtleties and insights are not inferior to those we are accustomed to find in the writings of aestheticians and literary critics.

This goes far beyond the examination of a work as only the product of or the appeal to a particular interest. Dominant themes are, of course, very important, but the newer view begins by accepting the work on its own terms as an artistic entity and not simply as the sum of its tendencies.

Psychoanalysis is able to do this by virtue of such concepts as secondary autonomy in ego functions and the conflict-free sphere of the ego, which are based on relatively new hypotheses of energic origin and activity. No longer are sexuality and aggression the sole determinants of psychic acts. Psychoanalysts now postulate a third kind of energy, either neutral in origin or coming from the other two sources but partially neutralized, and thus available for higher mental functions.

It is time we realized that students of the ego do not see the artist as the prisoner of his impulses nor his art as an uncontrolled form of psychic explosion. Neither do they regard their therapeutic task as simply helping the individual adjust to whatever situation he happens to find himself in. What they are concerned with is establishing an appropriate relationship between individual and environment and this sometimes requires creative adjustment of the latter to the former. Therefore, both as therapists and as students of the psyche, they are interested in the kind of imaginative invention and reconstruction which is characteristic of the artist.

Rooting itself firmly in classical psychoanalysis, recent ego psychology sees creativity as a natural expression of the psyche with its basic dual and reciprocating motive forces, but it has now reached a stage of sophistication in the formulation of theory which is no longer satisfied with merely accounting for the polar interaction of libidinal and aggressive drives.

A phenomenon so complex as creation requires something less simple than the concept of alternating counter-tensions leading to the dominance of one or to a compromise which fully satisfies neither. Eros and Thanatos remain the foundation of the new theories, but on them is built a superstructure which permits psychoanalysis to achieve a new understanding of large areas of psychic life which lie beyond primary involvement with instinctual drives. By the introduction of a third set of psychic motives the theoretical means have now been made available to examine psychoanalytically a large number of mental acts—including creative thought, with which this discussion is concerned—and to extend significantly our knowledge of them. This new theoretical aid is the concept that psychic energy may be used for purposes independent of its origin in instinctual sources.

The mystery of creativity is still a mystery, but new light is being shed into some of its darkest corners. By looking in a direction away from its biological orientation, psychoanalysis is increasing its ability to cope with certain social aspects of human life on terms which approach more closely than ever before the assumptions of non-psychoanalytic thinkers—philosophers, critics, artists. In these areas of study the emphasis is shifting from problems of genesis and development, viewed historically, to those of present process and production, from expression to communication, from individual elements to entire wholes, from the necessary satisfying of instinctual demands to what may fairly be called higher pleasures.

In what is to follow I shall survey the findings and hypotheses of the outstanding workers in the field of psychoanalytic ego psychology as these apply to the problems of creativity. Some of the ideas were originally Freud's, some grew out of his suggestions, and some are new. But the importance of them now is that they dominate psychoanalysis today and seem to afford the greatest potential for its future development. Since this influence is a phenomenon of relatively recent years, the task is barely begun, and consequently the results are inconclusive. Although psychoanalysis is tending toward an all-inclusive theory—Freud made tentative proposals for one even before the publication of *The Interpretation of Dreams* —it is still a young scientific discipline and has a long way to go. It is too soon to tell what will actually happen to some of the suggestions I shall discuss, but their possibilities will, in most cases, be quite evident.

One of the most interesting revisions of earlier thinking which is emerging from the newer studies in ego psychology is the conception of the artist as a person with a strong ego rather than a weak one. Part of this comes from endowment, part from development. Individual differences prevail throughout life, and they take their pattern from the particular psychic potential with which the individual happens to be born.

The artistic gift, for example, depends in part upon the capacity of the ego to submit itself temporarily to the power of the id, to disengage itself, and to utilize id material for its own higher purposes. If the ego's innate potential is less than such capacity, then the id will simply not permit itself to be used in this way; on the contrary, it will constantly threaten the ego with domination. Presumably, in such a case, the individual concerned could not become an artist, or at least not a very good one. This recognition of the importance of endowment, though it raises new problems, increases the possibility of further scientific understanding of the uniqueness of the artist, both as a person and as a creator.

This "flexibility of repression" works hand in hand with another endowed ability, the artist's capacity for "multiple and mobile identifications." The latter refers to his power of establishing meaningful emotional connections between himself and other (psychological) objects. It is plain that these two inborn abilities, when they occur in significant strength in one person, make possible a degree of availability and control of psychic material which must be extremely serviceable to any artist.

To these ego psychology has added the study of the innate capacity for sublimation, the transformation of psychic tendencies from forms suitable for the satisfying of basic needs to those which are appropriate for use by the higher mental processes, including creative thought. An important aid in understanding the role of sublimation in art is the concept of neutralization of psychic energy, which, though it derives from a suggestion made by Freud as far back as 1922, is only just coming into general use. It refers to the process by which psychic energy can be more or less freed from its original libidinal or aggressive matrix and thus be made available for other purposes. Some theorists even argue that the individual is born with a store of such uncommitted energy which may be added to later from instinctual sources. Not only the "amount" of creativity but its nature as well may be powerfully affected by the ratio between the three kinds of energy which exists at birth.

The investigation of the specific ways in which psychic endowment contributes to artistic talent has only just begun, but some progress has already been made in two areas: the determination of vocational choice, and the composition of the psychic apparatus which is especially talented in performing functions that facilitate artistic work. The question of why a particular person becomes an artist and the related question of how good an artist he can become are thus being asked in terms which make it possible for psychoanalysis to begin searching for answers. As might be expected in this stage of development, most of the current approaches are theoretical, though based on clinical experience. The suggestion has been made that there are innate differences in the ability to let in or to keep out stimuli, the so-called stimulus barrier. One study indicates that these differences are related to precocity in ego development generally and to the early development of special gifts in particular. The ability to neutralize psychic energy, also partly a matter of endowment, facilitates the development of the artist's capacity for successful activity.

Besides the potential present at birth, the course of the ego's development is of great importance to the study of the artistic psyche. Recent views emphasize the higher, i.e., the non-instinctual, kinds of mental acts. These include problem solving, reality testing, and creative thinking, all intimately related to art. The role of the instincts in all of these is well-known; for that matter, the knowledge that satisfaction may be gained from the functioning of the psychic apparatus itself is not new. What is new is the focusing of attention on the latter, another instance of psychoanalytic interest in those activities of the psyche which transcend instinctual conflict. It is a matter of some moment that pleasure in artistic form can be sufficient unto itself and that it serves as more than a mere facade for what has been complacently called the "real" psychic content behind it. Conflict is not simply masked; it is joined by non-conflictual forces to help produce the complex we speak of as the aesthetic experience.

Some of this can be recognized in the relation of preconscious thought processes to the secondary process. Preconscious thoughts are those which are repressed, i.e., kept unconscious, not out of psychic necessity but simply for mental convenience. There is no particular objection to their becoming conscious; there is just not enough room on the stage of consciousness for all of them at once. Consequently, they remain unconscious until attention is directed to them, thus providing them with the energy necessary for emergence.

Since one of the reasons for the slight degree of repression of such thoughts is the fact they are not involved in instinctual conflicts, they are readily available for use in "just-below-the-surface" (preconscious) thinking and in conscious thinking as well. Their relative freedom from instinctual domination makes them particularly useful in constructions or inventions whose psychic value is on the higher levels of ego performance.

As described in *The Interpretation of Dreams*, the secondary process (unconsciously) brings a kind of order to the mass of seemingly chaotic dream thoughts, connecting similar elements, providing logical and chronological sequences, and otherwise giving enough form to the dream to enable it to pass the relaxed censorship, which is not nearly so demanding as the waking consciousness on matters relating to correspondence with outer reality. Nevertheless, this process does represent the first rudimentary influences of reason and external experience upon the direct expression of the id impulses. As such it is the prototype of the later conscious elaboration to which these and similar fantasies may be subjected in art; in its primitive fashion it foreshadows the achievements of artistic form.

The ego is, in fact, the agent which enables psychic expression to emerge from the process of raw catharsis and to assume forms which are useful and pleasing. In 1922 (in the preliminary draft of *The Ego and the Id*) Freud noted that sublimation takes place when energy is desexualized. Four years later he stated that the ego works with desexualized energy. These two concepts are among the bases for modern research into creative thought processes. From them comes the view of the ego as "the psychic system that controls perception and motility, achieves solutions, and directs action" (Hartmann and Kris). Adequate performance of these functions is possible only when a sufficient degree of freedom from instinctual involvements is attained. For technical reasons this is never actually complete, although it may be so great that the residual conflict is negligible; more frequently than is generally recognized, the conflict, though present, is pretty thoroughly under

229

control. Hartmann therefore speaks of the "conflict-free ego sphere," by which is meant the range of ego activities conducted with relatively little interference from id sources or, to state it less negatively, those which transcend instinctual origins or whose base is in "higher" mental processes. As indicated earlier, this includes the whole range of synthetic ego functions such as problem solving, reality testing, and creative thinking together with their vast numbers of minutiae many of which go into the production of works of art and the transmission of the aesthetic experience.

Current psychoanalytic views of creativity gain much from the recognition that it may be regarded qualitatively as well as quantitatively and from the providing of a conceptual means of accounting for both kinds of attributes. This is best seen in the recent formulations of the nature of sublimation, one of the earliest psychoanalytic concepts now being re-examined in this connection. The technical hypotheses now being offered concern themselves with the character of psychic energy, the motive power of the psychic apparatus. So far has psychoanalytic theory come from the purely quantitative view that one investigator, Edward Glover, even suggests that "some qualitative change in energy may prove to be the only metapsychologically valid criterion of sublimation."

In order to clarify the two aspects of the problem, it is probably better to adopt the proposal of Kris that "the term *neutralization* could be conveniently used to designate the relevant energy *transformations*, and that the term *sublimation* be reserved for the displacement of goal." This has the merit of retaining the familiar usage of *sublimation* and referring to the newer concern with energic changes by a distinctive term. Sublimation basic to the psychoanalytic study of art may thus be seen as related to intention. This emancipates it from mechanistic conceptions while at the same time allowing for the necessary quantitative considerations. Both are relevant to the understanding of the link between sublimation and such familiar psychic processes as displacement and identification, but the focus is now upon the correlation between change of mode of energy from instinctual to non-instinctual and the change in the aims of the objects. This provides part of the theoretical basis for psychoanalytic study of artistic problems which it formerly lacked the means of handling conceptually.

Creativity, then, may be regarded as a special form of sublimation in which natural endowment facilitates the development of the ego toward mastery of its psychic environment and toward an increasing ability to devote itself to activities which are relatively independent of conflict. The part played by sexuality in this process has long been an object of study; currently, increased attention is being paid to the role of aggression. As basic forces in the psyche, they must both be involved significantly in creativity. According to the newer conceptions, there are actually three sources of psychic energy. Besides the sexual and aggressive instincts, there is, as I have mentioned, a stock of neutral energy helping to activate the ego.

Not only is this available for higher psychic functions, but exchanges and enhancements also are possible between it and the other two. This neutral energy "may stem from and may be retransformed into either libido or aggression," according to a study by Hartmann, Kris, and Loewenstein. A tremendous reservoir of energy is therefore available for creative thought, some of it neutral and some of it tinged with sexual or aggressive characteristics. The artist, with his strong ego, i.e., one that can neutralize large quantities of energy from instinctual sources, is most fortunately equipped to bring maximum psychic resources to bear upon his artistic work. He also has a great deal to "invest" in the product, permitting it to attain a high degree of independence (secondary autonomy in ego functions), since he can tap the instinctual reservoir for replacements at need.

Ordinary ego activities are carried on by means of transitory shifts in the distribution of energy, the "energy flux." What makes creativity possible is the ability of the artist's ego to neutralize energy from the instincts and to commit it to the created thought or object. In this way the "secondary autonomy" of ego functions may be brought about. The corollary to this rather technical matter is that the artist, with his special capacity for neutralizing energy, is well fitted to master many situations in everyday reality as well. The primacy of sexual forces in this process has long been taken for granted, but recently a distinction of considerable importance has been proposed. Hartmann, Kris, and Loewenstein suggest that aggression plays a greater part in creativity than might be expected. In their view, it manifests itself in such fundamental activities of the psyche as the control of the body, the formation of psychic structures, and the mastery of outer reality. By the same token it takes part in the creation of artistic forms, and the possibility now exists for a theoretical integration of the phenomena of form and content which can now be seen to have an even more intimate psychic relationship than had been previously supposed.

Few of the motives for artistic creation which have so far been identified are well understood. Psychoanalysis has no comprehensive theory to account for them all. The inadequacy of the earlier cathartic theory has long been recognized, but as yet there is no agreement on its successor; even the restitution theory has its critics. Of the approaches to this problem which have been made by ego psychology I shall briefly describe the most promising.

One of the newest is Erikson's concept of *ego identity*, which has not yet received its full formulation. It attempts an accommodation of psychoanalysis and gestalt psychology that seems to hold considerable potential for the scientific understanding of complex mental acts. Erikson conceives of the process of psychic growth as moving through three major stages: the beginning awareness of separate selfhood in infancy and early childhood; the placing of that self in a dynamically satisfying relationship with some form of the family; and the evolution of this identification into a new configuration (Erikson's word) resulting from the recognition by society of the young individual as "somebody who had to become the way he is, and who, being the way he is, is taken for granted." It is a theory of growing autonomy, of development toward an ever more sharply delineated self-image. By the end of adolescence it is, for all practical purposes, complete.

The process is largely unconscious in both society and the individual, but accompanying it for the latter is what Erikson calls "a sense of psychosocial well-being"—usually just below the threshold of awareness but sometimes emerging into consciousness—a feeling that one is "at home in one's body," that one's course and destination are clear, and that the world, or at least those people in it who matter, will acknowledge one's gifts and achievements. This feeling is brought about by a series of extensions of horizons during genetic and social development, by a series of relationships with desired objects, and by a series of investments in the possibility of accomplishment which attain the status of convictions, almost of "givens."

Such an assumption of what amounts almost to destiny, coming to fruition at the time of life when the individual is ready to take on adult responsibilities, can be a powerful influence in the decision to become an artist. It is precisely at this time that the impulse to artistic creation is so strong in many people, a time when the realization of special abilities also often occurs. Erikson's theory, as applied to motives for creation, has comprehensiveness to recommend it. In the process of finding themselves, some people find that they are artists.

Psychic conflict is involved in the motivation of creative thought not only in the familiar sense that it supplies themes and energy but in other ways as well. Ego psychology now sees it as a necessary component in the development of the personality and not simply as a hazard which must be surmounted in order to avoid pathology. Thus the artist and his work are related even more intimately than before. By the agency of conflict the aims of both libido and aggression are modified and brought within the control of the ego so that it may be said psychoanalytically that the artist taps his own inner resources and shapes them to his own purposes rather than being driven helplessly by them into actions and thoughts not of his own choosing.

There are times, however, when creation may be motivated by a conflict situation in a fairly direct fashion. Like some psychoanalytic patients who talk a great deal about autobiographical details in order to avoid talking about the immediate psychic problem, an artist might contrive a work of fiction in order to mask a conflict. Kris. gives a striking example of the feeling of protection which such an invention may give both creator and audience. A captain of marines on a Pacific island in World War II came upon one of his men on duty alone in a solitary outpost listening to a short-wave radio tuned to an American station. "The captain reported that he hardly had time to ask himself whether or not such listening, while on outpost, was permissible; he found himself within a short time engrossed in the story. It dealt with outposts of marine detachments waiting on a Pacific island for a Japanese attack. . . . Safety in the aesthetic illusion protects from the danger in reality, even if both dangers should be identical." This is so even when the danger is psychic rather than external. In this connection ego psychology says nothing about the production of a particular form; it is concerned here only with motivation.

234

Another widely held theory of motivation involving conflict stresses restitution rather than protection. The artist creates because he has unconsciously fantasied the destruction of certain objects. To overcome this psychically felt loss, he restores them by putting them into a work of art. Or he has (again unconsciously) entertained a forbidden wish, and his artistic fantasy enables him to atone for it. The relation of this theory to the basic conflict of Eros and Thanatos will readily be seen. Creation is the artist's way of frustrating the triumph of the death tendency: he brings into existence an object which cannot die. (This theory is, of course, not exclusive with psychoanalysts. See, for example, Keats's "Ode on a Grecian Urn.")

The restitution theory has been objected to by Bychowski on the ground that it is not inclusive and must be counted "only as one of the possible unconscious mechanisms of creation." As an example of another he cites the case in which the artist has abandoned the world because of unconscious conflicts and then felt the need to become part of it once more. Creation can thus become, as Freud said earlier, a way back to reality.

Further support for the theory that creation is motivated by the simultaneous wish to destroy and to make restitution for the wish lies in the earliest stages of ego development. The child, when it becomes aware of itself as an entity different from its surroundings, is able to transfer emotional values to other human objects. This, however, is not a simple transfer. The child's parents or their surrogates have caused it to experience both gratification and deprivation, and the feelings, therefore, are a mixture of positive and negative, or what psychoanalysis terms *ambivalent.* Moreover, this quality persists throughout life, though it varies in strength. In this way any later impulse to create may well take on the character of an act to undo a destructive fantasy. This act consists not only of the alternation of feelings just mentioned but also of simultaneous experiencing of both kinds at once. The creation is accomplished by reconstituting the object according to the artist's aesthetic conception, and this means that the image of the object in its natural context must be destroyed. Thus gratification at partial satisfaction of the destructive impulse is achieved, guilt at the destructive wish is alleviated, and pleasure at the new creation is felt, all being experienced concomitantly, and the combined, complicated value of the whole is invested in the created object. To this is added the pleasure which the ego feels in solving artistic problems and in the operation of the psychic apparatus itself. A statue, a novel, or a concerto each constitutes a world with its elements better ordered than they might have been in non-artistic external reality.

But another motive exists, counter to these and stemming from the urge to master the actual environment by learning about it. From childhood on, curiosity serves this purpose. One looks, hears, investigates, tries out new things, and does over and over those which have special appeal. When this is done not merely for pleasure but for the sake of mastery it is said to be motivated by the repetition-compulsion, the habit of repeating an act until its accompanying affect has been assimilated into the psychic equilibrium. It obviously influences the choice of the conflict which is to be represented symbolically through theme, plot, and characterization, and it is related to the phenomenon of recurrence in the work of some authors. When a first novel is followed by a series of others in which variations are played on the same theme, it may be guessed that the author is still striving to master the situation from which the series took its genesis. Conversely, fresh, independent books argue for successful early handling of the material, leaving the author free to go on to other things.

The clues may be more subtle than those afforded by theme, plot, and characterization. Studies of imagery, for instance, may reveal striking patterns showing the author's attitude toward certain aspects of his work. Repetition, or its absence, and the relating of otherwise disparate elements through similarity of image clusters may provide useful hints toward the understanding of the psychic motives of a work and its appeal to certain types of audiences.

What underlies all these motives for creation is the fundamental drive of the ego toward mastery of its environment. Creativity must be seen as a special instance of this necessity. At the very least, the organism must survive; this is the ego's first responsibility. Beyond mere survival, however, there is the need for effective functioning, and here the ego's capacity for selecting, analyzing, organizing, and controlling elements from both the psyche and the exterior world provides not only solutions to problems but also rearrangements of situations which serve to maintain the dynamic equilibrium. Aesthetic activity grows out of the regular functioning of the psychic life processes.

For the artist the most important mastery is mastery of his material, and here the ego plays its part. It regulates the blind power thrusts of the id, helps determine which unconscious trains of associations shall receive the essential energic strength, and contrives consciously the patterns within which they shall be displayed and to which they give life. In these ways, among others, it arranges the transmission of experience from artist to audience. Artistic conventions, currents of taste, the demands of the medium and the genre—all these are incorporated by it into the grand design which serves the creator's purpose. For the most effective work, not only innate talent is required but ego strength as well.

Creation may be characterized psychoanalytically as a process having two phases, inspiration and elaboration. In the first, impulses from the id attained a high degree of expression, but this occurs only under the close control of the ego which receives

237

their powerful manifestations, shuts off the supply when it chooses, and turns them to its own uses. The primary process is thus channeled into organized patterns of expression at the direction of the reality-controlling, problem-solving agency, and this is no less true because the id impulses may be perceived by it as coming from the outside. That is, the individual is aware of an idea or flash of insight which appears to have originated elsewhere and of which he is only the gifted receiver, his gift consisting precisely in the ability to receive such "messages." The impulse has, of course, not actually been external to his psyche but only to his ego.

A certain amount of preconscious manipulation of it then takes place during this inspirational phase, but the product is far from a finished work of art, for the modifications, as described in *The Interpretation of Dreams*, are just enough to soften the forbidden elements and make the whole admissible to consciousness. There have been various attempts to bring to light such creation as takes place during this phase, e.g., automatic drawing, surrealism, and to place a high artistic value on the product on the ground that it came directly from the "true" artistic center of the psyche. This romantic misreading of psychoanalysis is, of course, directly opposed to its real concern which is with the value of the higher thought processes, and it is easy to see why Freud was at some pains to repudiate those enthusiasts who claimed that his discoveries had established the id as the seat of the artistic personality and the sole source of art.

Instead of emphasizing the crude origins, Freud insisted rather that the essence of artistic creation was the reworking of the elements into consistent artistic wholes, and in this it is necessary to go beyond even the second phase, that of unconscious elaboration. To be sure, in producing a work of art, the artist builds upon the partial alteration of the fantasy which has occurred unconsciously, but at least as significant a part of the work is conscious. The impulses, having achieved partial expression, are no longer in a position to exercise control, and the work of art may acquire greater independence from their demands, i.e., secondary autonomy. Another way of saying this is that the unconscious psychic mechanisms are satisfied and that the conscious perceptions and acts of the artist can now deal with the material according to aesthetic rather than psychic considerations. Though this statement is an oversimplification, perhaps it may help to clarify the actual process.

From an energic standpoint the emergence of an idea which may become part of an artistic work occurs in this fashion. A part of the energy which was formerly employed in repressing a given forbidden impulse is shifted to another, perhaps a more threatening one. This increases the possibility that the first impulse might drive past the barrier of counterforce. If the energic shift is of sufficient magnitude, then the "upward" movement may be accompanied by feelings of relief, elation, and similar sensations which then become a part of the pleasure of creating. But the mere removal of a fraction of the opposing force is not enough; the drive so far is only preconscious (that is, free of repression or countercathexis) but not yet conscious. It must compete with a great many others for the limited amount of attention which is available at any one time. Extra energy is necessary to assure the center of the stage (the technical term for the acquisition of this extra energy is hypercathexis). It comes from quantities of energy which have been engaged in repressing other drives of lesser significance but which are now attracted to the emerging one by its accompanying elation or relief and which thereupon enter its service, thus increasing the pleasurable feeling.

It is presumed that such increase is felt to be greater than the risk of the actual liberation elsewhere in the psyche of other material accompanied by negative, i.e., unpleasurable, feelings, or else the emergence of the impulse in question could

239

not take place. Conversely, if the danger of the negative feelings should be greater, then presumably the rise of the pleasurable ones would be restrained and the process of creation thereby inhibited.

This dynamic equilibrium of feelings, actuated by shifts in cathexis, abides by the rules of the primary process in what Rapaport calls the "inventive" phase of creative thinking. In many essentials this is identical with what I have been calling here, after Kris, "inspiration." That is, it is characterized by primitive thinking and largely controlled by feeling which depends in turn on relative quantities of psychic energy. As yet this does not involve cerebration in any significant way. As the idea rises into consciousness, it may consist of "a vague general 'feel,' a sense of relationship, a schematic pattern, a verbal or visual fragment, and so on" (Rapaport). In the beginning it has few or no relationships with other conscious thoughts. The elaborative phase of creation follows, and it is then that such relationships may be established. Connections are made, patterns are created, and communication is possible. From an internal, idiosyncratic process, operating almost automatically, a product emerges which is modified or even transformed into something which can be received and understood by another person. Having passed through the primary and secondary processes, the material is now subjected to a much higher degree of conscious control according to an entirely different set of rules, the requirements of society, of communication, of art.

In view of the belief held by some that authors are primarily concerned with externalization of their inner conflicts and that their books may therefore be read simply as embodiments of such conflicts, it is necessary to understand the interest which ego psychology takes in this aspect of the creative process. It is true that some books come close to answering this description, but it may safely be said that most do not. A distinction must be made here between origin and result; the genetic fallacy must be avoided. Although a book may be written under the influence of psychic conflict, this does not necessarily determine its form, its message, or its impact. This is so simply because conflict is not the only force at work in creation. In fact, if it assumes too prominent a role in motivation, it may well vitiate the result, damaging or even destroying the book as a work of art. Psychoanalytic ego psychology stresses control by the artist. Emergence from conflict plays a part in every creative process.

The functioning of the ego is significantly influenced by the fact that it originates, in part, outside the sphere of instinctual conflict altogether. In so far as the creative process utilizes this primordial uncommitted energy, the work of art is also independent of conflict and its vicissitudes. This may be true as well of those contents of the ego which originated in conflict, as a defense against an instinctual drive, for example, and which develop thereafter into ideas having no further connection with their origins. In ego-psychological terms these "aims, attitudes, interests, structures of the ego" (Rapaport) have entered its conflict-free sphere. Together with the ones which were free of conflictual influences from the beginning, these constitute the greater part of those mental acts which take place during the elaborative phase of creative thought. They are therefore of supreme importance for our understanding of that aspect of artistic activity from a psychoanalytic standpoint.

They are largely under the control of the artist, but this is because they have already passed through the secondary process just as ordinary ideas libidinally or aggressively influenced have passed through the primary process. In secondary-process thought, memory governs. We are speaking here of unconscious memory with a conceptual organization based not simply on sensory memory-traces but on the activation of these by quantities of energy, that is, by cathexes. In contrast with the primary process, in which cathexes are quite mobile, shifting readily from one train of associations to another, the secondary-process cathexes are relatively stable. They are bound, i.e., more or less permanently committed, to a given idea or cluster of ideas. It is rather difficult to shift them, and the ideas they give power to are not striving—as primary-process ideas are—for immediate and total discharge. Consequently, this portion of the ego affords the safest channels for the release of tensions. Such release can take place at a rate and in a direction both of which are subject to a large degree of unconscious ego-control, depending upon the quantity and intensity of pleasure attained by the ego in the process. As Rapaport remarks, secondary-process thought, although it sustains the goal of the pleasure-principle, reaches it "not on the path of least resistance but on that of greatest advantage." Surely this effectively destroys the notion that psychoanalysis regards the artist as the prisoner of his emotions and the victim of his conflicts and that it reduces his art to "nothing but" the automatic, helpless response to them.

The increasing sophistication of psychoanalytic thought raises its potential as an instrument for the scientific study of creativity. Its actual value for this purpose is difficult to assess at present because psychoanalytic ego psychology may be said to be in its formative stage. Much more information needs to be gathered, and the various contending hypotheses must undergo the test of time. In view of this, it is well for us to be patient. All that it has given us so far are some insights and an expectation. Perhaps the insights will be added to and deepened; perhaps the expectation will be fulfilled; perhaps not. The only relevant question for us is whether we can make use of what is now available.

The answer is that we can, but it must be on a tentative basis. The concern of science with the mind as an entity functioning in ways appropriate to the contexts in which it finds itself, or which it invents, parallels the speculative thinker's view of literary thought. The ever closer approximation of these two modes of conceptualization affords promise of greater usefulness as their translatability is enhanced. What is crucial is that more attention is being given to psychoanalytic studies of mental phenomena on higher and higher levels beyond the instinctual. The intellectual and the imaginative are being studied on their own terms, and psychoanalysis is gaining the power to deal with problems of configuration and milieu and, consequently, of art.

1961

▣ A THEORY CONCERNING FREE CREATION IN THE INVENTIVE ARTS

Harry B. Levey

The mystery of the mental processes underlying the gratuitous creation of beautiful things is rarely considered for itself. The artist, the inventor, and the scientist are unable to explain their creative processes satisfactorily, and have relatively little to say upon the subject. In fact, the interest of most of those who write about the creative imagination is secondary to their major concern in something else, and so expresses itself in a wish to explain artistic creativeness by stretching about it, via introspection and speculation, the generalizations they have devised, or accepted, toward a particular philosophic, scientific, economic, or religious system as an orientation to life; they have dealt with the artist, so to say, *in vacuo,* and without observing his mental processes according to the rules of science. This secondary interest, and the unscientific attitudes searchers after truth have shown toward the mystery, are inconsistent with the cardinal importance they, as well as the man-in-the-street, place upon art as an individual and a social good.

Oscar Wilde remarked upon the devotion to art in the following words:

This devotion to beauty and to the creation of beautiful things is the test of all great civilized nations. Philosophy may teach us to bear with equanimity the misfortunes of our neighbors, and science resolve the moral sense into a secretion of sugar, but art is what makes the life of each citizen a sacrament immortal. For beauty is the only thing that time cannot harm. Philosophies fall away like sand, and creeds follow one another like the withered leaves of autumn; but what is beautiful is a joy for all seasons and a possession for all eternity.

Havelock Ellis commented:

But it is only in art that the solution of life's problems can be found. Life is always immoral and unjust. It is art alone which, rising above the categories of morality, justifies the pains and griefs of life by demonstrating their representative character and emphasizing their spectacular value, thus redeeming the pain of life by beauty.

. . . It is highly probable . . . that no civilization can be worthwhile unless it is rich in creative genius and unless the population generally exhibits a sufficiently cultured level of education out of which such genius may arise freely and into which the seeds it produces may fruitfully fall.

John Dewey wrote:

Aesthetic experience is a manifestation, a record and celebration of the life of civilization, a means of promoting its development, and is also the ultimate judgment upon the quality of a civilization. For while it is produced and enjoyed by individuals, those individuals are what they are in the content of their experience because of the cultures in which they participate.

The importance of the free inventive arts for our culture, and their dignity and prestige, are quite generally accepted facts, but men vary more in their opinions about how art is produced, and as to which art productions are worthy of appreciation by themselves as well as by others, than they vary in respect to most other topics; their behavior in defense of their prejudices and beliefs about art is often as deeply subjective with too much piety and blind faith as are their convictions about religion. People who are fairly reasonable even about religion and psychoanalysis are likely to be touchy with respect to their opinions upon art, the artists, and the arts. Those who hold nothing else sacred hold their love of, and beliefs about, art sacred. Writers upon the subject of art creation too often behave as if a worshipful love of art for its own sake, or else the exquisite avoidance of this attitude, were a sufficient credential for speculating *ad lib* about the mental processes governing art production. This is true alike of aestheticians, critics, sociologists, psychologists, and psychoanalysts. In the present inquiry, I shall try to avoid this subjective error, and to season my own love of art with some scientific temper in attempting a new and more objective approach to the truth —one fully based on the foundations previous investigators have given me, and one which might inform some of their apparently erroneous conclusions with more than the proverbial grain of truth contained in all theories of aesthetics.

My use of the term "art" is very broad; it refers to the exercise of every inventive art, and includes those original expressions of the creative imagination which we are accustomed to classify as fine art, scientific discovery, and invention. I limit the scope of this study to the creation of original art from some purely personal need of the artists, that which Ella Sharpe has described as "pure art"—"dictated only by the inner laws and urges of the creator. They serve no practical end, and have no public criterion. The public bows to them. The goal of their endeavor is neither worldly wealth nor ease"; or which Roger Fry referred to in writing of the pure artist: "but, at all events, he will have an impulse to 'free' unconditioned creation which he will try to satisfy at all costs. If this impulse is so overpowering that the artist is quite incapable of modify-

247

ing his imagery in any way in order to satisfy the exigencies of other people, we may call him a pure artist"; and which R. H. Wilenski pictured for us in stating that: "The originality of a work of art consists in the attitudes, motives, and procedure of the man who made it; . . . if the artist sets out to enlarge his experience by his work, and in fact does so, his work is original . . . and he regards as fit material for his art only such emotive fragments as have in fact enlarged his own experience."

I believe that the terms "pure art" and "the pure artist" are undesirable, being as poorly descriptive of gratuitously creative activity as is the term "sublimation," and because they carry certain subjective connotations it would be better to discard because some philosophers have given them an intellectual construction, and because the pure artist has become too closely associated in our minds with Parnassus, the tower of ivory, *la poésie pure*. Accordingly, I suggest that we adopt in their stead the terms "free art" and "the free artist," which are really descriptive and are not handicapped with the connotations mentioned. Throughout this paper I shall use the terms "free art" and "the free artist" to indicate what are ordinarily described as pure art and the pure artist, or as original art and the original artist.

The problems of why certain persons, mostly men, have the power of expressing themselves in inventive ways, of why they are capable only at certain times of creating beauty which satisfies them, of why their work is more a completely absorbing passion than that of most men, of why they are relatively disinterested in producing primarily for applause, monetary gain, or for utility, of what the especial nature of their fantasy life consists, and of how their creative fantasy is transmuted into creative activity, have always impressed thinkers as important to understand since art is so vital to culture. In fact, to try to understand the mental processes by which art is produced is a temptation too powerful for most of us, including the writer, to resist. Yet, the problems surrounding the phenomenon, the free artist, are regularly approached with either a denial of their existence, or else with the same awe and wonder we experience when we behold a marvellous work of art. Thus, aestheticians, artists, philosophers, sociologists, academic psychologists, physician-psychologists, psychiatrists, and psychoanalysts react most often to these problems with subjective attitudes and theories echoing those of our childhood and of the myth-making ancients when curiosity engaged the problem of human reproduction. This subjective fault in scientific attitude is due partly to the same feelings as those which determine both the individual appreciation and cultural valuation of art; and it moves those who intend to write about the creative impulse to apologize for so doing, and to evade their announced intention in a typical manner. This subjectivity in approach is, of course, facilitated by the real difficulties the problem presents.

Otto Rank and Hanns Sachs estimated the status of psychoanalysis with reference to understanding the problem of the process of artistic sublimation in 1913:

The question whence the artist gets the psychic material previously unknown to him is not difficult for psychoanalysis to answer. It is otherwise, of course, with the problem of the course by which the transition from conscious to unconscious is put into the work and the mechanisms by which this transition is brought about. How the mode of utilization of this method differs from that which the neurotic prefers, for which exactly the same formula holds, is still little investigated.

In *A Psychoanalytic Study of Hamlet*, 1910, Ernest Jones wrote:

Psychologists have as yet devoted relatively little attention to individual study of genius and of artistic creativeness, and have mainly confined themselves to observations of a general order.

249

They seem to share the shyness or even aversion displayed by the world at large against too searching an analysis of a thing of beauty—the feeling expressed in Keats's lines on the prismatic study of the rainbow.

In the writer's opinion, the literature of psychoanalysis testifies that these estimates both of our lack of knowledge about the process of artistic sublimation, and of our subjective attitudes toward the problem, are as valid today as in 1910 and 1913.

The objects of the present paper are to avoid the tendency usual to philosophers, aestheticians, critics, and scientists to obfuscate the problem of artistic creativeness with that of aesthetic appreciation; to avoid the evasion of the problem regularly observed in writings about the creative impulse . . . to correlate what seem to me to be the most valuable efforts of others toward solving the problem; and, by going to the ant to learn her aesthetic ways, to contribute from clinical observations of the creative process as it occurs in free and original artists some tentative generalizations for a frame of reference about the mental processes actually observed in the free invention and creation of art.

1940

◻ THE CREATIVE ARTS

AS THERAPY

Mary Huntoon

The modern concept of psychiatric treatment emphasizes the fact that the cure of the patient does not depend upon the physician alone, but upon the combined efforts of all the members of the psychiatric team, and upon the therapeutic atmosphere created in the hospital by this point of view. Recovery in the psychiatric patient means the discharge of his negative and destructive feelings in a harmless way, and a reinvestment of his positive and constructive feelings in the world of reality about him.

The recognition of the part that art can play in the modern psychiatric hospital has come, largely, from the medical and psychological profession, and not from the artist—a fact which I find significant. Freud was interested in the therapeutic role played by the creative process in the man of genius. It is becoming increasingly clear that by means of the creative process the individual is able to keep his destructive tendencies in abeyance, and that this is applicable, not only to the man of genius, but to any individual.

It seems logical, therefore, that it would be possible to aid

251

selected patients by stimulating their creative faculties. The selection of patients for this type of therapy, however, seems to depend more upon the patient's deep need for a mode of expression which will synthesize his inner states of mind, and upon his latent creative faculty, than upon any superficial facility in the different media of art. A statement attributed to Picasso claims that a painting worthy of the name of art takes charge of the painter at a certain stage. In other words, when the creative process is aroused in a person, it acts as a liberating agent for unconscious material in his mind.

A department of art was incorporated in the original setup of Winter Veterans Administration Hospital, Topeka, Kansas, and from the beginning it has been immensely popular with both the patients and the staff. It has been progressively used by physicians who saw their patients finding release and joy in the creation of inspirational material, and in the projection of their feelings upon canvas. Patients who had failed to respond to other specific modalities sometimes began their recovery in the studio. Other patients graphically portrayed their emotional problems, conflicts, and sometimes the solution or evolution of these in a form understandable even to the artistically unsophisticated doctor. Patients who had no conscious need to express themselves in art blossomed into creditable artists to the astonishment of doctors, nurses, therapists, and friends—and always to the amazement of themselves. Such phenomena are now so familiar to the therapists and doctors in this hospital that the place of creative art is unquestioned. This has led us to attempt to describe and analyze our work more specifically.

In the studio, many discussions arise as to modes of expression. So-called realism, surrealism, naturalism, classicism, romanticism, impressionism, as well as expressionism and non-objective art, all find their place in the studio. A catholicity of taste is maintained. The only prerequisite is the existence of the sensitive faculty through which the individual has collected impressions. He may have no conscious wish to communicate his thoughts, but if he is willing to work in the studio we know that he is making an effort to understand some segment of experience. The tools with which to work are given to him, and he is taught how to use them as any other skill is taught, but the important part of creative arts therapy is that he has an idea which he wishes to express.

Ninety per cent of those patients for whom art is a prescribed therapy at Winter VA Hospital have had no formal training in art. In spite of this, many first works show an amazing dexterity. This was the case with one patient who had shown no dexterity in the psychological tests which had gone before. Through a need which amounted to an inspiration, the emotional material was artistically expressed. This would seem to indicate that we have not, as yet, found an adequate test for the individual's potentiality in the use of art as treatment.

The patient may or may not be aware of the ideas that he is expressing through his artistic production. In many cases it is necessary for the physician to interpret the patient's painting to him before he understands its implications. Sometimes the meaning of the painting becomes clear to the patient after he has finished it, and this process, which we call "art synthesis," may be dramatic and revealing. In some cases, when the patient shows no indications of any conscious realization of what he has painted, he may, nevertheless, show a clinical improvement and his behavior may indicate that he is working out an unconscious conflict through his painting. This seems to be a self-limited process which often results in a psychological resolution, and incidentally in a most interesting series of paintings through which the patient's progress can be traced.

This means that the patient needs the constant help of his doctor as he goes through these experiences in self-expression. It has been those patients whose doctors came into the studio frequently, following each step in the studio milieu and aiding in the integration of all material expressed, who profited most directly from art therapy.

In organizing the studio for the use of art as treatment, we had excellent guidance and material aid. Dr. Karl Menninger's insight into the possible function of art as treatment, and his unfailing encouragement were fundamentally important. Our consultant from The Menninger Foundation, Dr. Edward Greenwood, gave us suggestions and criticism. The physical medicine rehabilitation service of Winter VA Hospital furnished the supplies, equipment, and organization. The studio was planned to afford the best possible atmosphere for creative work, with opportunities for both expressive and vocational art, so that the patient could be guided, through suggestion and availability, toward the physician's prescribed aim.

In over three years of experience in the use of art as treatment at Winter VA Hospital, more than a thousand patients have been sent to the art shop by their physicians. More than a dozen media were made available, but the principal ones used have been oil painting, modeling in clay, and engraving. The patient, or student, as the patient is called in the studio, was given individual attention in order to discover in what manner art could function to bring about the prescribed aim, and in what medium the individual could best handle his emotional problem. In each case, the art productions were studied and placed in groups or categories according to their therapeutic function for the individual.

The categories which follow are not given in the order of their value, nor are they associated with particular illnesses. Any patient may use all or only one of these categories. They merely indicate some of the functions of art for the individual.

Group one includes the use of fantasy, or wish fulfillment. The attitude of this group usually seems rather casual. The need may and usually does spring from deeper levels, but the productions are not indicative of this underlying dynamic, although they may give a key to the doctor which will help him aid the patient to an understanding of his problem. Sometimes the fantasies expressed may lead the patient to considerable verbalization, and this verbalization which was formerly impossible to the patient may aid in his cure. Sometimes the patient expresses fantasies which are a prophecy of what is to come as, for example, when a bedridden patient, who was only able to come to the studio in a wheel chair, painted himself out of doors in a daisy field.

The second function is that of dexterity, by means of which the patient builds up a facade against a threatening reality. This function is similar to the function of any skill by means of which the ego gains strength and security, with the exception that it offers the exclusiveness of the studio, the ivory tower behind which the ego can withdraw for contemplation. It must be remembered, however, that in art the individual does not withdraw into the ivory tower to become inactive, but to make an effort toward self-understanding. The facade of dexterity may become permanent if the ego cannot mature beyond this point, or it may be temporarily used until the ego has built up enough strength to adjust itself to life on a more adult level.

This dexterity facade was made use of temporarily in the case of a young unmarried white patient, formerly of the navy, who first developed a serious case of tuberculosis. The tuberculosis was cured, but a severe psychosis took its place, the psychosis centering on the use of the hands for masturbation. His doctor interested him in painting and followed his progress in the studio closely. It took several months before the patient felt confident enough to try a complete painting, but as he became more and more interested, and found himself capable of very excellent painting, he found the solution of his masturbation preoccupation. As he made progress in the studio, he showed marked clinical improvement. He became adjusted enough to take part in many hospital activities, recovering, or at least becoming well enough to make adequate reality adjustments.

The third function which art may fulfill is that of relief of anxiety through the patient's representation of conflictual material. Graphic expression seems to escape the vigilance of the superego more easily than verbal or written expression, so that the aggressive and traumatic material may be depicted without the artist's feeling culpable. However, after it has been put down graphically the artist may be able to recognize it because it is rendered in his own symbols (art synthesis). It is sudden, and may be too much for the maker to tolerate without the constant help of his doctor.

If the meaning of a painting is not understood, it may be made clear to the patient by the doctor. This process was followed in the case of a young single male with the diagnosis of psychoneurosis, and anxiety state, with character disorder. His first painting depicted conflictual material which aided the doctor in the solution of his problem. Discussion of paintings and their interpretation never takes place in the studio until after it has been brought out in the patient-doctor relationship, as any interpretation in the studio makes the patient self-conscious and restrains the creative process. With the insight gained from his first painting, this patient's choice of color changed completely and his behavior also changed for the better.

There are several ways in which patients deal with an upsurge of aggressive material. Some paint their aggressions out quite frankly in the form of knives, monstrous faces, animals, and bleak landscapes. Others obscure their aggressions by using surrealism, abstract and non-objective art, or a combination of these. Others paint out recurrent dreams. These have a peculiar power which may be due to their use of "dream language" or universal symbols. They are reminiscent in their style of such painters as Marc Chagall.

Others transform their anxiety into moral, social, or philosophical subjects and entitle their works "Death," "Loneliness," "Good and Bad," etc. This objectification of inner and largely unconscious conflicts is often helpful to the patient and for that reason the artist is urged to title his work.

This leads to the fourth function of art therapy—that of externalization and mastery of subjective thoughts and emotions. A young married male with the diagnosis of psychoneurosis, anxiety type, was said by his doctor to be on the borderline of a more serious break. The doctor hoped to interest him in painting to turn his preoccupations from himself and from too much reading. He had no interest in art but came because his doctor asked him to. He was too self-conscious to paint the first day, but spent a little time looking around. On the second day he was given materials and a place to work, his attention being turned toward the use of equipment and the setting up of a still-life subject. He was told to try putting paint on the canvas just to feel the medium without paying much attention to subject matter, to start him toward "making" rather than "thinking." He painted that first still life with so much inward stress that it resembled the subject very little, and he was permitted to change the colors as he wished.

Color appeared to have special significance for him even at this early stage. He tried several still-life subjects, and a scene from memory. By this time he had become accustomed to the studio, and his manner was less tense. The first thing he painted as if it had reality significance for him was a trash can. This marked a turning point. From this time on he began to experiment with paint; it became fun. He became more friendly and sociable. He was given two weeks' leave and brought back some very creditable paintings. He was far from well, but this was the beginning of a slow, steady improvement. His doctor followed his progress and came to the studio frequently, aiding the patient in understanding each step taken graphically. Through his paintings this patient was turned toward the expression of his emotions in a socially acceptable way, thus gaining some mastery over them, so that he was no longer at their mercy. When to this process of self-healing is added the understanding of the therapist and doctor, the experience becomes of conscious emotional value. This clinical progress is gradually reflected in better rapport in the studio and then in other social contacts.

It is interesting to see that the patient works out his problems not only in his choice of subject matter and his method of representation, but also in color. In the beginning he may reject color completely, preferring black and white, but as he improves, and concurrent with his clinical improvement, color may become acceptable to him. It has been observed often enough for comment that if a patient is going toward the acceptance of color, or is regressing away from color, there will appear at an intervening stage a flaring-up of red through the black in the former, and a receding through the browns to red and then to black in the latter case. In receding through red to black the patient will express anxiety about his work.

It has been noted also that the creative faculty tends to remain on the same level in an individual, whether he is acutely ill or well. If it can be aroused in the acutely ill, it may be only in the field of color dynamics that the illness is most apparent in most cases. This means that the acutely ill patient, if he can be persuaded to work, can produce as good work then as he will when he is oriented to reality.

There are many other uses of art as therapy than those I have indicated in describing the work in the studio. For example, there are patients who are acutely ill and have no specific creative ability who may be benefited by the use of art on the primary level, going back to that stage at which almost every child shows a desire to draw. By calling upon this latent tendency the ill adult may be drawn out of his preoccupation with his inner thoughts and, by the use of still-life objects, or by other pictures which he is told to copy, be led to observe the world around him. He may be encouraged but must not be given false praise. If a therapeutic benefit results he will soon become aware that his art work is, as one patient expressed it when he became better, "lousy," and this is the point at which he may be directed toward a field in which he has better qualifications.

1949

◘ CREATIVE THERAPY

Edward Liss

The troubadours contended that poetry was The Gay Science. Hobbes classified poetry among the sciences. Kant insisted that art is an experience which furthers life, in contrast to pain, which in a sense hinders it. Modern psychiatry would agree with Kant. Artists and scientists, originators in their fields, find a common denominator in all creativity. Disputation has been long, and at times acrimonious, as to the goal of an art.

There is a general agreement that knowledge has had a dramatic upsurge in recent years, and with it has been released concomitantly a significant, malign destructive process, as if construction and destruction were companionate. The lay public is well aware, by enlightenment through various channels of information, of these changes. As is natural, some changes have received more emphasis than others. A short survey would indicate how common is the knowledge as to progress made in medicine, particularly in the field of nutrition, and in therapy through the use of vitamins, glands, and new drugs. Increasing utilization of modern advances in physics and chemistry has resulted in more accurate techniques of diagnosis and treatment. Essentially, this growing body of knowledge has been applied in the healing of physical disturbances.

However, much advance has been made in the handling of psychic disturbances.

An important step in progress is a fusion of thought and action, and this is reflected in the growing acceptance of the human being as an entity, or, as the physicians call it, a psychosomatic unit. This concept travels in cycles; it is not new, for it has been the subject of philosophers' and scientists' debates for centuries. A characteristic of the growth of the story of man, it is fundamentally an amplification of Plato's concepts and probably of cultures older than the Greek. In students of man, it naturally follows that exploration and investigation of man's growth lead to an inspection of his institutions and practices, which are symbolically represented in the arts and sciences. The body-mind concept brings with it acknowledgment that there cannot be any major physical disturbance in the human being without the accompaniment of mental disturbance and, vice versa, significant mental disturbances bring with them evidences of physical stress. This leads to the conclusion that in the evaluation of an ailment it is a matter of emphasis rather than an exclusion of mind or matter. In such circumstances a splitting into separate categories is not only undesirable but impossible.

There have been as striking and dramatic changes in the handling of the mentally ill as in the treatment of the physically sick, and through increasing skill in diagnosis there has been a growing utilization of knowledge as to available therapeutic agents. Unfortunately, a much neglected area is the use of the arts in the healing process. This, again, is by no means new. We are apt to forget that man's means of expression is not confined to words. In actuality language had its genesis in some form of graphic expression; the pictograph preceded the alphabet. This, in our culture, which glorifies the word, has been glossed over and quite forgotten.

Man's inner world changes slowly, and that which is expressed on the surface is by no means accepted within. The truth must out through some form of expression, and the Seven Arts have their say in spite of barriers which can and often do limit verbal expression. Science is at times vociferous, but the arts spring from a silent, still, inner voice and will be heard. When words fail, this voice speaks out to him who will listen and can understand. Its very directness and its simple truth are often too much for many of us to grasp.

The arts have been used to bring comfort and peace to those under stress, they have been and still are utilized in religious ceremonials, and in so-called primitive cultures art is a part of the healing rites. In our contemporary culture we refer to it as "occupational therapy." The timeliness of an exhibit to demonstrate this valuable instrument in healing is beyond question. Our responsibility is to gather and summarize our present knowledge and utilize it to the utmost, to apply it more intensively and investigate with zeal its potentialities, always with the healing of human beings in mind. Within the last two decades, as part of finer applications of knowledge in all aspects of medicine, there has been an increasing use of the arts, not just the graphic arts. This has been particularly so in education and in research with our very young. A pooling of the resources of all fields of activity is essential, for one must offset some of the by-products of specialization (which are not always satisfactory); one must break down the compartmentalization of knowledge which at times leads to an unfortunate isolation from other practitioners. It is important that we fuse these areas, which are apt to remain remote from each other, and break down artificial barriers.

Investigation of the arts will serve many purposes, not alone the elements of expression and release, not alone the evaluation of aesthetics, but also the refinement of an instrument which will help us to diagnose what ails the inarticulate human being. Each aspect of this work has a definite purpose and function, and that purpose is the healing of the sick and the keeping well of the healthy.

There are, of course, different means of approach. Some of the sick find great comfort in the stability and fixity of certain finished products; others, however, find this is inertia and for them, comparatively intolerable. For those individuals a freer self-chosen medium is conducive to accomplishment and brings with it the comfort which comes from creativity. It is implicit that, as our knowledge grows, we shall become more exact in our prescriptions and that, likewise, we shall become more flexible and more dynamic. With pioneering in any area there comes great comfort in the establishment of routines. That aspect of occupational therapy is the springboard to further growth. Armed with the experience of the educators and the pioneers in the medical arts, particularly in psychiatry, we now expand the techniques of approach. Through the flexibility which comes with familiarity and use, we meet each individual's specific problems not with a set formula but according to each one's need. This is by no means an easy task, but one which challenges the inventive genius of the American mind.

We are now faced with the problem of a sick world and increased responsibilities to our armed forces and civilians who are striving to bring about a betterment in man's lot. Just as they, through unlimited sacrifice, have drawn upon every resource available to accomplish their purpose, we too, who have their health as our responsibility, must draw upon all our resources. Let us prepare fully now so that we may be ready to return in part—for who can return in full?—our obligation to them.

The institution of the future for the casualties of life, whether the illness be mental or physical, shall be an institution whose faculty will represent the best in man's knowledge. Medicine and education must be conjoined, for there is no borderline between art and science. It is not too utopian to think of such an institution as an educational one which prepares the sick and ailing for the art of living when they become well again.

1943

CREATIVE DANCE

IN THERAPY

Lauretta Bender and Franziska Boas

The newborn child cannot sit or stand up. However, it reacts to changes in the position of the head in relation to the body and also in relation to space. One speaks of righting reflexes and postural reflexes which are either in connection with the neck-righting reflexes or with the labyrinthine postural and righting reflexes. There are also body-righting reflexes acting upon the head. An asymmetrical stimulation of the body surface, for instance, influences the posture of the head. There are also body-righting reflexes acting upon the body, and there are optical-righting reflexes. It is true that these reflexes are not always obvious in the human individual after infancy unless there are lesions in the central nervous system.

The whole system of postures is fundamentally different when an individual is lying on the ground, or when he is standing. The usual dances keep the individual in the upright position. They restrict the possible varieties of postural experiences. Even when standing in an upright position, the muscle tone is very different when the head is turned forward or to the side. The whole distribution of tone changes with every change in the position of the head as described by Magnus and De Kleijn, Goldstein, Hoff, and Schilder. Turning around the longitudinal axis done voluntarily in play or at order stimulates the semicircular canals and there will be a great number of changes in postural responses in connection with the vestibular irritation. Such turning may also occur involuntarily under pathological conditions. Turning around the longitudinal axis and rolling on the floor have very different effects, since the tone when lying on the floor is changed by the body-righting reflexes. Furthermore, there is a change in the tone since the head has a different position in space. Everything which disturbs or changes the relation of the individual to the vertical plane (gravitation) affects the motor mechanism of the whole body. Put the head in a different position in space and you have changed the world of the individual. One sees that the usual forms of dance, such as folk, social, and ballet, utilize only a small part of the physiologically important variations of body postures.

From the point of view of posture, the following points are important: (1) whether the body is in the horizontal, vertical, or inclined plane; (2) the relation of the posture of the head to the posture of the body; (3) whether the body is or is not supported on one surface; (4) the rotation (and speed of rotation) of the head on the body.

Fundamental changes in the postural motility take place in relation to the four possibilities mentioned. It must be kept in mind that with these variations in motility, significant modifications in sensory experiences are also perceived. The orientation concerning one's own body is completely altered when the different postural and righting reflexes occur. Changes in one's perception of the outward world take place when one is turned around the longitudinal axis. One also gets a completely different picture of one's own body. The vestibular irritation leads to important changes in the vaso-vegetative system. Simply, the man who lies and the man who stands are different in their somatic reactions. There are also important changes in the mood and in one's total personality, depending upon one's posture.

Dance routine of the usual type is a rhythmical motion in which many of the fundamental physiological actions are neglected. Walking on all fours is a very primitive reaction. The posture itself probably brings with it a great number of primitive attitudes. Compare, for instance, the book *Children Who Run on All Fours and Other Animal-Like Behavior in the Human Child*, by Hrdliĉka. Jumping belongs to the important primitive actions. It is obvious that many important psychological changes take place when physiological mechanisms of such type are brought into action in a dance technique. These physiological points have been particularly stressed. However, it should not be forgotten that they will be especially effective when combined with the well-known forces of rhythmical movement, and particularly when all of these factors are integrated purposefully with the fantasy life.

We must also consider the relationship of the single dancer to other dancers in the group. There is the problem of the direct contact between two bodies (for instance, one riding on the back of another). The form and duration of contact may determine the relation between frankly sexual and only latently sexual contacts. The contact will in turn be dependent upon factors of aggressiveness and body curiosity.

All these actions are not only taking place in a specific group but also in a specific space which will determine the problem of the actions of the single individual. The relation to the space in dancing is not merely psychological in the common sense, but we know that optic impressions have a definite influence on the postural reactions. Besides the primitive wriggling reflexes, the optic situation will be fundamentally altered by the optic experience of the moving body of the other, which invites imitations and reactions. In addition to these physiological problems there is the inter-human relationship to the leader of the group, and the relations of the members of the group to each other. These will be dependent upon the individual life history of the participants. From all these points of view the problems of modern dancing offer great interest to the psychologist and physiologist, and it is to be expected that modern dance technique might have an important influence on the psychological attitudes of children. From such a point of view the following experiment was undertaken.

Groups of six to eight children from the children's observation ward of the psychiatric division of Bellevue Hospital were utilized. These children were twelve years of age and younger, and represented all types of behavior disorders and psychiatric problems, although only a small part were mentally defective. They included underprivileged children of New York City with a wide range of characteristics determined by race and environment. Many, though less than half, were Negro children. The groups were unselected except that boys between six and twelve or girls of the same age, or a mixed group of boys and girls of six years or under, made up separate groups. On some occasions these classifications were ignored.

Any arbitrary group of children moves in a world of everyday life experiences. Accordingly, they have resistances to more primitive types of experiences and one has to overcome these inhibitions in order to allow for the breaking through of the deeper-lying impulses of rhythmic action and dance. This can be done particularly effectively by having the children lie on the floor and encouraging them to do cart wheels, somersaults, leapfrog, and childhood stunts which have deep-lying physiological and psychological meaning. In the same category belongs rolling on the floor and crawling on all fours, or running in circles. All of these activities have in themselves a tendency to reiteration and rhythm. The use of percussion instruments is a decided help in provoking reactions and re-enforcing them when they start to appear. The influence of rhythmic sound is very soon felt on the motility, since it is well known that every sensory impression carries with it a command to a specific action. It is possible that percussion instruments, which seem to be felt all over the body, may have a particularly deep psycho-physiological influence.

It proved advisable to use the percussion drum continually. Sooner or later the rhythm will dominate the group and produce a discharge into rhythmical movements. If the leader interrupts the rhythm, the coherence of the group activity disappears. The same thing happens if one of the children takes the percussion drum and handles it in a more or less arbitrary fashion.

The cymbal is used in a double way. It is useful for holding tensions on the medium level. It is then beaten in a rather steady way. It can also be used in a crescendo which increases tension to an almost unbearable extent, is finally released in a sudden loud sound, which leads to jumping or falling with vocal outbursts.

In the course of these group activities, children very often jump at the physical surroundings, windows, walls, etc., and whatever can be climbed on. Then they pile on each other, ride on each other, and finally jump at the leader. This represents experimentation with the physical environment and with each other. They finally look to the leader for many new technical ideas, greater strength, and more daring ventures. More venturesome and stronger children may imitatively take the leader's part and are so used by the smaller children.

One way of releasing dance activity in children has been to use a circular formation with some rhythmic or dynamic activity, such as skipping, leaping, running, and "Indian steps." Another method was to place the children on their backs on the floor and proceed with such stunts as back somersaults, rolls, shoulder stands, and forward somersaults. From these exercises the usual development is to go into animal fantasies with their characteristic movements of crawling on all fours, propelling the body across the floor without the use of the hands or feet, rolling over one another, and jumping like frogs. Certain of the children prefer to retain their human characters. This leads to dramatic dance games of shooting animals or of animals attacking humans, or horse and rider games. During this early activity there is a sudden interest in movement in different heights. From the activity on the floor the children begin to climb on each other, first on the backs of crawling children, then riding piggyback. Finally they attempt to ride on each other's shoulders or climb three high on each other's backs. There seems to be no consciousness of the necessity of a small child climbing onto a larger one. Often a very large boy will try to ride on the shoulders of a very small boy. When this is frustrated through the interference of a leader or through failure of the experiment, there is usually a reaction of disinterest and a break in the continuity of group work. Soon the climbing activity is taken up again in relation to objects about the room, with the development of all kinds of jumps from various heights with different resulting fantasy activities, such as diving into water and swimming, animals jumping from trees onto people, etc. Also various jumps from the ground onto and over objects and each other are undertaken. These are soon combined with more complicated rhythms such as cart wheels and somersaults which have been remembered from the work on the floor.

They soon begin to feel the need of help in these more difficult activities and look to the leader for technical aid. Here, then, is the opening for the leader to place the children in all sorts of unaccustomed positions in relation to space. They are encouraged to lie on their backs and are lifted by their feet so that they must put their hands on the floor. They are then told to look between the legs of the leader and walk through on their hands. Their final position is lying flat on the abdomen. Usually the child is so astonished and pleased that this must be repeated over and over. Similarly, the child jumps and sits on the haunches of the leader. Then, holding by his feet, he drops over backward and crawls through between the legs of the leader. The child lies on his back on the floor with his arms outstretched above his head. In this position he is swung around the leader who holds him by the hands and turns around his own axis. As the momentum increases, the feet leave the floor. There are usually outbursts of pleasurable excitement and verbal descriptions of sensations felt while "flying" through the air. Since all of these activities require two persons, often one or two of the stronger, more courageous, imitate the leader, and again the relation of child with child is established.

During activities requiring the physical help of the leader there is no set rhythm. However, at all other times there is the constant beating rhythm of a drum, gong, or cymbal. The atmosphere created by the repetition of sound and the quality of tone seems to provoke movement reactions. It also causes a group reaction which seems to force even the more difficult children into participation with the group (example 1). The feeling of unreality seems also to be established, since it is seldom that an aggressive activity is carried to its realistic conclusion. If the rhythm is discontinued, the group begins to fall apart. If one of the children takes the drum and plays, there is a tendency for the dance activity to change into rivalry over the instrument. Only when a child is able to play well and steadily will the children tolerate his continuing. Sooner or later, however, others will demand their turns. So far, the problem of having the children accompany themselves has not been solved, since playing the instruments is an attraction far greater than dancing.

273

The drum may be used either as a steady pulse beat or with rhythmic figuration. The intensity of activity may be regulated through the use of the crescendo and accelerando or the diminuendo and retardando. Sometimes especially susceptible children will develop their own dynamics over a steady quiet bass (example 2), or they may create all kinds of dramatic situations (example 3). The gong and cymbal may be used to quiet an especially unruly group and hold tensions at a soft or medium level. This is accomplished by playing a steady low tremolo. The crescendo of the cymbal may be used to heighten tensions to an intolerable point of suspense which is broken by a tremendous crash and muting of the cymbal. This leads to jumping or falling, usually accompanied by vocal outbursts. The gong may be used to create a swinging atmosphere which causes swaying of the entire body and leads to pendulum movements of the torso and arms and legs, finally to a feeling of suspension in which the child allows the body to be carried through space in curved sweeping lines, and to spin and turn (example 4).

It is of importance to note that the children are constantly talking and explaining their fantasies without interrupting their activity. For this reason the dance can be a very fertile field for gathering material on the child as well as a field for his own release. Before giving examples of some of the material obtained we will briefly present case histories of each child involved.

1. Patsy, a nine-year-old boy, could never accept the fact that he was not wanted by his inadequate alcoholic parents. Although abused in his own home, he was miserable in a Catholic institution where he was sent after frequent attempts to run away from home. In the Catholic home he developed a severe anxiety state with numerous phobias reactive to his compulsive masturbation, and colored with religious lore.

2. Carrol, a nine-year-old American Negro boy of almost unknown antecedents, lived with an aged couple variously referred

to as grandparents and uncle and aunt. He had been exposed to most of the social traumas: gross abuse, neglect, poverty, alcoholism, and sexual attacks. He displayed a distressing hysterical anxiety and believed, both when asleep and awake, that he was chased by the devil. He could readily be thrown into a state of hysterical terror by the simple suggestion that the devil was behind him. Terror was associated with feelings of guilt for past sexual experiences, many of which were probably fantasied. He was capable of ecstatic experiences as well as terrifying ones, but was apparently equally afraid of both.

3. Ralph was a nine-year-old Puerto Rican Negro boy who was too wild for public schools. While hitching on a car he had fallen off and injured his head, and the question had been raised as to whether a brain injury did not account for his hyperkinesis. However, there were equally serious social factors. The father had deserted the family and the mother had moved from Puerto Rico to New York only two years before. Ralph had none of the supervision and help he needed in adjusting to a new social situation, as the mother worked. His quick responsiveness to the training and socializing influences on the children's ward argued against any serious brain damage.

4. Fred, a dull ten-year-old Italian boy, lived on the lower East Side of New York City, and was a member of a gang. He was caught stealing with the gang and was sent to Children's Court. Because it was evident that he was the dullest, most passive and suggestible member of the gang he was sent to our children's ward for study. He had a vivid but confused fantasy life colored with the lore of the underworld.

5. Benjamin was a five-year-old boy from a boarding home, where he was placed by one of the child-placing agencies. He was very bright but had been the source of a great deal of trouble in several boarding homes where he had lived. Abandoned by his mother when he was a baby, he never stayed in any home long enough to feel he belonged to anyone, nor have the ability to make himself the part of any home. For that matter, he did not seem to feel that he belonged in any social situation, either in a home or in a school, or among a group of children. His emotional reactions all seemed of the negative sort. He was always unhappy and at odds and even spoke of suicide or turning on the gas to kill others in the home. At best he was reckless in dangerous situations

such as entering traffic. What the child actually needed was the love and attention which neither his mother nor any mother substitute had ever given him.

6. Jerry was a bright nine-year-old boy whose home had been made unhappy by a father who deserted, and a mother who could not carry the burden of supporting and caring for a large family. She was both too busy and unhappy to give Jerry anything but a sense of futility. Such children often find satisfaction and human warmth in schools. But here he was doomed to failure because he had a severe reading disability in spite of being bright. He spent weeks away from school, living in an empty shack he had found. He was a precocious child, sadly aware of his problems and with an almost adult hopelessness in regard to any happy solution of them.

Example 1: The group was dancing to the even, steady beat of the drum. Two boys sat in the corner weeping because they did not want to dance and desired to go out of the room. Patsy, who always seemed to take the part of the negativistic group, supported them by beating against the door with his fists and feet and throwing his shoes at it. The two boys joined him and suddenly all three started to march in a circle, chanting: "We want to go home! We want to go home!" Their feet moved in time with the drum beat. When they were convinced by looking through my purse that I had no key and could not let them out, Patsy began to work with the group and the other two sat quietly watching the dancing.

Example 2: Ralph was always active. He was proficient at turning cart wheels and somersaults, and turning around his own axis. He had no fear unless he was being held or carried by someone. On this day, a steady pulse with a repetitious pattern was beaten on the drum. The children were crawling and rolling on the floor. Ralph rolled over Carrol, grasping him around the neck. Carrol became frightened, and, losing control of himself, attacked Ralph. Both became extremely upset and Carrol had to be taken from the room. The steady rhythm of the drum began again. Ralph gave himself up to an orgy of cart wheels and turns. When he fell to the floor, he continued his movement by rolling and turning somersaults without interruption for at least ten minutes. When the class was dismissed Ralph stayed behind and, taking the drum, began to tell the story of "King Kong," which he had seen in the moving pictures. He punctuated his words with drum beats and occasional explosive sounds and gestures of his whole body. When the next group of children came he participated in the work in a much less spectacular way.

Example 3: The class was playing "Indians," dancing around in a circle to the steady beat of the drum. Fred decided to be the fire and sat in the center of the circle making hissing sounds and darting movements with his arms and hands. When the class left Fred was asked to stay. His fire dance was praised and it was suggested that he repeat it and let the fire spread. The drum beat was resumed. He started his fire dance as before, sitting in the middle of the room, twisting his arms and legs and darting them out from his body. Gradually he began twisting and swaying more in his torso and the fire spread through the room with rolls and cart wheels. He became dizzy and tried to stop, but he must have felt the movement continuing for he said, "The house is going up." Following this, he rose from the floor, stretching up as far as he could until he was on his toes. Then he started to jump, always reaching up toward the ceiling. He became tired from the jumping and rested. Suddenly he found a small toy pistol with wooden cartridges that one of the boys had hidden under a radiator and began shooting the doctor and me. When we had been killed he danced a dance of triumph and then killed himself. His next game was to throw the cartridges at the wall and pretend he had blown up the building. He acted out very realistically and dramatically the collapsing of the walls and his being buried under the debris. He dug himself out again, only to place the cartridges between his toes and blow up his feet.

Example 4: A gong was being played with slow, steady beats, producing a swinging tone. The children began to sway back and forth. Patsy, who no longer resisted the work, began to swing his arms and legs. As the gong tone became more insistent and faster, he turned slowly first to one side, then to the other, rising on his toes, then dropping his body onto the whole foot with knees bent. The gong beat increased in speed to a steady tremolo. He swung his arms more violently and turned very fast around his own axis, so lightly that his feet seemed to leave the ground.

The following notes on Carrol were taken over a period of about one month. On his first day in class, the incident described in example 2 occurred. Carrol became terrified when Ralph grasped him around the neck. He lost complete control of himself, screamed and kicked and tried to get at Ralph. He had to be held by the nurse who finally took him out of the room. Later he was brought back in a much quieter condition.

The group was playing at being animals. Several children began to ride on my back. Carrol was very much amused but did not take part. He played at being a buffalo and butted the children and me. Then he tried to make a double animal by putting his arms around the waist of a crawling boy and crawling behind him.

Benjamin was a chicken attacking children. The chicken was killed by a child; it came alive and was killed again. Finally it was really "dead" and should be buried. The children "dug" a grave and "covered" him up. They all wanted to step on the "grave" and then left him. Carrol did not take part until Benjamin was buried. Then he crouched next to him, closed his eyes and performed a kind of sorcerer's dance. He had a slight vibration in his body and passed his hands back and forth over Benjamin's head and over his body. When the children came back he pushed them away. Finally he slid away of his own accord when the chicken decided to become alive again and attack.

On May 17, Carrol made another double crawling animal, this time between the other boy's legs.

On June 14, Carrol is more active. He tries cart wheels. He started a very good Indian skip. He is very self-conscious and must be coaxed into working. For the first time he really tried some of the stunts. He allowed me to take him by the arms and swing him around parallel to the floor. He was extremely thrilled by the flying sensation when his feet left the ground. He kept urging the other boys to try it. He also jumped up and sat on my haunches, letting himself down to the ground backward until he could walk on his hands between my legs. It is characteristic of him that he works for only short intervals. He sits quietly in a corner or on a bench between working periods and dreams. He knows he is dreaming but says he does not know what it is about. He has many impulses to start dancing but stops himself.

On June 1, Carrol alone. An animal that "can walk through walls." He crawled around the room at the very edge, so that his body touched the walls at all times. The third time around he closed his eyes, dropped his head between his arms, and felt the ground with his "forepaws" before moving ahead.

Sitting with his legs curled up under him: "Oh! I am sinking in the water, way down! Now I am down on the bottom." This was accompanied by a great many changes of facial expression; then he closed his eyes and lay down.

As a result of the cymbal sound, Carrol was an airplane. He landed in the water and became a hydroplane, moving on his abdomen, legs held quiet, the arms pulling him forward.

I reminded him of his "sorcerer's" dance. He asked for one of the boys to dance with, since he said he could not conceive an imaginary companion. While waiting for the other boy he played with the cymbal and listened to its undertone. He accompanies everything with facial expressions and sounds. Many expressions are like African masks.

Jerry came. The boys played lions; they were sleeping lions dreaming. Carrol: "I am in a straitjacket. I am wild." He lay perfectly still, arms at his sides, making faces. He crawled around and then lay in the straitjacket again, sleeping, dreaming. To Jerry: "You'd better watch out when I wake up. I'm wild." He began to talk of being a buffalo, then turned into a rooster. "I'm a rooster laying eggs in my nest. It is a very big nest." Climbed on Jerry's back and stayed there quietly while Jerry tried to crawl, protesting that he was no nest.

Jerry played the cymbal as Carrol lay on his back on the floor. He asked Jerry to hold the cymbal so close to his face that it was practically touching it. He lay still, listening and making faces. Suddenly he said: "Oh! where does that sound come from? I wonder where it is! I must find it." He looked at me and smiled about his joke. Before this he had said the same thing after he had been dancing for some time to the sound of the drum. He is perfectly conscious of the origin of the sound, looks at me to see whether I take him seriously or know he is playing.

"I am a monkey. See, I am climbing on you. You are a tree." With that, he pretended to climb, holding on to my clothes. He gave up very soon and lay down.

Carrol alternates activity with sitting or lying down with closed eyes, making faces and saying all kinds of things, sometimes snatches of stories, sometimes just sounds. He is full of fantasies, any one of which would be good dance material. He plays good rhythms on the instruments, not for noise but for quality. His periods of activity are only short fragments of his prolonged fantasies. The animal crawling through the walls was continued for the longest period.

This must be looked upon as a preliminary report of an experiment in the use of spontaneous dance and music in the study, therapy, and training of children who present deviations in behavior in the social, psychiatric, and neurological fields. It has been carried on by an exponent of the modern dance movement and a child psychiatrist.

Spontaneous dance and music proved to be of special significance in such an experiment because it represents a manifold form of expression for the individual and the group.

It calls for the utilization of primitive motility reflex patterns, auditory reactions, optical patterns, and spatial relationships (vestibular, gravitational, and optical). It permits of many types of movements, especially repetition.

It stimulates and finds expression for primitive and deeply buried fantasies, allows the individual to give expression to personal aims and capacities and also to personal conflicts.

It reveals the individual's social problems and allows new social experiences.

It gives the individual the satisfaction of the expression of deep instinctual drives, of new inter-human contacts and of original aesthetic experiences.

1940

CREATIVITY

AND ENCOUNTER

Rollo May

In this paper I shall not use our usual psychological language. I am not inclined to apologize for this since I believe that most of our approaches to creativity in psychology have been strikingly inadequate. Essentially we have come up with what the artists and poets smile at and say, "Interesting, yes. But it has next to nothing to do with what is actually going on within me in the creative act." There have been notable exceptions to this tendency, of course: the works of MacKinnon, Frank Barron, Crutchfield, and Harold Anderson, for example, and the insistence of Allport, Rogers, and Maslow that creativity be studied not merely as an aspect of neurosis, or reductively, but in its own right as a positive aspect of personality. But, in general, we have come up with truisms or irrelevancies.

It is not that I believe that the ideas which I will put forth cannot be phrased in psychological language; I think they can, and also can to some extent be tested and understood by empirical methods. However, I believe our pressing problem

283

at this stage is that we have not grasped the nature of creativity as such.

I wish, therefore, to propose a theory, and make some remarks about it arising largely out of my contacts and discussions with artists and poets themselves. The theory is: *Creativity occurs in an act of encounter, and is to be understood with this encounter as its center.*

Cézanne sees a tree. He sees it in a way no one else has ever seen it. He experiences, as he no doubt would say, a "being grasped" by the tree. The painting that issues out of this encounter between a person, Cézanne, and an objective reality, the tree, is literally new. Something is born, comes into being, something which did not exist before—which is as good a definition of creativity as we can get. Thereafter everyone who has the experience of encounter with the painting, who looks at it with intensity of awareness and lets it speak to him, will see the tree with the unique powerful movement and the architectural beauty which literally did not exist in our relation with trees until Cézanne experienced and painted them.

The very fact that the creative act is such an encounter between two poles is what makes it so hard to study. It is easy enough to find the subjective pole, the person, but it is much harder to define the objective pole, the "world" or "reality." Since my emphasis here is on the encounter itself, I shall not worry too much at the moment about such definitions. Archibald MacLeish, in his book *Poetry and Experience*, uses the most universal terms possible for the two poles of the encounter: being and non-being. He quotes a Chinese poet: "We poets struggle with non-being to force it to yield being. We knock upon silence for an answering music."

MacLeish goes on: "Consider what this means. The 'being' which the poem is to contain derives from 'non-being,' not from the poet. And the 'music' which the poem is to own comes not from us who make the poem but from the silence;

comes in *answer* to our knock. The verbs are eloquent: 'struggle,' 'force,' 'knock.' The poet's labor is not to wait until the cry gathers of itself in his own throat. The poet's labor is to struggle with the meaninglessness and silence of the world until he can force it to mean; until he can make the silence answer and the non-being be. It is a labor which undertakes to 'know' the world not by exegesis or demonstration or proofs, but directly, as a man knows apple in his mouth."

One of our most serious errors in psychoanalysis has been the attempt to find something within the individual which is then projected onto the work of art, or something in his early experience which is transferred to the canvas, the poem. Obviously, early experiences play exceedingly important roles in determining how the artist will encounter his world; but this subjective data can never explain the encounter itself. Even in the case of abstract artists, where the process of painting seems most subjective, the encounter is present and may be sparked by the artist's encountering the brilliant colors on his palette or the inviting rough whiteness of his canvas. Mark Tobey fills his canvases with elliptical calligraphic lines, beautiful whirls which seem at first glance to be completely abstract and to come from nowhere at all except his own subjective processes. But I shall never forget how struck I was to see strewn around in Tobey's studio books on astronomy and photographs of the Milky Way. And I knew that Tobey experiences the movement of stars and solar constellations as the external pole to his encounter.

Out of the encounter is born the work of art. W. H. Auden once remarked: "The poet marries the language, and out of this marriage the poem is born." How *active* this makes language in the creating of a poem! It is not at all that language is merely a tool of communication, or that we only use language to express our poem—it is just as true that language uses *us*. Language is the symbolic repository of the meaningful

285

experience of ourselves and our fellow human beings down through history and, as such, it reaches out to grasp us in the creating of a poem. Thus the original Greek and Hebrew words meaning "to know" meant also "to have sexual relations." One reads in the Bible, "Abraham knew his wife and she conceived." The etymology of the term demonstrates the prototypal fact that knowledge, as well as poetry and other creative products, arises out of the dynamic encounter between subjective and objective poles.

The particular form these offspring take are "symbols" and "myths." (I do not use *symbols* in the abstract sense of mathematical symbols—these, accurately speaking, are signs, not symbols.) The symbol and myth are the living, immediate forms which emerge from encounter, and they express the interrelationship of subjective and objective poles. Symbols (like Cézanne's tree) or myths (like Oedipus) express the relationship between subject and object, between conscious and unconscious experience, between one's individual present history and human history. They are born out of the heightened consciousness of the encounter we are describing; and they have their power to grasp us because they require from us and give to us an experience of heightened consciousness.[1]

Thus, one distinguishing characteristic of the encounter is some degree of intensity, or what I would call passion. Hans Hofmann, venerable dean of abstract painters in this country and one of our most expert and experienced teachers, remarked that art students these days have a great deal of talent but what they lack is passion, commitment. Hofmann went on to say, interestingly enough, that his men students get married early for reasons of security and become dependent on their wives, and that often it is only through their wives that he can draw out their talent. The fact that talent is plentiful but passion is lacking seems to me to be a very important facet of the problem of creativity in many fields in our day, and our ways of approaching creativity by evading the encounter have played directly into these trends. We worship technique (talent) as a way of evading the anxiety of the direct encounter.

Kierkegaard knew this so well! "The present writer, . . ." he wrote about himself, "can easily foresee his fate in an age when passion has been obliterated in favor of learning, in an age when an author who wants to have readers must take care to write in such a way that the book can easily be perused during the afternoon nap."

We see at this point the inadequacy of the concept commonly used in psychoanalytic circles to explain creativity: "regression in the service of the ego." In my own endeavors to understand creative people in psychoanalysis and to understand the creative act in general, I have found this theory unsatisfactory not only because of its negative character, but chiefly because it proposes a partial solution which diverts us from the center of the creative act and therefore away from any full understanding of creativity. I grant that creativity often seems to be a regressive phenomenon because it brings out archaic, infantile, unconscious psychic contents. But this is a result rather than a cause and when these archaic elements have genuine power to move others and a universality of meaning—that is, become genuine symbols—it is because some encounter is occurring on a more basic, comprehensive level.

Ernst Kris, in supporting the theory of "regression in the service of the ego," cites the case of the minor poet A. E. Housman who, in his autobiography, describes his way of writing poetry as follows: After a full morning of teaching his classes in Latin at Oxford, Housman would have lunch, with which he drank a pint of beer, then take a walk. And in this somnambulistic mood of the walk his poems came to him. Kris, in line with this theory, correlates passiveness and recep-

tivity with creativity. It is true that most of us find an appeal
in such lines of Housman as these:

> Be still, my soul, be still,
> The arms you bear are brittle . . .

And the appeal does have a nostalgic, regressive mood.

If, however, we take as contrast some lines from one of
the major poets of our day, W. B. Yeats, we find a quite
different mood. In his poem, "The Second Coming," Yeats
describes modern man's condition:

> Things fall apart; the center
> > cannot hold;
> Mere anarchy is loosed upon
> > the world. . . .

He then tells us what he sees:

> The Second Coming! Hardly
> > are those words out
> When a vast image . . .
> Troubles my sight; somewhere
> > in the sands of the desert
> A shape with lion body and the
> > head of a man;
> A gaze blank and pitiless as
> > the sun,
>
> Is moving its slow thighs. . . .
>
> And what rough beast, its hour
> > come round at last,
> Slouches towards Bethlehem to
> > be born?

Our experience of this last symbol is one of tremendous power, revealing in a new way, with beauty but with terrible meaning at the same time, the situation we modern men find ourselves in. The reason Yeats has such power is that he writes out of an intensity of consciousness which includes archaic elements because they are part of him, as of every man, and will emerge in any intensity of awareness. But the symbol has its power precisely from the fact that it is an encounter which also includes the most dedicated and passionate intellectual effort. As MacLeish has told us, "The poet's labor is not to wait until the cry gathers of itself in his own throat."

Obviously, poetic and creative insights of all sorts come to us in moments of relaxation. They come not haphazardly, however, but come only in those areas in which we are intensively committed and upon which we concentrate intensively in our waking, conscious experience. It may be, indeed, that the insights can break through only in moments of relaxation; but this is *how* it comes rather than explaining its genesis. My friends who are poets tell me that if you want to write poetry, or even read it, the hour after a full morning of teaching and a full lunch and a pint of beer is just the time *not* to pick; choose rather the moments in which you are capable of highest, most intense consciousness. If you write poetry during your afternoon nap, it will be perused that way.

The issue here is not simply which poets you happen to like. It is much more basic—namely, the nature of the symbols and myths which are born in the creative act. Symbol and myth do bring into awareness infantile, archaic, unconscious longings, dreads and similar psychic content—this is their regressive aspect. But they also bring out new meaning, new forms, disclose reality which was literally not present before, a reality that is not merely subjective but has a second pole which is outside ourselves—this is the progressive side of symbol and myth. This aspect points ahead: it is integrative; it is a progressive revealing of structure in our relation to nature and our own existence; it is a road to universals beyond discrete concrete personal experience. It is this second, progressive aspect of symbols and myths that is almost completely omitted in the traditional Freudian psychoanalytic approach.

This heightened consciousness which we have identified as characteristic of the encounter, the state in which the dichotomy between subjective experience and objective reality is overcome and symbols which reveal new meaning are born, is historically termed ecstasy.[2] It is highly interesting that in psychology we dodge that problem, Maslow's work on the peak experience being a notable exception. Or when we do study ecstasy we are implicitly pejorative, or assume outright that it is neurotic.

The experience of encounter brings with it anxiety. I do not need here to remind you of all the testimony by artists and creative people of their "fear and trembling" in their moments of creative encounter. They also use the word "joy," or an equivalent, which illustrates the positive aspect of anxiety. The myth of Prometheus is the classical expression of this anxiety. W. H. Auden once remarked, in answer to my question, that he always experiences anxiety in his writing of poetry except when he is "playing." Playing may be defined as encounter in which anxiety is temporarily postponed.

According to the theory proposed in this paper, anxiety is an understandable concomitant of the shaking of the self-world relationship which occurs in the encounter. Our self-system and sense of identity are literally shaken; the world is not as we experienced it before, and since self and world are always correlated, we no longer are what we were before. Past, present, and future form a new gestalt. Obviously this is only rarely true in a complete sense (Gaugin going to the South Sea Islands, or Van Gogh becoming psychotic) but it is literally true that the creative encounter does change to some degree the world-self relationship. The anxiety we feel is temporary rootlessness, disorientation; it is the anxiety of nothingness.

This is why I have been so impressed by Frank Barron's studies of creative persons. Presenting cards, some with orderly and symmetrical designs, and others, disorderly and irregular, he found that the average person liked and chose the orderly, symmetrical cards. But the creative persons, both scientists and artists, much more frequently chose the disorderly cards. They chose the "broken" universe; they got joy out of encountering it and forming it into order. They could accept the anxiety, confront it, and use it in molding their disorderly universe "closer to the heart's desire."

The creative person, as I see him, is characterized by the fact that he can live with this anxiety, even though he may pay a high price in terms of insecurity, sensitivity, and defenselessness for his gift of the "divine madness," as the Greeks called it. He does not run away from non-being, as MacLeish tells us, but by encountering and wrestling with non-being, he forces it to produce being. He knocks upon silence and meaninglessness until he can force it to mean.

1964

NOTES

1. Thus in the history of culture artistic activity precedes other forms. As Sir Herbert Read puts it, "On the basis of this [artistic] activity, a 'symbolic discourse' becomes possible, and religion, philosophy and science follow as consequent modes of thought." This is not to say that art is the more primitive form in a pejorative sense, reason the more civilized—an egregious error unfortunately often found in our rationalistic Western culture. It is, rather, to say that the creative encounter in the art form is "total," expresses a wholeness of experience; and science and philosophy abstract partial aspects for their subsequent study.

2. I do not, of course, mean ecstasy in the popular sense of hysterical. Like passion, ecstasy is a quality of emotion (or more accurately, a quality of relationship one side of which is emotional) rather than quantity. Ecstasy is *ex-stasis*, a temporary transcending of the subject-object dichotomy.

THE GOAL OF CREATIVITY IN PSYCHOTHERAPY

Edith Weigert

Psychotherapy is, like other therapies, a creative art which applies the findings of biological, psychological, and sociological science to reach the goal of mental health. This goal depends on the subjective values and philosophies of patient and therapist. They may or may not arrive at a consensus about these goals, and an outspoken discrepancy of overt or covert goals will, of necessity, hamper a successful collaboration.

Thomas Szasz has written a book on the *Myth of Mental Illness*. However, we could also talk about the "myth of mental health" as a goal of psychotherapy, since not only the psychotic and the neurotic patient, but also every human being is liable at times to fail, to some degree, in reaching his goals of satisfaction and security in collaboration with his human and non-human environment. Where is the human being who reaches full maturity and mastery of his fate, who in all contingencies rises, with ever renewed force, to reassemble a creative synthesis of his unique identity in harmony with his environment, actualizing the optimal potentialities of his growth and development? And usually when he grossly fails in this attempt, the label of a psychopathological diagnosis is fastened on him. Such a diagnosis is different from the diagnosis of pneumonia or appendicitis. In an organic illness the total personality need not be disturbed, nor the patient's interpersonal relations. Burdened with an organic illness, the patient feels entitled to receive treatment and support from his fellow men. The mental patient also often reaches out for help, but he is frequently insecure about his claim. He may feel that his integrity is being attacked by his community on which he depends or against which he rebels. He may feel accused as a non-conformist with a more or less disturbed conscience. His guilt feelings may increase the opposition and resentment of the family, the more fiercely the more unstable the family is. When the patient in this struggle loses faith in the potentialities of reconciliation, of reintegration in the groups in which he has sought his security and belonging, he often turns to the psychotherapist, with exalted hopes or with doubt and distrust, leaning on his prestige and authority as a physician and mediator between himself and his community. The aim of perfect mental health, of undisturbed harmony between the patient and his community frequently remains a myth, an unreachable utopia. Yet the psychotherapist can often help the patient to reach a tolerable compromise. To be committed to an absolute ideal of mental or interpersonal harmony can make both therapist and patient ungrateful to the reasonable compromise solutions that can be worked out in the rehabilitation of the patient.

Rado and Goldman have distinguished between reconstructive and reparative psychotherapy. Reconstructive therapy, or psychoanalysis, implies a complete reorientation of the total personality; it is indispensable for optimal training in psychotherapy. The patient who consciously as well as unconsciously accepts the goal of creative reconstruction must not only be willing, but also able, to face all the unconscious anxieties from which each human being automatically recoils. He needs the courage and the flexibility to relax and regress, to let go of his habitual defenses. Kris has called this regression, which is the precondition of all creativity, "a regression in the service of the ego." It represents a *reculer pour mieux sauter* (to recede in order to take a higher jump). In reconstructive therapy the patient must ultimately be abandoned to his own sense of responsibility. There is increasing detachment in the sympathetic attachment of the doctor to the patient; thus the patient feels supported but sufficiently on his own so that he can express even the most contrary, hostile, bitter, disdainful emotions which would destroy all relationships other than a therapeutic one. The creativeness of the psychoanalytic process is tested when all the masks of hypocrisy and accommodating conformity can be dropped. When infantile guilt feelings can be replaced by a true sense of responsibility, then new horizons of understanding and alternative decisions are opened up. The psychoanalyst must be a truly sympathetic listener, tuned in with the most personal, unique needs of the patient, so that he can support the patient through the revelation of the darkest suspicions about others and himself, and through the self-accusations of cowardice and despair which threaten the patient's identity. The therapist must have a creative understanding that sees the light behind the shadows, the saving grace in the desolation and forlornness of human nature, so that the patient can give up the defenses of hypocritical obedience and conformity and regain the authenticity of being true to himself.

Creative reconstruction is characterized by a re-evaluation of values. Success does not depend only on the skills and efforts of the therapist, but also on the stamina of the patient, since all change in values arouses deep anxieties in human beings.

A patient may only seek support in a transient crisis and not want to get through an anxiety-arousing upheaval. Other patients—either constitutionally or because of early traumatic experiences—may be so deeply damaged that they cannot afford a change in their precariously maintained equilibrium. The psychoanalyst must be able to respect the limits of his art when a patient can, at best, only tolerate a compromise between his inner needs and external reality.

Every patient lives in a reality of his own; there is no standard reality for all. The analyst must enter into the patient's reality with him. In times of political upheaval, the psycho-therapeutic goals change rapidly due to eternal pressures. I experienced drastic examples of such pressures when I worked with private patients during the beginning of the Nazi regime in Berlin. In the course of a morning, I saw a patient who pondered whether he should join the party to save his career and his family. He was followed by a Jewish student who was struggling against great odds to prepare himself for agricultural work and immigration to Israel. The next patient was a social worker who tried to abreact the shock of abuse and humiliation by storm troopers. She was followed by a Communist who doubted whether he could trust me enough to reveal, via his free associations, plans of revolt and destruction which might be incompatible with the neutrality of an analyst.

At that time, I wondered how we could possibly work toward the goals of mental health in an insane society shaken by an upheaval of traditional values. However, as Redlich and Hollingshead have demonstrated, in a relatively stable society, the needs of patients often are at variance in different classes and under different economic conditions. Classical analysis which avoids all parameters may be of insufficient help to a patient who is involved in an unmanageable external situation, for example, a patient who must return from a protective hospital to an emotionally impoverished or unbearably hostile home. The therapist may have to step out of the one-to-one relation and engage in marital therapy or other forms of group therapy to expose a fuller view into the complexities of the patient's maladaptation. Additional management through drug, sleep, or shock therapy may become advisable. Winnicot and Guntrip have indicated that the psychoanalyst must find in each given situation the optimal equilibrium between mothering management and interpretive confrontation.

Reparative psychotherapy that is adapted to a variety of needs in the patient demands a high skill and greater flexibility on the part of the therapist than traditional psychoanalysis. The boundaries between reparative and reconstructive therapy are fluid. What started as reparative therapy may turn into reconstructive therapy and vice versa. At present, reconstructive therapy or classical psychoanalysis seems to have a higher prestige value than the reparative form of psychotherapy. Freud spoke of "mixing the pure gold of psychoanalysis with the copper of direct suggestion in the future application of our therapy to the masses." But the psychoanalyst may be entrenched in unyielding theories and his need to verify his philosophy may outweigh his ability to adapt to the needs of the patient. Not every analyst is as flexible as Freud; he referred to his theories as a "scaffolding" adaptable to ever-broadening experience. He even called his instinct theory a mythology. The controversies inside and outside the psychoanalytic association bear witness to how difficult it is for all of us to reconcile the need for interpersonal professional solidarity of a shared theoretical orientation, with the need to create individual improvisations in the art of psychotherapy.

I would like to illustrate an attempt at reparative psychotherapy which was too short-lived to reach the depth of authentic reconstruction of a deeply damaged personality. We sometimes learn more from a failure than from a success. This treatment experience was more than twenty years ago, yet it stands out in my memory because of what I learned from it. In this case the limitations to therapy lay not only in adverse external circumstances but also in an unfortunate emotional development.

In a hospital setting I treated a thirty-five-year-old German refugee woman who was married to a Russian-Jewish scientist. She was diagnosed as schizophrenic; her main symptom was a destructive rage that made around-the-clock special nursing care necessary. The patient had married shortly before their immigration. She could not have children; her husband was absorbed in scientific research, had become unreachable in his egocentricity, and the patient had lost her devotion to him. They were worlds apart in temperament and interests, and this alienation interfered with the primarily good sexual adjustment. Without goal and direction and having to adapt to a new country, she was overwhelmed by a sense of futility and despair. She had come from a home impoverished in emotions. She did not know her father, who had divorced her mother in her infancy. The stepfather was cold and aloof. The mother, conventional and sentimental, was unable to tame her only child's temper tantrums. As a child the patient adopted a veneer of good manners, but in adolescence she broke away from the cold conventionality of her home. In spite of good intelligence, charm, and good looks, she was not able to commit herself to extended professional training. A largely negative identity—not to be like her conventional mother—led her into a bohemian milieu where she drifted from one love affair into another, mostly with narcissistic intellectuals for whom she developed a kind of sentimental hero worship. Through identifying with the man's ideals she found sexual gratifications, and her rich gift of empathy permitted vicarious satisfactions in the man's intellectual interests; she was inclined to establish a mimetic type of identification with her lover, but she was unable to commit herself to a relation of mutuality. Whenever she fell out of love, she experienced a loss of identity and a crisis of frustration and rage which brought her to the verge of disintegration. However, the crisis would pass when she fell in love again and identification with a new lover gave her weak ego a new identity. Under the pressures of the political situation, she rather hastily married a man who had been a relative stranger to her. In her middle thirties, facing the challenges of adaptation to a new country and to a man unable to show real understanding, she was thrown into despair by the aimlessness of her existence. She acted out her rage without squarely facing her despair. Her guilt feelings sounded unconvincing; they were the borrowed guilt feelings of a heteronomous authoritarian morality against which she rebelled. In her agitated depression accompanied by hallucinations and delusions, she would have acted out her impulses in a frenzy of assaultiveness and self-destruction had she not been prevented by hospital precautions. In daily interviews the picture changed dramatically; the patient became calm, reasonable, friendly, cooperative. There were no more assaults or fits of self-destruction, no more hallucinations and delusions, but her improvement was not trustworthy. Her rage was only tranquilized. The patient felt supported by my empathy and had fallen in love again. This love for me furnished her with an escape into a borrowed identity, and it soothed her frustration and despair. Her attachment was that of a suffocating dependency; she was improving for my sake. She voiced good intentions of being reconciled with her husband, to endure the inevitable limitations in this relationship, and to work out a better adjustment. The treatment lasted only five to six months and, during my absence, the patient was discharged to her home town on the basis of her spectacular improvement. She was not able to establish a similar attachment to the therapist to whom I referred her, and when the identification with me and the adoption of my goals wore off, she killed herself by throwing herself out of the window. The fact that I had suspected the possibility of such a tragic outcome did not offer any consolation to my distress about it. I had become intimidated by empathizing with the violent rage reactions of the patient, and I learned from this distressing experience that empathy is not enough. My empathy had lured the patient into a soothing positive identification which could not give her sufficient opportunity to work through the rage reactions and overcome her low self-esteem based on a negative identification with the parental authority. My empathy had not been able to convey to the patient a vision of a fuller integration of her potentialities. She had repressed her rage reactions for the sake of her positive identification with me which promised peace and harmony. When this soothing identification wore off, the frustration rage broke through with mortal force. I had not succeeded in strengthening her endurance of frustrations or her ability to visualize the creative goal of a self-actualization by which she could establish an authentic identity and meaningful interpersonal relations. The persisting infantile dependency and defensive identification were the main obstacles in the patient's creative maturing process.

This patient's ego weakness was based on emotional deprivation in early childhood. Though she had reached the level of orgastic genital maturity, emotionally she remained an insecure, impotently rebellious child. She suffered from so great an emotional starvation (which David Levy called "primary affect hunger") that she was willing to sell body and soul for any token of love and security. She fell in love with extremely self-centered male partners so that she was exposed repeatedly to a frustration rage that assumed increasingly destructive proportions. She aimed at magic transformation in psychotherapy and accepted me only as a parental authority. As long as she could harbor hopeful illusions of being passively saved, she was docile and ready to identify with me in a symbiotic surrender that left no room for the development of her own authentic identity. When she felt deserted, she was overwhelmed with frustration rage. Her low self-esteem did not permit a relation of mutuality which would have given her the courage to endure the inevitable frustration of loneliness and self-reliance, and so she yielded completely to despair.

It must be the goal of the psychoanalyst to make himself gradually dispensable just as the goal of every responsible parent is to make himself increasingly superfluous so that his growing child may learn to work out his own destiny on a self-reliant and aspiring level. The creative goal of psychotherapeutic reconstruction demands a long-term dedication so that the symbiotic tendencies of transference and countertransference can be truly outgrown. Transferences are fostered by empathic, symbiotic identifications with authority. Defenses against the existential anxiety of loneliness represent a harbor of pseudo-security for the patient while he leans on the therapist's presence to satisfy his infantile dependency needs. Only the full relation of the "I" of the patient and the "Thou" of the therapist, within the social limitations of the therapeutic situation, permits a maturing process of creative collaboration in which existential anxiety and frustration rage can be fully faced, constructive alternative solutions to present-day conflicts can be found, and the risks and challenges of the uncertain future can be accepted with the enduring courage of self-reliant and aspiring hope and trust.

I have attempted to illustrate by my example the limitations we face when we strive for the goal of creativity. These disappointments can become discouraging for the psychotherapist and he must find in his own philosophy the solidity of endurance which will enable him to accept the frustrations of his daily work. His philosophy may, in more fortunate situations, awaken the resonance of mutual understanding and carry the patient to the goal of creative reconstruction, but the psychotherapist cannot force his own philosophy on the patient.

In trying to clarify the goals of creativity in psychotherapy an orientation in the psychotherapist's philosophy and value systems seems indispensable. The Swiss psychiatrist Ludwig Binswanger, a lifelong friend of Freud, introduced into psychotherapy the phenomenological viewpoint and, later, the *Daseinsanalyse* orientation. Another Swiss psychiatrist, Medard Boss, has further developed the influence of modern philosophy on psychotherapy. Karl Jaspers began as a psychiatrist and became an existential philosopher, but remained rather inaccessible to psychoanalysis. Martin Heidegger and Jean Paul Sartre have become interested in the development of psychoanalysis, and their ideas have penetrated European and American psychotherapy. (They were introduced into American psychotherapy by Rollo May and his collaborators.) American psychotherapists have also become interested in Martin Buber and Max Scheler. All these philosophers show great differences in their approach but they have some trends in common: they all emphasize the intentionality of human behavior in contrast to a mere rational determinism. Intentionality is the precondition of creative reconstruction. The existential philosophers stress the integrative power of will, with a limited freedom to collect the diverse strands of motivations in ever new and unique creations of adaptation. The decisions of will, as far as they are spontaneous responses of the unique individual to a unique now-and-here situation, are unpredictable. The existential philosophers stress the historicity of the human being that rises above the plane of his biological existence into the awareness of his destiny.

Heidegger, like Dewey and Bergson, revolts against the rational world view of Descartes' *cogito ego sum*. Heidegger agrees with Bergson that man is *homo faber* before he is *homo sapiens.* Man is thrown into a world with others beyond his willing; in handling, manipulating, understanding, organizing material, tools, opportunities, this world is his own—world and self, subject and object are inseparable. This is expressed in the hyphenated term "being-in-the-world." The psychoanalyst originally was inclined to study the development of the individual in the context of his most intimate relations. The later Freudian and neo-Freudian development of ego psychology has opened broader vistas for the study of the individual in the context of his total cultural environment. In psychopathology, the psychiatrist discovers a simultaneous transformation of the ego and its world. In a depression, the ego and its world are shrunk, while in a manic mood-swing the ego and its world are overextended; the ego and the world of the schizophrenic are uncannily transformed by alienation, and we find different ego and world transmutations in the hysterical and the obsessional patient.

American psychotherapy was influenced by Dewey's philosophy which conveyed the buoyancy of pragmatism and an assurance of making a better world by sheer force of common sense. American psychotherapy stresses the values of adaptation while the influence of European philosophy, guided by Heidegger's vision of being-in-the-world as a being-to-death, emphasizes the value of authenticity. Jaspers sees in death a "boundary situation" which elicits the basic human mood of dread since the vision of death confronts man with his irrevocable and unutterable loneliness: man's enduring vision of death marks, as nothing else can, the integrity and independence of his life.

At the time of the First World War, Freud wrote a paper on war and death and described the helplessness of the unprepared, civilized man in the face of the catastrophe of war. He concluded this paper with the advice: *Si vis vitam, para mortem* ("If you want life, prepare for death") in an analogy with the old proverb *Si vis pacem, para bellum* ("If you want peace, prepare for war"). Freud defined the basic human anxiety as separation anxiety, castration anxiety, or superego anxiety, biologically determined by the pleasure-pain principle. Heidegger's influence has led psychotherapists to a more basic acknowledgment of anxiety or dread as it was defined by Kierkegaard. Heidegger sees man not as the victim of biological forces but as the active guardian of his experience. In being, he is concerned; he cares for his being. The dread of non-being is not only a biological anxiety; man may prefer death to the loss of what he loves, his values, his ideals, or he may survive like a vegetating nonentity when deprived of these goals of integration.

The human child is dependent longer than any animal, and the adult, in times of stress and strain, falls back into the dependency of the child. He then loses sight of his far-reaching goal of happiness through love and work. Happiness through love and work which permits an enlightened hedonic control of behavior on the level of self-reliance and aspiration has been well stated by Rado as being the creative goal of psychotherapy. But work may degenerate into drudgery or slave labor, and love can regress from the level of sympathetic mutuality to that of empathic defusion of ego boundaries and borrowed identity. Under the pressure of unbearable frustrations an overproduction of emergency emotions (fear, rage, guilty fear, and guilty rage) throws the organized behavior patterns of self-reliance and aspiration into the chaos of despair. Since frustrations are inevitable in human existence, it seems to me that an important goal of psychotherapy is to help the patient learn to endure frustration. This implies that he learns to understand and accept his destiny, his very own unique identity with its biological and social limitations. However, in the constant flux of change the analysand may easily become bewildered about his identity.

The topic of identity is taking on a growing role in modern psychoanalytic literature. This interest is reflected in the writings about psychoanalytic ego psychology. The individual is a goal-directed being. A patient who is overwhelmed by the meaninglessness of existence asks: "Who am I?" and "Where am I going?" Thomas French has demonstrated that man's intentions and goals for the future are important facts in the integration of his behavior.

Insight into the past is important for the analysand in order to understand his destiny, how he has arrived at the present stage of his development. Freud's ingenious invention of the method of free association has opened up the past to introspection by the self and to participant observation by the analyst. In an atmosphere of sympathetic understanding the analysand becomes able to drop some of his traditional prejudices and defenses that have barred memories, impulses, fantasies, and emotions from any awareness that can be reported and shared in communication. A broadened awareness mobilizes psychic energies that were bottled up and the analysand becomes able to arrive at new conflict solutions and decisions.

However, not all insights into the past lead to foresights and firm intentions that take up the challenge of the future with hope and confidence. At times, many an analysand complains: "I see the chains of cause and effect that have led me into the present impasse, but I still find it impossible to change." He cannot make the change from despair in the past to trust in the future. Freud has postulated that constitutional factors—for example, the untamable character of instincts—are responsible, in some patients, for the interminable state of their analyses. While not denying the importance of hereditary factors in the condition and prognosis of mental illness, it is doubtful that the instinctual endowment as such must make us pessimistic about the prognosis.

When we turn from the study of human behavior to that

305

of animals, as has been done by modern ethology, we encounter a broader concept of instincts and their constructive
role in adaptation. Ethology defines instincts as stable, though
quite complex, innate behavior patterns that respond to internal
and external stimuli in a form adequate to guarantee optimal
possibilities of survival not only at the level of the individual
but also at that of the species. The following example is taken
from an observation by the ethologist, Adolf Portmann. When
in a pack of wolves a contest for supremacy breaks out, the
battle is fought out until the superior strength of one wolf is
established, but this fight does not lead to the destruction of
the weaker rival. In a gesture of humility the vanquished
wolf exposes his jugular vein to the teeth of the victor, but the
victor does not bite. This instinctive behavior pattern guar-
antees the survival of the individual as well as the solidarity
and hierarchy of the group.

Man seems to be in conflict between his trend toward individuation and his need for solidarity with others. In human
groups the motivation to eliminate a rival in the hierarchy is
not left to an instinctive releaser automatism which dictates
whether to kill or exercise mercy. Man uses foresight which
mobilizes anxiety or guilt feelings, and he anticipates retalia-
tion or punishment, which counteract and repress the mur-
derous impulse from awareness. But the conflict between
impulse and foresight continues undecided in the non-reporting
parts of his brain (Freud's unconscious), threatening to return
from exile and upset man's equilibrium by an outbreak of
uncontrolled rage when his frustrated egocentric impulses over-
run his need for group solidarity. Why is man's reasoning
power so relatively weak in taming the frustrated impulses?
In the introduction to Goethe's *Faust*, Mephistopheles, the
devil, bemoans the fate of man before God the Lord: "Man
would live a little better, had you not given him the shine of
heaven's light. He calls it reason (*Vernunft*) and he uses it

only to be more brutish than any brute." Man's instincts are as innocent and free of guilt as the animal's instincts, as long as the needs which guarantee his survival are not frustrated. But man's capacity of foresight, his gift of imagination which anticipates the consequences of his behavior and actions, frequently lead him to overreactions in response to the danger signal of fear or anxiety. The human being is the only animal that is aware of his destiny to die, though he does not keep this knowledge in the focus of his awareness. Yet, in his imagination he may die a thousand deaths, and when this foresight triggers off unmanageable fears, his adaptational behavior may be thrown out of kilter.

Selye and others have described the physiological responses of the human organism to the danger signal of fear. Under stress, man's preparedness for fight or flight mobilizes a whole array of primitive weapons of defense: acceleration of respiration and circulation, evacuation of intestines and bladder, increase of blood sugar and clotting. Man is not as well endowed for flight and fight as many animals; his diencephalic physiology has equipped him rather poorly in his precultural condition to encounter danger. However, in the course of cultural development man no longer relies mainly on his muscle strength, but on the vast defense systems of civilization that the human cortex has invented and developed. The paleontologist, Jesuit Father Pierre Teilhard de Chardin, has described the trend of evolution as that of integration of ever-increasing complexities. The reliance on these defense systems enriches the potentialities of adaptation but they have become immensely complicated. Dr. A. T. W. Simeons, a British internist who has studied psychosomatic diseases, has described in a book entitled *Man's Presumptuous Brain* the discrepancies between the diencephalic preparedness for danger, and the cortical overreactions to the precariousness of human existence which have built up elaborate technical devices of security.

These devices can become unmanageable when the organism is flooded by primitive emotions. Men under continuous stress and strain may become victims of psychosomatic ailments. The awareness of danger does not always work to the advantage of man's survival. The drowning man sometimes can be more effectively saved when he is knocked unconscious and no longer fights frantically and inappropriately for his survival. The experience of mortal danger may leave the overreacting individual with a sense of helplessness in the throes of a traumatic neurosis, but it may kindle in others the elation of triumph and renew the zest for living.

Kardiner has described how, in a traumatic neurosis, the ego and its world have changed: the ego has lost the confidence in organization and mastery; its world has become permanently changed into a more dangerous place. Bettelheim's experiences in Nazi concentration camps and Lipton's analysis (which has been elaborated by Chinese communism) in *Thought Reform and Psychology of Totalism* have demonstrated that there are limits to human endurance of pain and continuous threat to survival under circumstances of deprivation and isolation. The sturdiest individual may lose his sense of identity and the dignity of personal self-esteem and, therewith, the ability of creative adaptation when, under extreme pressures, he has to submit to physical and mental cruelties. Those individuals who have some prevailing interest, some hope or trust in the future, some goals to which they can remain committed despite frustration, have the best chances to survive and maintain their integrity. Such maintenance of goals provides the optimal strength of defenses as well as a flexibility of adaptation, but overwhelming force and violence of attack on human integrity sets limits to the most stoical endurance. Lilly and others have described various degrees of ego disorganization in states of isolation and sensory deprivation. It seems to me that the disintegrating effects of boredom, monotony, and the loss of aim and purpose are almost certainly important factors in these experiments.

I want to return to the influence of existential philosophy on the goals of creativity in psychotherapy. In Heidegger's terms, the call of conscience is more than the incorporated parental authority—it is man's anticipation of his own possibilities. Man is an historical being, he tries to understand the past and to project his destiny into the future. He grasps the contingencies of his present situation as a challenge to his own power of becoming what he *may* be rather than what he *must* be. This is his limited freedom as well as the source of psychopathology. This basic concern of becoming an authentic self—"To thine own self be true"—is frequently in conflict with values of adaptation which may foster a non-authentic duplicity not only in the region of psychopathology. The defeat of adaptation frequently occurs in very richly endowed personalities, and many so-called normal individuals may lose their authenticity in the struggle for survival. The concern for man's total integration and authenticity is at the mercy of his moods and passions of the moment; drowned in forgetfulness, it gets lost and dissipated in self-alienation, lost in the thousand little cares of everyday living, in trivialities, in the restlessness of being busy, distracted by meaningless pleasures, by trading in empty curiosity and gossip or vegetating in boredom. Through self-alienation the human being becomes the other-directed person of Reisman in the indifferent, anonymous crowd that Heidegger calls *man* (the German impersonal pronoun for everybody or anybody), playing the role that society expects him to play, more being lived than living.

Heidegger's concern is not a psychological but an ontological concern. He does not talk about individual man, but about *Dasein*, being-there, a clearing in the chaos of human experience through the intuitive grasp of being-in-the-world, being with others, caring for one's *Dasein* and that of others. Heidegger bridges the gap between subjective, emotional experience and objective, mathematical-physical constructs. Other existentialists, such as Jaspers and Sartre, who are more interested in individual psychology, relapse into subjectivism. Jaspers professes a philosophical faith in encompassing being. Sartre expresses a defiant solipsism when he says: "Man is the being who wants to be God, but the idea of God is contradictory and therefore man is a useless passion." Nietzsche's idea of the superman and his all-encompassing will to power is dictated by a similar defiant individualism. In its extreme forms this overreaching passion may result in the creative achievements of a genius or the chaos of a psychosis.

The psychotherapist who traces the patient's development back to childhood in order to understand the unique destiny of the individual is necessarily guided by a sense of value, the pragmatist's value of adaptation and the existentialist's value of authenticity. The creative integration of both values can only be approximated in a state of maturity, when the individual has acquired the skills, the knowledge, and the mastery necessary for optimal survival among equals. The helpless child still depends on the authority of the superior adults; he is directed by ideals and guilt feelings borrowed by empathy, as long as his survival depends on parental gratifications and protection. Parental care can be crippled by excessive anxieties which the child adopts by empathy. Excessive parental anxieties may lead to a misuse of parental authority through punitive domination, exploitation, neglect, or overindulgence, thus hampering the maturing process in the child. Punitive domination, neglect, and exploitation tend to produce frustration rage and envy as well as persecutory anxieties in the child, while parental overindulgence fosters self-inflation, filial ingratitude and/or anxieties of being abandoned in a state of dependency. Due to the failures in parental care, the burden of excessive anxieties and inappropriate defenses can be carried from one generation to another, militating against the maturing process and the individual's creative adaptation to his destiny. The goal of creativity in psychotherapy, the integration of traditional ideals and freely chosen commitments and responsibilities on the level of maturity, can only be reached when the vicious cycle of empathically experienced anxieties can be reduced to a tolerable degree. Among equals able to truly sympathize in mutual respect, there is room for a limited freedom in authenticity and spontaneity in self-actualization as well as for the adaptation through solidarity in interpersonal relations.

Among the existentialist philosophers Martin Buber and Max Scheler have particularly emphasized the interpersonal aspects of human development. Martin Buber has established the contrast of I-Thou relations and I-It relations. Under the stress of fear or dread, interpersonal relations remain arrested at, or regress to, the level of I-It relations in which man uses force, may even explode in violence, and misuses his fellow men as a means to his own ends, be it by domination, manipulation, or submission. Max Scheler's concepts of empathy and sympathy are necessary tools of psychotherapeutic understanding. But empathy is not enough; it is the outgrowth of infantile symbiotic dependency. The bond of sympathy is more than a tool of psychotherapy—out of the bond of sympathy grows a reverence, a respect for man as man which, in the words of Whitehead, "secures liberty of thought and action for the upward adventure of life, the progress from force to persuasion." This reverence discloses the potentialities of creative reconstruction, the goal of psychotherapy.

1962

311

THREE CREATIVE PHASES IN PSYCHOANALYSIS: THE ENCOUNTER, THE DIALOGUE AND THE PROCESS OF ARTICULATION

Charles R. Hulbeck

I do not intend to add anything new to the different methods of psychoanalytical work. I will talk about some creative aspects of psychoanalysis, not because these aspects are in themselves creative, but because they impress me as suitable material to be related to the problem of creativity. These aspects are found in any analytical work. They are the working parts of any analytical effort from the side of the analyst as well as from the side of the patient. There is no sure method by which psychoanalysis brings about creativity. By creativity I do not mean merely the creating of art works or

313

works of genius, but also the true human nature which is given to growth.

It would take another paper to make clear what I understand as growth. In this case growth is, of course, not growing in size; it is not related to success nor to any other outside quality or value. It is something quite different indeed, namely, the ability to live, to survive, and to face the world against the evidence of failure, death, and other misfortune; it is the quality to possess and keep the vision of justice against all evidence to the contrary. Growth is a quality *against*, which means that an individual possessing this quality is able to see the deeper realities of life, though they are covered up and distorted. Growth is therefore something to learn, to find, to understand, something to act on. Growth is also the understanding of the even deeper structure of the world, by which I mean the understanding that life and the human being in life are faced with irrational powers trying to distract and divert us from our path and trying to destroy our direction—what we call the meaning of our life.

I have selected three stages or phases of analysis—the encounter, the dialogue, and the process of articulation—because they are important and related to the creative work of the analyst and the creative possibilities in the patient. There is no logical sequence applicable to these three phases.

To start with the first: I consider the encounter with the patient a most revealing creative process for the two participants. Patient and doctor meet under special circumstances, though these special circumstances enter the picture only secondarily. They are two human beings meeting under special circumstances in the doctor's office. The patient is willing to pay a certain amount of money and comes to the doctor to get help because of an ailment, in this case an emotional disturbance. There are many forms of emotional disturbances. I shall leave out the psychotic patients; I would rather think of a patient coming to the doctor for minor disturbances. In this case, patient and doctor meet like two other human beings on a normal level to talk out certain problems, the solution of which is expected from a collaboration between the doctor and the patient. The atmosphere of such a meeting is definitely non-medical but it is definitely also more than a meeting or should be more than a meeting.

It is for this reason I call this first meeting an encounter. The first meeting can also be a series of first meetings serving to settle certain questions between two persons who are intent on accomplishing a special kind of work. The fact that they intend to accomplish a special kind of work gives such a meeting or series of meetings a special coloring, though it is also not more than a meeting between two human beings. A meeting between patient and doctor in the office of a psychoanalyst is different from a medical meeting in the sense that no distinct diagnosis is expected. The patient does not come to be subjected to any unusual form of scrutiny. The patient is simply there and the doctor is simply there. Such a meeting is an encounter in the sense that two persons of different personality and often cultural background come together to find a level of communication without knowing whether their search will be successful.

The encounter between doctor and patient is of the greatest importance to the course and the subsequent possible success of the analysis. The encounter is actually a collision of two different worlds: the world of the patient and the world of the doctor. To reach a level of communication is the aim of a proposed and planned process, called psychoanalysis. Therefore, what is mostly wished for is the readiness of two greatly different human beings to co-operate in reaching a common goal. Consequently, the encounter should arouse in the doctor as well as in the patient a creative curiosity not unlike the creative curiosity felt by an artist before he starts painting, writing, or composing. Thus, right at the start, there is a distinctly felt, immediate reaction. The patient quickly knows whether he likes the doctor or not and this like or dislike colors his whole attitude during the analysis. The collision of two worlds of reality creates the immediate need for an evaluation of the first meeting after which both parties ask themselves about the possibility of continuance.

They come to the conclusion that the differences which will always be there are either tolerable or not. They feel clearly and painfully that there is no equality in such a meeting on a commercial, or rather professional, basis. The possibility of continuance, to extend the talks beyond the first meeting is either there or not. If the patient decides to continue, he has given the first proof that he possesses a potential amount of transcending ability. He then probably will be able to see the differences between himself and the doctor as a mirror of his own differences with other persons. Consequently he will see the nature of conflict and the nature of complexes. The second, third, and the following meetings— all will have the quality of the encounter. There will be, from both sides, an evaluation and re-evaluation of the differences of two worlds of reality. Patient and doctor are thus pushed toward the hard facts of being, and obliged to leave the world of abstractions. The need to take the world as it is, as a sequence of experiences and changes, hits the patient as well as the doctor in these series of interviews, but mainly in the first interview.

I would call the first interview the decisive encounter, when, as I said, the two different worlds or realities of the patient and the doctor meet in collision. The doctor as well as the patient, but the patient more than the doctor, are like two adventurers traveling into unknown countries. Consequently the encounter takes a great deal of its realistic impact from the anxious psychology of exploration. Both parties find themselves ready to proceed with certain plans but there is complete uncertainty as to how well the plans will work. The problem of chance and the irrationality of life are distinctly and intensely present in the encounter. Therefore, as Tillich has said, and as I have also asserted when I spoke about the human situation and "acting against evidence," man in any situation, but mostly when he is faced with another human being, unknown to him, acts somewhat "in spite of."

In the encounter, the course to take, the analysis as a scientific process, the success which depends on money, duration, and the procedure, emotionally and psychologically, of not yet present events—all these are possibilities and not more than possibilities. The creative process is very much a possibility and we never know whether possibilities can be transformed into realities. The element of chance present in the described situation is an element of not knowing. The encounter is therefore a creative vacuum, a form of emptiness that may be filled with knowing later in the process of treatment. It may be or it may not. The awareness of uncertainty surrounding the encounter, so deeply felt by both parties, makes it a creative stage in the sense that no preconceived formulas can be conceived. An analyst's ability to experience the creative vacuum of the encounter makes him different from an adviser, as for instance most marital counselors are, who know all the answers before they even see the persons coming to them for help.

The dialogue is the second creative activity between the patient and the doctor which can be identified. One cannot really call it a stage or a phase of the analysis as it accompanies the analytical work from the beginning to the end. The ontological meaning of the dialogue is seen in an advance of the participants toward the reality of communication. The dialogue replaces the purely impressive state of the encounter, the mutual seeing, evaluating, and measuring, by a different form of creativity. As I indicated, a greater effort is made toward finding a common level by using words instead of using only the senses. The changing of the meeting atmosphere toward the dialogue atmosphere is an important moment of the analytical work. It takes the two persons who have come together for a definite aim out of one situation and places them into another, though both efforts or situations or stages work and happen simultaneously. It is nevertheless a fact that a decision has been made in the sense that both parties find and use new means for mutual understanding.

There are many forms of dialogizing and I would say that creative dialogizing in analysis is a special sort of creative ability. Some dialogues come from one person trying to convey a definite opinion to another person, either because the situation may require it or because one person finds his opinion to be more important than the other person's opinion. In contrast, the analytical dialogue originates from silence. It actually is the transformation of silence into words after recognizing the fact that other means are necessary to cope with a different world. The use of words is definitely a stronger instrument toward understanding than the use of the senses.

In primitive times, for example, when language was born, the use of words most likely came from the earnest will to overcome differences. It soon then becomes obvious that the use of words and of language is not an ideal means to find a common level of understanding. If, for instance, the analyst would say: "Put yourself on your own feet. Become independent," or use similarly well-known phrases, it might mean anything.

Each time one speaks, one has to take oneself into account, evaluate one's own ideas, one's own subjective approach as it is conditioned by former parental and present cultural influences. In orthodox analysis this caution is very much neglected. Since the system is strictly adhered to, the meaning of the system is conveyed even in small conversation. The fact that the analyst sits silently behind the patient neither denies nor distracts from the fact that a dialogue is taking place. Free association is only a specific form of dialogue. The possible directing by the analyst, his influencing of the patient, is as great as if they were facing each other.

On the other hand the silence I talked about is a preceding phase; the dialogue is a cautious waiting, an intention to reduce one's own influence to a minimum. Only if the influence of the analyst upon the patient and the possible influence of the patient upon the analyst through words or simply through the impact of personality are reduced to a minimum, can dialogue arise as a creative phase in analytical work.

Then in the course of analysis the dialogue becomes more intense and as time goes on it becomes clear what every dialogue is, namely, a proposition for reason. But even so, when it has become clearer that reason, as a possible remedy for anxiety and guilt, is proposed, there is no defined system for doing so in creative analysis. It is simply that between two persons reason, as such, has appeared as a possibility for the settlement of the patient's ailment. It becomes clearer what reason is, namely a category of thinking which, in contradistinction to intellect, is able to transcend. Reason is then recognized as a means to relativize facts and hindrances. It finally becomes clear to the patient that the doctor has something in his mind pertaining to logos, or to the meaning of that part of the patient's existence that he lost through his neurotic sickness.

The proposition for a reasonable settlement of the patient's problems has nothing or very little to do with the contents of the neurotic difficulties. In the appeal, as conveyed by the dialogue, the logos refers to the meaning of the patient's life in a special and in a general way. What I said by implication is that the loss of the meaning is the real problem, and the contents, whether they are in the area of the patient's occupation, his marriage, or anywhere else, are secondary. As soon as the reluctance to talk is overcome, the patient leaves the area of detachment—his hideout, his frozen attitude toward his own person. He puts himself again into life, though, of course, it is only a semblance of life, a small part of life, the doctor's office, which then gains in significance. The doctor's office reveals itself as a form of enclosure, different from the enclosure with which the patient surrounded himself in his detachment. While the doctor's office is away from the reality of life, it is at the same time already a part of life, and it offers certain aspects of real life that the outside imposes on the patient to a much greater extent.

The dialogue, as it gradually progresses in the analytical process, is a creative experience between the doctor and the patient. It becomes, therefore, a sort of rehearsal of real life. It is a substitute but, at the same time, a near to real experience for the patient who, after his cure, is supposed to be in life again. In the dialogue, the patient learns to speak and to regain confidence in the possibility of defining himself and his environment, the objects surrounding him, including the persons he has to deal and cope with in his individual existence. He regains confidence in the fact that there is a method (whatever method this may be) to approach his problems and, therefore, he is able to lose the attitude of disgust and utter despair characteristic of so many patients in the beginning of the analytical process.

As the dialogue puts the patient into the perspective of logos, a new conflict arises in him. He now becomes keenly aware of the paradox between the possibility of a reasonable settlement of his problems and the nature of the unreasonableness of his own world. Through the quiet imposition of the dialogue carrying the suggestion of the logos, the patient, as a last refuge, tries to flee into his neurosis and its gains. This is the period of vehement arguing about what is "right" and "wrong." The patient not only displays a sort of artificial morality while trying to prove his case, but he also criticizes the value system of the doctor. It sometimes takes a long time before the patient sees through the fact that the cure consists not of the acceptance of the doctor's values but of the insight into the nature of values or the logos. To put it differently, resistance is caused by the difficulties in understanding the need to accept values or the logos in spite of its relative value. The patient, finally losing his rigidity, also loses the trend to absolutize his "truth." Only then, when he is willing to transcend his truth without giving up the idea of truth, can the cure really make progress. Only then is the patient willing to leave his state of isolation.

I decided to call the creative phase relating to the persuasion of the logos the "phase of articulation," because it consists of a constant attempt at the definition and redefinition of the patient's and the doctor's standpoints. The phase of articulation appeals to the ability to accept the paradoxicality of life and its inner contradictions. The process of articulation is the phase when the patient finally accepts not only the possibility of the meaning of his life, but also the possibility of giving life a meaning. Articulation, transcending the simple search for communication, examines the basic tools and instruments in the possession of the patient with the help of which he may put himself into the position of being a person or an individuality.

In *Winston's College Dictionary* I find the following definition for "articulation": "The act of forming sounds, enunciation, utterance as regards its distinctness, also that which is pronounced distinctly." Then, under the same heading, it says: "A point of juncture or of union between parts of bones or plants." Articulation as a creative psychoanalytical process is not the forming of sounds, but just as the sounds underlie words and language, so are they the first primitive attempts to form means of speaking. Thus, articulation forms the means of understanding the human situation of the patient. Articulation, by bracketing the contents of a person's life, by going through all the different expressions and all the consequent conflicts, is listening to the sounds of personality.

In modern poetry and literature the principle of reducing the aesthetic elements to a minimum without which the work cannot be done goes through a process similar to what psychoanalysts have to do with their patients. Just as the sound poems reflect such basic emotions as hatred, love, etc., so are basic emotions and attitudes, as we find them in the psychoanalytical work, revealed in the process of articulation which is an analytical and creative process at the same time.

All of us know to what extent these emotional attitudes of a patient can be covered up by rationalizations and intent to mislead the analyst as well as the patient. To teach the patient to see his basic attitude toward life, to make him aware of the fact that these basic attitudes determine his being-in-the-world, is the task of the process of articulation.

In art, the reduction to mathematical symbols, such as Mondrian did, and in poetry, the sound poems as they were produced, are accompanied by the wish to start again. This is the positive side of the process of articulation and its specific creative side, namely to arouse the earnest wish to start again through simplification.

This is not the place to describe the various aspects of the articulation phase of psychoanalysis. It seems arbitrary to select the problem of simplification but still, to my mind, simplification is one of the most important aspects of articulation in psychoanalysis. By going through the contents of a person's life the analyst is involved in the process of personal history. The contents in such analytical activity assume a symbolic character as they are subjected to the aim of the analyst to simplify and relate them to the basis of a person's character structure. In a person's life the different events revealed in analytical activity are comparable to a play on the stage in which the patient plays most of the roles simultaneously and, as we ask ourselves about the plot after seeing a play, about the story, about the meaning, so we ask ourselves and the patient about the plot, about the story and the meaning of his life. We find out in the material of his life, what makes him tick.

We see, through the reducing and desymbolizing, what Sartre calls the primary choice. The patient, in the process of articulation and with the help of the analyst, will find out about his primary choice and how his life was taken away from his primary choice and why, as Sartre puts it, he dwells in the state of bad faith. Why did he lose the ability to make new choices, and so why did he lose the ability to be in life instead of being beside life, next to life, or above life?

Let me close this short description of three creative stages in psychoanalysis with a quotation from Maimonides which refers to the self and which I think has much to do with the primary choice. Maimonides says, or is supposed to have said: "If I were not interested in myself what would the others be able to do for me, and if I were not interested in myself, what would I be able to do for the others?"

1964

▣ THE GROWTH OF ARTISTIC CREATIVITY THROUGH THE PSYCHOANALYTIC PROCESS

Paul Lussheimer

In the beginning of this century, there was a well-liked comedy in which one of the characters is interrogated by a policeman. When he is asked what he is doing, he replies: "I am an artist." "What kind of an artist are you?" asks the policeman, and the man says: "I am an umbrella maker," whereupon the policeman wants to know: "Is that an art?" The man replies: "Can you make an umbrella?"

We join the skeptic policeman and submit the question: Has that man the right to call himself an artist? My answer would be that he can call himself an artist, but not a creative artist.

My presentation, stimulated by Karen Horney's study on creativity in her book *Neurosis and Human Growth*, will have a clinical approach. It will concern itself with the interrelationship between artistic productivity and the individual's movement in the direction toward self-realization.

I am limiting myself to those cases where there is no doubt about genuine artistic creativity. I have in mind the artist who is able to create something from nothing: the painter with an empty canvas; the writer with a blank pad of paper; the sculptor with an unformed slab of marble or clay or with a raw piece of wood or metal; the musician with his blank music paper. I am thereby including all those artists who, in their creative work, call exclusively upon their inner resources. Artists who are re-creating, even if their performance may be formidable, cannot be included in this study because their approach toward their work requires a different prerequisite. A separate investigation would have to clarify the psychological problems of this latter category, it would have to be devoted above all to the study of all the many kinds of performing artists and to such artists who produce their work along lines which have been outlined for them by others.

The creative artists to whom my study is devoted come into treatment for all kinds of reasons, such as marital difficulties or psychosomatic problems, but very seldom out of the awareness that strong forces stand in the way of their creative work. Each one of my colleagues, however, has gone through the same experience with which I was confronted many times: artists, whether painters, sculptors, writers, or composers, expressing the fear that with the progress of their psychoanalysis their creative faculties might be impaired. It can be said immediately that this fear is unjustified. In certain instances, people have given up their artistic endeavors in the course of an analysis, but in all these cases the discontinuance of their artistic work was the result of their insight into the fact that their creative talents were not significant enough to warrant all the effort they had put into their work.

The really creative person creates not because he wants to

but because he must; something in him forces him to work, but this "must" is a healthy force only if his whole life structure is balanced properly. Many creative artists have no real awareness that something is wrong with their creativity; others may sense it, but difficulties in other areas of their personality predominate to such an extent that the inhibition of their artistic growth is overlooked. They come to see an analyst for all kinds of reasons and with a great variety of symptoms. Often there is no mention of their artistic creativity unless a specific question by the interviewer elicits some information about this subject. I remember one patient who did not mention his work as a sculptor until after a long period of therapy. He had come to therapy because of marital difficulties and serious problems in dealing with people in general. While working in an office, he had used his spare time to take courses in sculpture and his progress was initially very satisfactory. Some of his sculptures had been in an exhibition and had been favorably reviewed. A short time later, his interest in his artistic work decreased and he found that he did not make any progress; he discontinued his studies and thereafter he tried only occasionally to do some work on his own. But eventually he gave it up completely and his unhappiness about his creative inhibition was overshadowed by his ever-increasing difficulty in interhuman relationships. He must have practically repressed all thoughts about his creative work and limited himself to a very narrow kind of life. In the analysis, his tendency for self-belittling gradually was removed, and as he achieved closer and better contact with others, he slowly reached the point where he found it possible to talk about his former need to express himself artistically. With the improvement of his general condition, particularly with the increasing degree of self-acceptance, his desire to return to sculpture became strong enough to enable him to take it up again and make his life richer and more satisfactory.

It is worthwhile to ask the question about the significance of artistic creativity when we first interview a patient; it is also worthwhile to keep that question in mind as we proceed in therapy. And it would also be interesting to see, if possible, what artistic creativity means to a person after termination of the treatment. At the beginning of the treatment, some of the most frequent explanations given for the need to be artistically creative can be incorporated in a statement such as: "I just must." This statement may mean many things. It can be, as I indicated before, the healthy desire of an individual to create and express himself. However, we discover that in many instances it is not a voluntary act that brings the individual to his creative endeavors but compulsive drives, the need to please himself or to please or impress others. Not infrequently artistic creativity is the result of a need to escape, that is, to run away from the unpleasant reality of the closer environment or of the world at large. Some individuals use their artistic creativity in an attempt to "abreact," just as other persons go to a gym, work on the punching bag for a while, and feel better afterward. Some others attempt to solve problems without outside help. They do not want advice of friends or relatives and are against consulting experts in difficult situations; they try to paint or write their problems out of their system or, if music is their medium of expression, do it by means of composition. Beethoven, for example, demonstrated this when he wrote his *Wut über den verlorenen Groschen* ("Fury About a Lost Dime").

Some of the statements I have made above can be studied, and others added in the following case history. The patient, a thirty-six-year-old man, came to see me on the recommendation of his wife, a social worker. When asked about his occupation, he described himself as a laborer who worked in a warehouse. His wife had observed that he was increasingly irritable and that his alcohol consumption had increased during the previous months. He added that he was suffering from a great restlessness so that he could not stay at home and was going out alone in the evening and on weekends without any special goal and purpose. In the course of the first interview, I asked if he had any hobbies. He described his hobby as being that of a writer, that he wrote short stories and had even written a novel which had been published in paperback form. He spoke in a rather belittling way about his writing, commenting that it was "not worth very much." His irritability came to the fore even during the first interview when our conversation was interrupted by incoming telephone calls. He said, with some hostility, "Don't you have anybody who takes care of your telephone when you are seeing your patients?"

In calling this manifestation "irritability," I should add that it was an expression of arrogance which was contained in the way he made the statement, almost as if he meant to say: "This is my time and nobody else's." In a later session, another telephone interruption brought him back to the first statement that he made about the telephone, and he then said: "Don't you think I am right? Do you think I'm making undue demands?" It took a while before he saw that maybe his demand was not completely justified. In discussing what was justified or not, he offered for the first time some details about his writing. He explained the idea of his novel and the "philosophy" which motivated him to write it. He was disturbed about the petty injustices which occurred in everyday life: experiences such as being pushed around in an overcrowded subway car, having to wait for the next elevator because the first was overcrowded, or inadequate service in a restaurant. Such experiences made him angry, unhappy and gave him such feeling of frustration that at times he was afraid he could not stand it any longer. But at that time of his life, something happened to him that he had never observed very clearly before. Suddenly, his fantasy was mobilized to such an extent that during his spare hours, or in the monotony of his work in the warehouse, he began to daydream almost continuously. In his daydreams he experienced a world in which all the annoying factors of everyday real life had been eliminated, and all the frustration with which he had to cope in his daily life disappeared.

We can recognize that his daydreams became for him an escape from the unpleasantness of real life and, temporarily, the daydreaming was helpful enough to let him overcome the painful experiences of everyday life. Slowly his daydreams increased, and what had been previously only small pieces of daydreaming became what has been called a "continued story." Living with the daydream which has become a "continued story" may have two kinds of effects: an escape mechanism which becomes a substitute for artistic creativity; or a precursor of artistic creativity which finds its precipitation in one of the artistic forms to which the individual is most inclined and for which he has a special talent. Kris has talked about "socialization of daydreams." His assumption, as well as that of other authors, is that daydreams become pieces of writing, painting, or music. I feel, after a long series of observations, that most if not all products of artistic creativity are preceded by daydreams. That even real dreams may be the instigators of pieces of art has been repeatedly described.

The patient whose case I am describing offered a wealth of daydreaming material as well as most interesting dreams. He was very conscientious in coming to his sessions, and as progress was made in our work he started to talk more and more about his bad luck to have to earn money as a laborer, rather than spending all his time writing stories or novels for which he had a wealth of material. In contrast to the somewhat flippant attitude which he had shown toward his writing in the beginning of his treatment, he began to respect artistic work as being something more than superficial entertainment.

The idea of respect—toward others as well as toward himself—grew simultaneously with his growing respect for art and for his own artistic activities.

At about the same time, a change took place which can easily be ascribed to the profound changes just mentioned; it was like an awakening from a lethargy and his resigned attitude began to subside. The first manifestation of the patient's new attitude was his decision to make writing the most important part of his daily life. Fate was with him; through a lucky streak, he became acquainted with a man who had just started a publishing venture. This man hired him as a proofreader on a full-time basis but under conditions which permitted him to have ample time for free-lance writing. He was then able to exploit the resources of his fantasy. He proved in his prolific writing that he was different from a large number of writers who, after they have written their first book, are lacking in further literary resources.

This phenomenon of a lack of further resources is not only observable in writers but in many other persons who pursue creative endeavors. Painters, as well as sculptors and composers, may create an outstanding first work of art, only to become repetitive in every subsequent work. In many instances the analytic process helps such persons; with their general growth, the increasing insights and the widening of their horizons, they learn to change their outlook in general, to overcome inhibitions, and to modify their artistic approach.

In the case of our patient, there was no need to liberate his inhibitions as far as productivity was concerned. His output was tremendous even when he had just started in his new job. But whatever improvement was necessary had more to do with quality than with quantity. We should not overlook the problem of lack of productivity. We find that patients who have an outspoken need for creative activity work slowly and against tremendous resistance within themselves, but we

331

analysts are aware of the lessening of resistance as analysis proceeds. In this patient a considerable change in the quality of his work could be observed. Figures in his stories, which one could barely call more than presentations in two-dimensional form, became three-dimensional—instead of marionettes, they became human beings. The patient's own experience and awareness of his emotions started to penetrate into the characters of his fiction. What originally had been a cold, descriptive presentation of man and nature became warm-blooded, and it is interesting that one reviewer of a novel which he had written after this change had occurred, said: "What a change! He must have become human. . . ."

As the analysis made further progress he gained greater and greater insight into himself. Externally things changed insofar as he was promoted from proofreader to managing editor. One phenomenon, often observed at the time of the inner change of the patient, was easily observable with him: he paid more attention to his appearance and was very glad when somebody commented on this improvement. His outbursts, which had been an essential factor in his coming to therapy, became less frequent and, when they did occur, were milder and of shorter duration. It is interesting to note that his need to talk about his daydreams in his analytic session disappeared almost completely, and I had to learn about his daydreams by reading his stories.

I have devoted considerable space in this paper to a discussion of this case material, since I see it as a standard case from which we can learn a great deal. His neurosis, generated at an early age and through complicated circumstances which are not essential for this presentation, reached a level unbearable to his environment and to himself at the age of thirty-six. In his interhuman relationships, as well as in his reactions toward himself, he met with great difficulties, but he had only slight insight that a serious disturbance in him created the trouble which he experienced and to which he reacted most violently.

He was unable to extricate himself from these difficulties and neither his prolific daydreaming nor his writing enabled him to find liberation from his disturbances. Dissatisfaction with his work as a laborer, inability to make the shift to writing, doubts of the quality of his literary work, and the final general reaction of how badly this world treated him were the essential sources of his irritability and of fantasies which often came close to and frequently had the quality of paranoid manifestations. The therapist had to keep in mind the basic tenets of proper psychoanalytic treatment: in all areas of his personality, the patient had to gain awareness of his constructive forces; the main task here was to strengthen the patient to come closer to his real self. A "Walter Mitty" fiction had to be destroyed and an acceptance of the valuable self had to be inaugurated. The other task that met with greater resistance was the liberation of the individual from the retarding forces, from his self-belittling, self-destructive trends, the doubts of himself and of his fellow men.

This pattern of procedure, while more or less a standard one, can be and has to be applied to a creative personality in a most delicate manner; care has to be taken that the existing values of artistic creativity are kept alive and that no blockages prevent the real artist from paralyzing himself in his creative work. The artist wrestling with himself on the couch about the question of acceptance of his past artistic endeavors and the possible expansion of his artistic work in the future, has to gain knowledge of blockages which are a general pattern in him and involve his creative development. The daydreams which an individual with artistic gifts experiences may be his blessing or a curse. They are a blessing when they can be translated into a painting, a sculpture, a novel, or a musical composition; they may, however, be a curse when the driving force is missing to permit him to transform the daydream into

333

a real piece of art. The analytic process has to try to mobilize the forces by removing the blockages.

I think it is necessary to stress that the work of an analyst with the creative artist is not that of a teacher or art reviewer; it does not include value judgments. Basically, it is not fair to discourage a minor painter because he is not a Picasso. I have made it a principle in my work with creative patients to encourage, rather than to discourage, if their creative talents are truly essential parts of their personalities. Only in a case where I feel that it is obvious that the patient is motivated exclusively by the neurotic need of self-glorification, do I try to make the person realize the futility of his artistic endeavors.

It is my firm conviction that no other area of psychoanalysis requires so much tact and taste on the part of the analyst than when trying to change the patient's outlook toward his own artistic work and to make him find another avenue of self-expression. In the analysis of a really creative person, forces will be mobilized that lead to change in the artistic approach without the encumbrance of the neurotic retarding forces. I have observed such changes in my patients whose ways of expressing themselves developed in different directions, and where even the techniques they applied changed considerably. These changes are always running parallel with changes in the personality, and this confirms the opinion that creativity is only *one* segment of the total personality.

The patient who enters psychoanalytic treatment changes his orientation the moment he begins therapy. We cannot generalize and say that his artistic creativity is involved immediately. The therapist who would instantly place emphasis on working on the problems of active creativity may make a serious mistake. It is much more desirable to let things first fall into place—and I have learned that even without a premeditated concept, all segments of the personality structure will be taken care of in a properly conducted psychoanalysis.

Even in a very successful analysis, there may be more growth in one area than in another; however, it is not the parts that decide, but the sum total of them. What we are striving for has been very well expressed in a statement by Dr. Schneider: "Psychoanalysis is not simply a set of explanations and interpretations; it is a work of transformation in which the real self—the ego—[is] strengthened."

In closing, I want to summarize my observations. While it is a natural thing that a successful analysis brings about growth, no matter what a person's position or occupation is, growth of artistic creativity has specific manifestations. The really creative person has the gift for expressing himself most powerfully in that field of art to which his specific talent predestines him. During and after a successful analysis we observe in the creative artist an increase in the depth of his approach, and the change in his personality often brings about new techniques and modes of expression. The mobilization of constructive forces and the removal of blockages through the analysis will bring a true talent to its full fruition.

1963

CREATIVITY

AND FREEDOM

Antonia Wenkart

Creativity is an exquisitely human faculty that is essential for the evolution of man and for his personal growth. Creativity and freedom are inseparable. Freedom—the internal as well as the external condition—is also exquisitely human, and it lays the foundation for creativity. Mental health hinges upon both.

Growth, development, evolution are processes governed by rules similar to the biological laws underlying all living matter. The most characteristic of them is the very sign of life itself, that it can copy and reproduce itself. Reproduction, regeneration, and creation are at the core of the most profound emotional and spiritual experiences in living. The complex multidimensional growth of the human being as a whole can be grasped in terms of creativity.

Culture is part of man's biological heritage, although it is passed along by society and not through the genes. Culture is so much a part of our psychological environment that it enters the world of objects around us. Cultural issues and values have a distinct impact on individual development.

Neither socially transmitted culture nor gene-transmitted biological characteristics can establish exclusive claim. The study of man becomes a comparative study of cultural differences within genetic sameness. Everything that is handed down either through heredity or culture is grist for the individual's creative mill.

Creation, in the Biblical sense, is full of wonderment at changes that are not directly explainable, immediately visible, or accountable for logically. Creativity, as perceived in its beginnings, is the inherent, innate essence of living matter—the living idea or passion full of marvels.

The creative impulse is a general characteristic of any human endeavor, be it directed toward bringing into existence something new, or reconstructing issues, or bringing to life what had been forgotten or invalidated. The primary zest or initial stirring is an enigma and remains so when we are confronted with it; there is no scientific explanation for it.

The primary creative impulse is frequently accompanied by the joy of discovery. While material values or social accoutrements may bring pleasure, creative work and love bring joy. And although joy may not be more intense than pleasure, it does have to do with a larger order of experience than is the case with pleasure.

There are some investigators who believe that artistic creativity is intuition and unprejudiced and direct perception. As defined by phenomenologists, in Spiegelberg's *The Phenomenological Movement*, intuition is ". . . the intuiting act in which a phenomenon is contemplated and explored directly." Eventually, ". . . it is always the intuiting of phenomena, particular as well as universal, in which all genuine knowledge finds its verification."

To know what one has intuited one has to name it, to bring a formulated version into clear consciousness. And since even naming it may be evanescent, one has to fix it, to organize it into meaningful connections. To give the thought independent existence, one has to express it, put it into formal language. Cocteau calls intuition a creative instinct of contradiction, by which he means opposition to old, well-trodden ways.

The effort needed to grasp, translate, and transmute the idea creates a feeling of achievement. Out of fog and confusion a meaningful experience finds its way into the clearing. Expression is a creative act for the one who does the listening or receiving as well as for the one who does the expressing. And what happens between two people as the expression takes place is still another creation.

Impulse, intuition, organization, and expression are stages in the individual creative process, and in psychoanalysis the creative process resembles the individual one. Viewing analysis from this special angle is of the utmost significance, in contradistinction to the past, when psychoanalysis was regarded as a predominantly reductionist process—a technique of elimination and adaptation. Karen Horney tipped the scales of this prevailing attitude toward the creative goal by placing the morality of evolution at the center of the distinction between neurosis and human growth.

The psychoanalyst is mindful that creativity is an attribute of life, that it is an unconditional and unreserved openness to stimuli. It is an acceptance that allows for a spontaneous, fresh response. A general disposition of freedom to full exposure in one's own being warrants creative living—one's very own unique experiences even in the most trivial matters. The opposite of this freedom—inhibitions, restrictions, and fears—keeps the individual in captivity and curtails and distorts the full range of impressions and expressions.

Another dimension of creativity is that of interpersonal relationships. In the struggle between the neurotic need and inclination, the opposition against submission to the first is creative in nature. We all know patients who insist that they

339

have to be as the others want them to be, or that the presence of others has such an overwhelming impact on their being that they feel squelched or paralyzed. The dynamic world of relationships reveals its creative aspects at various levels: active being, functioning, role playing, sharing. The emergence from any of these stages into the actuality of relating is a creative act. The essence of man is to be found not in the isolated individual as a static element of society, but in his dynamic potential to relate, to be related, and to have relationships.

Four phases may be distinguished in the creative act: (1) emergence from the potential of solipsistic being; (2) creation of relating principles—in the main, language; (3) establishing a relationship through sharing or opposing; and (4) reflection upon the relationship, with integration and synthesis taking place thereby.

Man is unthinkable as a unique entity confined to his selfhood but disconnected from his world and from the others. His relatedness to his world and to others is not separable from his own identity. Not only does the patient present himself with his neurotic distortions, but the embodiment of his activity reveals his world view. The confluence of his essential selfhood with otherness is an important source of creativity. The dimension of selfhood reaches beyond the self into the world and to the others. There is a between-ness which is created by relatedness to the other. Buber says: "Freedom provides the possibility for the true life to unfold." The unfolding is accomplished and fulfilled in the between-ness.

The creative dynamics of relatedness are extremely complex and many links are required in relating. Psychobiological links signify the entry of the human infant into the world. His first breath of air, the temperature of his skin, the initial outcry of his vocal cords are expressions of relating interchange. The parents, the family's anticipation, the acceptance and care of the infant start the emotional chain rolling, the endless procession of links in human belonging and social communion. Relationships are what establish each individual as an entity participating in the life of the world.

The function of each individual is to a large extent put on a social scale where it is weighed and compared with the function and position of other people. Role playing is a positional directive that is structured by societal organization. As in psychobiology, where the newest discovery of the molecular structure of the substance of heredity contributes to the understanding of the basic life process, so in psychic life the basic endeavor is the discovery of any and all means of communication and connectedness that originate and structure relationships.

Self-realization—the self coming into its own—becomes real in the sharing of experiences. The degree, intensity, modality, and level of sharing vary, of course. Significantly, the word for share in German is *teilen,* while *mitteilen* means to convey and communicate. It points to the relating links, the foundation of creativity. Every relation, every relating and connecting link, helps to establish the self.

Language is one of the strongest of these links. The first grasp, the intuition established in the reality of one's experience, can be translated into comprehensible language. The expressing of the experience is a creative act.

Language is the main tool in psychoanalysis; the relationship between patient and analyst is fulfilled through language. Everything that is given form in speech, from sound to symbol, acquires new life and creates a new bond between two people. In the *New Testament* the first words describing the creation are: "In the beginning there was the word." Jaspers wrote: "All that which cannot be known may be felt through telling." Language is truly the medium of sharing experience.

Language is the lifehood of a dual and reciprocal process. It has its arteries in one's own response to one's inner voice;

341

it finds its stirrings in the need to reach the other. The etymological roots are *spondeo:* I swear, I bear witness to the truth; *respondeo:* I react and answer. The history of psychiatry could be written in terms of what happens to language in mental illness—how the duality and reciprocity loses its spontaneity and freedom.

By entering into a discourse one knows one is trying to reach into the world. Reality is formed through language and the word is the most potent instrument for creating continuity. The experience of the fullness of life in one little instant of time is a gift of freedom. Split moments can create an entirety in freedom. A spiritual meeting through language can establish a relationship. If freedom is the foundation, language is the content and carrier of meaningful links of relating.

In psychoanalysis, the language of free association involving the patient and the analyst cannot be taken only as the expression of transference. Those unlived neurotic needs that repeat infantile patterns or give vent to repressed hostility are some aspects of relating efforts. They are also creative spurts by someone who for the first time has found an ear that is free to listen.

Just as the blood, conveyor of substance, is the body's artisan in repairing damaged tissue, so language is a natural means of re-establishing true communication. One's ability to convey is in direct proportion to one's inner freedom. If the continuity of experience and expression is established and preserved, direct communication is possible. If not, disconnectedness and distortion reign.

A relationship has a life of its own. Although for the sake of self-realization the identity of the individual has to be defined, a strictly personal foundation for his evolution lies within the matrix of relationships. Buber's "I and Thou," Erwin Straus' "opposition," and the old psychological quest for borderlines all point to the meaning and function of relationships in the development of selfhood.

The psychological investigation of man has been focused on the self and/or on others, or the relationship of an individual to himself, as it were, and to others. In the exploration of dynamics, inevitably penetrated is the motivation that prompted attitudes and led to certain kinds of relationships. However, the whole theme of the creativity of relatedness, the phenomenon as such, calls for special attention and needs to be probed further.

No psychic or emotional reality of an individual obtains in a vacuum. Vital contact through relating as a frame of reference is a *conditio sine qua non*. This applies to selfhood as well as to the community of others. All relating is a series of stepping stones into the world and toward others, and it opens the way to one's self. The synthesis of all human forces experienced and lived through in this world and in contact with others sums up and completes the individual and his personal life.

Although the individual personality is drenched in infinite subjectivity, it is not a permanent substance but rather a creative act. All creative activity consists of establishing relating links in the condition of freedom.

Every individual in possession of the right to be himself is free to relate. This exempts him from being driven by needs and hampered by restraints. In the world of others, he can meet a situation and attack a problem by finding out objectively that which is, and by knowing subjectively how he feels. When he is overwhelmed by inner and outer pressures, he loses his freedom; he falls into bondage to inner coercion and outer power.

It is when he reaches the limits of inner coercion that he undergoes the split which causes him to disregard dimensions, constituents, parts of himself, to be alienated and, therefore,

343

at odds with himself. He loses the ability to fathom true inner feelings and to bear witness to his inner truth. When he reaches the limits of what his particular traffic will bear in the way of outer pressures, he loses his social identity.

This theme is beautifully portrayed by two contemporary writers, Bertold Brecht and Max Frisch. Brecht's *Man Is Man* has as its main theme man's transformation through a series of outside pressures which flatten out and deteriorate the human element. The hero of Brecht's play arrives at the conclusion that ". . . right is wrong and might is right."

There is, of course, a relationship between the two kinds of pressure. Inner pressures respond to outer pressures. As Brecht proposes, "There are two of me: a man and/or a tool of me, malleable by pressures," or, a man versus ". . . nothing till somebody calls me something."

In his play *Andorra*, Frisch describes the fate of a man who is destroyed by the brainwashing of public opinion. It is the man's being-in-the-world, his plain and active role in his society, his wanting to share and contribute to the human community which is threatened and annihilated by the avalanche of public authority. In short, his hero has lost his human identity.

In a book entitled *Am, or the Journey to Peking*, Frisch describes a twosome of beings: the I and the Am, the outcome of the alienating process that divides the core of one's self from the active rest of existence. The villain of the piece, the cause of the alienation, is the coercion by inner pressures. Mr. Am travels through the world like a ghost. Only now and then does his "I" look over his shoulder to remind him that there is a possibility of merging, that he can stand up and say: "I am." When he does this his essences are united and his identity is established.

Such is the lot of man that he has to preserve his inner freedom while at the same time being concerned with his outer freedom. John Donne's line, "No man is an island, entire of itself," contains more than a grain of truth.

The relations and connecting links between the entity of an individual, his world and others are but another dimension in one's life and creativity. The patient needs to have this dimension examined and needs to be restored to a freedom from devastating pressures and a freedom for mutual exchange.

The problem of creativity and neurosis or psychosis has usually been ventilated only in connection with the output of an artist. The creative vein of Everyman seems to have been neglected. Is a neurotic or psychotic patient creative? The answer is yes. It is shown in the degree of destructiveness which is proportionate to the magnitude of frustrating failure to exist. "Destructiveness," says Fromm: "is the outcome of unlived life." It is common knowledge that neurosis and psychosis are webs of self-created defenses spun for wrong reasons toward an erroneous goal. But it is easily forgotten that the primary reason for those defenses is defiance against unlived life.

The struggle consumes all the freedom of will and action. Slavery to the unconscious binds the patient and prevents him from an all-round view. He loses autonomy and self-determination. The freedom that would enable him to preserve his integrity against the power of destructiveness is gone.

As freedom diminishes, so does creativity. The site of freedom is in the human spirit of the individual and of the society. The neurotic facsimile we see so frequently in defiance and delinquency is not freedom; this so-called freedom from social conventions amounts to slavery. Nowadays, youth looks for expression; while youth's vitality is restricted to movement but is lacking in endurance and meaning, the subjective element of expression is missing. The need for expression is an objectified freedom of movement and degenerates instead into license.

Creativity of the analytic process consists in the patient's liberation from slavery—not only delivery from bondage to compulsion, but also from the slavery of displaced position on the emotional scale. The problem for the analyst is to find the freedom to enter a relationship with the patient. It goes without saying that the clinical diagnosis is necessary. But the ostensible difficulty presented by the patient, as well as the analyst's knowledge or personal state of health, ought not to be permitted to stand between patient and analyst. While the objective and scientific evaluation is needed for didactic purposes, it would seem that comprehension of the person and contact with him are possible only after one has abstracted from the scientific aspects and suspended the logic of casuistry.

Two principles that prevail in the world and in the individual—freedom and connectedness—are found in a state of antagonism in the psychoanalytic situation. The analyst's creative freedom can reach beyond the cut-off stream or tangential convolution. He and the patient can join hands behind the lines of actual statement, ready to tap new reality.

A patient can find himself free at different levels of existence and in different fields of action. Freedom of speculation and great talent in organizational matters may be seen in many patients who are otherwise enslaved by fears and compulsions. The absence of freedom or slavery manifests itself in many ways.

Creativity of thought processes and organizational aspects of human relationships may be intact in otherwise disintegrated inner experiences. There is the example of the homosexual individual who seems to be connected with his outer world only by means of his visual perception. His awareness of colors, shapes, and design allows him to be actively creative. Often he excels in the fields of interior decorating, dress design, and the like. However, because of his inner fragmentation, he is not quite able to move from the visual perception to the abstract concepts. Freedom is only partially available to him. It is restricted to the fragment of his existence which appeals to his visual perception, while other broken-up fragments remain inert in the darkness of inner confinement, excluded from experience.

In the world of outer pressures lack of personal freedom, as in incarceration or imprisonment, can stimulate emotional and spiritual freedom and actually enhance creativity. Political leaders and great figures in history have given many memorable accounts of how they used their time while in involuntary confinement. Nehru claims that his most profitable time insofar as his personal growth was concerned were the years of imprisonment when he was left to his own devices.

Letters of famous prisoners even reveal an upsurge of emotional activity, as documented in stirring love missives. A woman prisoner, gazing through the bars in the window of her cell at the lonely night, cries out to her beloved, "Nobody can stop me from reaching up to the sky and snatching two stars to give you for cuff links!"

Freedom is far more than a birthright; it is something to be cultivated, activated, and, when necessary, fought for. Man has to exercise the courage to struggle for inner freedom out of the pain of oppression, and against the impact of power which restricts freedom and endangers its existence.

To be free is to be able to endure pressures, yet ride with them and transcend them, gathering strength enough along the way to fight overpowering adversaries while maintaining one's wholeness and inner autonomy. Pertinent and congruent freedom can only be a finite freedom, to use Tillich's phrase. Unrestricted freedom goes beyond the measure of what can be humanly expected.

We know that freedom and creativity are interdependent. Just as creativity is possible only in freedom, so freedom is the achievement of creativity. In psychoanalysis, acceptance of

347

the freedom to reveal, if nothing else, is at all times to expose an endeavor of creative transcendence. When the patient overcomes the shame and guilt of that which is destructive and harmful, a creative step has been taken. Later on there is a certain shyness about disclosing the real and authentic signs. All that is new and naked stands alone and unsupported. The analyst's creative intuition is made available as he stands by with compassion.

There is also the freedom to endure. In the artist the freedom to endure is connected with the vision of the completed work. He is even helped when he considers himself a tool in the hands of his vocation. A patient who is involved in psychoanalytic therapy lacks such vision. Only his faith and the vision of the analyst can help him endure his agony.

The theory and technique of psychoanalysis can always be examined, but the real concern of man's sanity and satisfaction demands immediate access to the creative essence of man. The healing, in the sense of becoming what one potentially can be, is self-creating.

The problem of creativity and freedom is of great concern to every analyst. He must be free to create his own true image and the image of man and not follow a pattern. It is not possible to be free and yet size oneself up against established models like the Madison Avenue type or the Bowery character, or the New England way of life, or life as it is lived in Mississippi.

The analyst has to be free to learn from any field of human endeavor and interest. Philosophy and physiology are both pertinent to the knowledge of man. The freedom of the analyst consists not only in freedom of mind—the degree of relaxation that permits one to listen unobtrusively—but also freedom from restrictive norms, from the technical skills in which one has been trained. Diagnosis, prognosis, fitting things into conceptual structures—all this has to go by the board to allow the freedom for a world view, the freedom and openness to life and its exigencies.

Recently, Pablo Casals, one of the greatest cellists of our time, appeared on television conducting a master class. While explaining the beauty of the music being played, he introduced many facets and innuendoes even experienced musicians would not think of. Yet, with it all, he advised his pupil, "Forget about the timing, forget about what is written on the sheet of music." He meant that all the highly skilled and rigorous training so necessary for every performer has to be banished from the conscious mind if he is to execute and reproduce the music artfully and creatively. What is more, Casals, while instructing his pupil, never once referred to the instrument, the cello, but always to the pupil's body, to the strong and free movements of her arms.

In the execution of a piece of art in creative activity, everything is incidental to the freedom and involvement of the performer. So it has to be with the analyst. The analyst must be free from anxiety in order to experience himself as a coexistent partner. The need to put himself in the category of the so-called mature person falsely elevates him above the level of the suffering patient.

Clearly, the analyst ought not to feel bound to the demands of rationality. The study of man's creativity has always been addressed to the search for the unknown, which, at times, posed as a magic force until a formula was found to place the unknown into a new order. The unknown is beyond rationality. Madness and inspiration have long been equated because both are of strange origin.

Freedom is victory over fear. The analyst is free when he is capable of indulging in creativity of his own, unhampered by false notions and prejudices. The responsibility of the psychoanalyst is a heavy one. The poetic and artistic freedom of intuition and imagination is always called for, while the ever-

349

present sense of observable reality constitutes the basis for this freedom.

In conclusion, it may be noted that human growth and the creative process are in the same category. The spontaneous primary growth as well as the recovery of secondary growth which takes place in and through psychoanalysis are also creative processes.

1963